Praise for *Tax Collector to G*

"Michael Kok takes readers through a fascinating piece of detective work as he seeks to answer the question of why a presumably initially untitled gospel came to be associated with the name of Matthew as its author. In exploring this question, no relevant stone is left unturned as Kok reevaluates the clues left by writers of early Christian texts, along with evidence from gospel manuscripts. The result is a highly engaging investigation and explanation of how this unnamed gospel subsequently became the Gospel of Matthew."

—Paul Foster, University of Edinburgh

"Nothing can be the last word because scholarship never stands still. But if you want the best word so far, this is your book: a meticulous, well-informed, and creative contribution on an important, truly fascinating question: How did Matthew become the author of Matthew?"

—Dale C. Allison Jr., Princeton Theological Seminary

"Already an established authority on the early reception of the Gospel of Mark, Michael J. Kok turns his attention to the contested authorship and reception of the Gospel of Matthew in *Tax Collector to Gospel Writer*. With a thorough command of the wide-ranging primary sources and the latest scholarship, Kok tells a detailed and engaging story of how the canonical Gospel of Matthew and the apocryphal Gospel of the Hebrews came to be attributed to Matthew the tax collector. Told with erudition and aplomb, Kok's fascinating and informative study is essential reading for anyone interested in gospel origins and their reception."

—Stephen C. Carlson, Australian Catholic University

TAX COLLECTOR TO
GOSPEL WRITER

TAX COLLECTOR TO GOSPEL WRITER

Patristic Traditions about the Evangelist Matthew

Michael J. Kok

Fortress Press
Minneapolis

TAX COLLECTOR TO GOSPEL WRITER
Patristic Traditions about the Evangelist Matthew

Cover design: Savanah N. Landerholm
Cover image: VESPASIAN. 69-79 AD. Æ Sestertius (25.77 gm, 6h). Judaea
Capta issue. Rome mint. Struck 71 AD; and Medieval manuscript fragments,
#6532. Division of Rare and Manuscript Collections, Cornell University Library.
Fragment in Greek from the Gospel of Matthew 21:1–19 describing the entrance
of Jesus into Jerusalem.

Print ISBN: 978-1-5064-8108-1
eBook ISBN: 978-1-5064-8109-8

To Alissa, my wife and the love of my life

CONTENTS

PREFACE

This is the third book that I have published investigating the historical development of the antique ecclesiastical consensus about the authorship of the four New Testament Gospels. The subject of the present work is the transformation of the apostle Matthew from a notorious tax collector to a celebrated evangelist in the early patristic traditions. By attaching Matthew's name and apostolic reputation to the canonical Gospel that is named after him, and much later to the *Gospel According to the Hebrews*, it bolstered the authority of these documents for the ancient Christian communities who treasured them. Indeed, the *Gospel According to Matthew* may have been the most popular Gospel for the majority of Christians in antiquity.

Getting a handle on the canonical and patristic data about the apostle Matthew is no easy task. I am grateful for the assistance of a number of scholarly peers such as Matthew David Larsen, Dean Furlong, Stephen Carlson, Chris Keith, David Sloan, M. David Litwa, Candida Moss, Matthew Ferguson, Andrew Gregory, Jörg Frey, and James Carleton Paget. They have helped me to locate certain publications, answered my queries, or provided constructive and critical feedback on select chapters. Of course, it is customary to issue the disclaimer that any blunders that I may have made are entirely my own fault. I did appreciate the opportunities that were afforded to me to test some of the theories advanced in this book at various academic conferences. This includes presentations on the identification of Matthew as a toll collector, the patristic reception of the elder John, the categorization of the Gospels in the writings of Justin Martyr, and the reconstruction of the Ebionites and Nazoreans for the *Centre for Gospels and Acts Research* established by the Sydney College of Divinity, the *Society of Biblical Literature* annual meetings, and the "Paul within Judaism Symposium," hosted by Ridley College. I could not have asked for better colleagues than the ones I have at Morling College, who allowed me to have the time and gave me the encouragement to complete this manuscript. I have benefited greatly from the editorial feedback of Carey Newman and would like to thank the team at Fortress Press for investing in this project.

Above all, I wish to express my gratitude to my wife Alissa, the one to whom this book is dedicated. It was a big change when I moved from Canada to Australia to take up my current position as a New Testament Lecturer, but my life was completely changed the day that I met her. Together we have journeyed through the whole Covid season and have been blessed with the birth of our baby girl, Amelia. Without Alissa's constant encouragement and support, this book would never have been written.

INTRODUCTION

The Tax Collector and the Gospel Writer

THERE WAS A tax collector stationed at a tollbooth on the outskirts of the Galilean fishing village of Capernaum.[1] His job was to collect duties on the goods transported between the tetrarchies of Herod Antipas and Philip, the local puppet rulers propped up by the Romans. One day, Jesus walked up to his tollbooth and issued the command, "Follow me!"[2] This chance encounter changed the course of his life. From that day forward, he ceased extorting money from his neighbors. He is identified as Matthew in the Gospel that is named after him.[3] This was the same Matthew who was hand-picked by Jesus to be one of his twelve apostles.[4] His reputation among Christians would no longer be that of a despised quisling. Throughout Christian history, he would also be acclaimed as one of the four evangelists whose Gospels were canonized in the New Testament.

Countless Christians, from the second to the twenty-first century, have taken the authorship of the *Gospel According to Matthew* for granted. Matthew may have been functionally bilingual or trilingual to strike up a conversation with anyone who stopped by his tollbooth. Some of the apostles were uneducated and illiterate,[5] but Matthew may have had rudimentary

---

1. I will stick with the familiar translation "tax collector" found in most English Bible translations, but in this instance, "toll collector" is a more accurate translation of *telōnēs*. See John R. Donahue, "Tax Collectors and Sinners: An Attempt at Identification" *CBQ* 33 (1971): 36–61, 42–49, 59; cf. Craig S. Keener, *The Gospel of Matthew: A Socio-Rhetorical Commentary* (Grand Rapids: Eerdmans, 2009), 292–93.
2. This story is found in Matt 9:9, Mark 2:13–14, and Luke 5:27–28. Note that the tax collector is named Levi in two of the three Synoptic Gospels.
3. See Matt 9:9; 10:3.
4. See Matt 10:3; Mark 3:18; Luke 6:15; Acts 1:13.
5. The term *agrammatos* in Acts 4:13 means literally "without letters." See Thomas J. Kraus, "'Uneducated,' 'Ignorant,' or even 'Illiterate'? Aspects and Background for an Understanding of ΑΓΡΑΜΜΑΤΟΙ (and ΙΔΙΩΤΑΙ) in Acts 4:13" *NTS* 45 (1999): 434–49.

literacy. His training could have been put to good use if he had volunteered to be Jesus's official note-taker.[6] On top of that, money is a recurring topic in passages that are unique to the Gospel of Matthew.[7] Jesus spun parables about an unmerciful servant who refused to cancel a debt that was owed to him and about laborers in a vineyard who were paid the same wage, irrespective of the hour when they commenced working for the landowner.[8] Peter miraculously caught a fish with a coin in its mouth to pay off the half-shekel tax for the upkeep of the temple.[9] A range of coins are featured in the Gospel such as the *kodrantēs, assarion, didrachma, statēr,* and *dēnarion.*[10] The twelve disciples are commissioned to minister to the surrounding villages in three of the Gospels,[11] but the distinctive wording in Matthew's Gospel stresses that they were not to bring along any "gold," "silver," and "copper."[12]

The traditional authorship of Matthew's Gospel may be defensible. Be that as it may, this Gospel remains formally anonymous. Its author is unnamed. Its sources are undisclosed. It opens by launching right into Jesus's genealogy and birth. It is fair to point out that there may have been no set conventions in ancient technical treatises, histories, or biographies for authors to include their names in the introductory prefaces or bodies of

---

6. See E. J. Goodspeed, *Matthew, Apostle and Evangelist* (1st ed.; Philadelphia: John C. Winston, 1959), 16–17, 74, 80, 86, 88, 99–100, 101–2, 105, 108–9; Robert Gundry, *The Use of the Old Testament in St. Matthew's Gospel: With Special Reference to the Messianic Hope* (Leiden: Brill, 1975), 181–83; Bernard Orchard and Harold Riley, *The Order of the Synoptics: Why Three Synoptic Gospels?* (Macon: Mercer University Press, 1987), 235; R. T. France, *Matthew: Evangelist and Teacher* (Grand Rapids: Zondervan, 1989), 67–68; D. A. Carson, *Matthew: Chapters 1 through 12* (EBC; Grand Rapids: Zondervan, 1995), 18–19; B. Ward Powers, *The Progressive Publication of Matthew: An Explanation of the Writing of the Synoptic Gospels* (Nashville: B&H Publishing Group, 2010), 28–31; John Wenham, *Redating Matthew, Mark & Luke: A Fresh Assault on the Synoptic Problem* (new ed.; Eugene: Wipf & Stock, 2020), 112–14.
7. The following examples are highlighted in Goodspeed, *Matthew*, 59–60, 92–93; Werner G. Marx, "Money Matters in Matthew" *Bibliotheca Sacra* 136.542 (1979): 152–57; Leon Morris, *The Gospel According to Matthew* (Grand Rapids: Eerdmans: 1992), 14n.46.
8. See Matt 18:21–35; 20:1–16.
9. See Matt 17:24–27.
10. See Matt 5:26; 10:29; 17:24, 27; 18:28; 20:2, 9, 10, 13; 22:19.
11. See Matt 10:1–42; Mark 6:7–13; Luke 9:1–6.
12. See Matt 10:9 (contra Mark 6:8; Luke 9:3). Matthew's Gospel has several references to "gold" (cf. 2:11; 23:16–17) and "silver" (cf. 25:18, 27; 26:15; 27:3, 5, 6, 9; 28:12, 15).

their works.[13] The authorship of a text could be communicated via oral tradition or other literary devices.[14] Even so, antique historians or biographers might speak in the first person when they participated in the events that they were narrating or let their readers know about their relationship to the subjects that they were studying.[15] The Gospel of Matthew is narrated in the third person by an omniscient narrator who never steps into the action. At the opposite end of the spectrum, the Gospel has been characterized as an evolving living tradition with a cacophony of voices from the different sources contained within it.[16] Varying instructions about restricting the Jesus movement to the people of Israel or embarking on a worldwide mission to the nations stand side by side in its pages.[17] It might be anachronistic to picture a single author or editor as responsible for the present form of the Gospel of Matthew.[18]

There are no clues within this Gospel that Jesus's biography was being retold through Matthew's individual vantage point. Matthew is not introduced as a character in it until chapter nine. Like the rest of the apostles, Matthew fled when Jesus was arrested. He did not witness Jesus's trials, crucifixion, and burial in the climax of the story. Notwithstanding his status as an apostle, he did not have as much prestige as Jesus's inner circle of disciples, consisting of Peter, James, and John.[19] This trio beheld the transfiguration of Jesus's appearance on a mountain. They heard the agitation in Jesus's voice when he pleaded with them to stay awake in the Garden of Gethsemane.

---

13. See Simon J. Gathercole, "The Alleged Anonymity of the Canonical Gospels," *JTS* 69.2 (2018): 455–59.

14. Gathercole, "The Alleged Anonymity," 459–60.

15. See Matthew Wade Ferguson, "Ancient Historical Writing Compared to the Gospels of the New Testament," *The Secular Modern Web Library* (2016), n.p. https://infidels. org/library/modern/matthew_ferguson/gospel-genre.html. See Polybius, *Hist.* 4.2.1; Dionysius of Halicarnassus, *Rom. Ant.* 1.7.1–3; Livy, *Ab urbe cond.* praef.1–4; Josephus, *J.W.* praef.1; *Ant.* 20.11.2–3; *Life* 1; Tacitus, *Hist.* 1.1; *Agr.* 3; Plutarch, *Oth.* 14.1; Suetonius, *Cal.* 19.3; *Otho* 10.1; *Dom.* 12.2.

16. In one scholar's assessment, "The Gospel of Matthew is a gathering point for a variety of existing traditions." See Edwin K. Broadhead, *The Gospel of Matthew on the Landscape of Antiquity* (WUNT 378; Tübingen: Mohr Siebeck, 2017), 110. This is the opening sentence of a chapter where Broadhead examines the conflicting viewpoints in Matthew's Gospel that stem from Mark, Q, M, or the Jewish Scriptures.

17. See Matt 10:5–6; 15:24; 28:19.

18. See the theses in Broadhead, *The Gospel*, XVII–XVIII.

19. See Mark 5:37//Luke 8:51; Mark 9:2//Matt 17:1//Luke 9:28; Mark 14:33//Matt 26:37.

Matthew appears just twice in the whole Gospel, once simply in the list of the twelve apostles.[20] Therefore, the internal evidence does not line up with the external evidence for the authorship of this Gospel.

The Gospel of Matthew is not the only Gospel to record Jesus's meeting with a tollbooth operator. The exact same episode is found in the Gospels of Mark and Luke, but the person at the tollbooth is named Levi in these two texts.[21] The Gospels are regularly harmonized on this point.[22] Some Christian readers distinguished Levi and Matthew as two separate individuals. When the philosopher Celsus demeaned Jesus's disciples as a ragtag bunch of tax collectors and sailors, the renowned Christian intellectual Origen of Alexandria (ca. 184–253 CE) protested that Matthew was the sole apostle who had collected taxes for a living. As for Levi, Origen noted that he was only listed among the twelve apostles in select manuscripts of Mark's Gospel.[23] There was indeed a textual variant in which Lebbaeus, the Latinized form of Levi, surfaces alongside Matthew in the list of the twelve apostles.[24] Other Christians regarded Levi and Matthew as two different names for the same tax collector. A few fourth-century commentators mused about Matthew's humility. Matthew contritely confessed that he had once earned his wages through disgraceful means in his own Gospel, while Mark and Luke protected Matthew's reputation by using his lesser-known name Levi.[25]

A third option is that the tax collector's name was intentionally changed from Levi to Matthew or vice versa. In deciding which Gospel(s) got the name of the tax collector right, many ancient Christians would have

---

20. See Matt 9:9; 10:3. E. J. Goodspeed (*Matthew*, 117) rationalizes Matthew's absence from much of the narrative on the grounds that Matthew "was the secretary, taking his notes. He performs no striking act, asks no questions, plays no leading part; that was not his role. He merely records."
21. See Mark 2:14; Luke 5:27.
22. For the *Rezeptionsgeschichte* ("reception history") of Matt 9:9 and 10:3, see Ulrich Luz, *Matthew 8–20*, trans. James E. Crouch; Hermeneia (Minneapolis: Fortress, 2001), 32n.12; Ian Boxall, *Matthew through the Centuries* (Wiley Blackwell Bible Commentaries; Hoboken: Wiley, 2019), 31, 172.
23. See Origen, *Cels.* 1.62 (cf. Mark 3:16–19).
24. The replacement of Thaddaeus with Lebbaeus in Mark 3:18 is attested in Codex Bezae, and this western reading influenced the textual transmission of Matt 10:3 as well. See Barnabas Lindars, "Matthew, Levi, Lebbaeus and the Value of the Western Text" *NTS* 4 (1957–1958): 220–22.
25. See John Chrysostom, *Hom. in Mt.* 30.1; Jerome, *Comm. Matt.* 1.9.9.

naturally turned to the Gospel of Matthew. This text was the most popular Gospel during the patristic period. Not only was it quoted more than the other three Gospels,[26] it was the one that was most frequently expounded upon in patristic biblical commentaries and recited in Christian liturgies.[27] There may have been a suggestion that the author of Matthew's Gospel set the record straight about the name of the tax collector because it was thought that he was the tax collector in question.[28]

---

26. See Brenda Deen Schildgen, *Power and Prejudice: The Reception of the Gospel of Mark* (Detroit: Wayne State University Press, 1999), 40–41. She calculates that there were roughly 3,900 citations of Matthew's Gospel, 1,400 citations of Mark's Gospel, 3,300 citations of Luke's Gospel, and 2,000 citations of John's Gospel. Excluding the assiduous biblical commentator Origen, she estimates that third-century Christian writers referenced Matthew's Gospel roughly 3,600 times, Mark's Gospel 250 times, Luke's Gospel 1,000 times, and John's Gospel 1,600 times. Factoring Origen into the picture, Origen cites Matthew's Gospel around 8,000 times, Mark's Gospel 650 times, Luke's Gospel 3,000 times, and John's Gospel 5,000 times. Her statistics are based on the *Biblia Patristica: Index des citations et allusions bibliques dans la litterature patristique*, 6 vols. (Paris: CNRS Editions, 1975–1995). The *Biblia Patristica* is an inventory of every potential reference to the biblical books in Greek and Latin Christian writers. There are more rigorous methodologies for detecting intertextual references to these Gospels in Helmut Köster, *Synoptische Überlieferung bei den apostolischen Vätern* (TU, 65; Berlin: Akedemie-Verlag, 1957); Donald A. Hagner, "The Sayings of Jesus in the Apostolic Fathers and Justin Martyr" in *Gospel Perspectives, Volume 5: The Jesus Tradition Outside the Gospels* (ed. David Wenham; Sheffield: JSOT, 1984), 233–68; Christopher Tuckett, *Nag Hammadi and the Gospel Tradition: Synoptic Tradition in the Nag Hammadi Library* (Edinburgh: T&T Clark, 1986); Wolf-Dietrich Köhler, *Die Rezeption des Matthäusevangeliums in der Zeit vor Irenäus* (Tübingen: Mohr Siebeck, 1987); Édouard Massaux, *The Influence of the Gospel of Saint Matthew on Christian Literature before St. Irenaeus* (3 vol.; trans. Norman J. Belval and Suzanne Hechte; ed. Arthur J. Bellinzoni. Macon: Mercer University Press, 1990); Titus Nagel, *Die Rezeption des Johannesevangeliums im 2. Jahrhundert: Studien zur vorirenäischen Auslegung des vierten Evangeliums in christlicher und christlich-gnostischer Literatur* (ABG 2; Leipzig: Evangelische Verlagsanstalt, 2000); Andrew Gregory, *The Reception of Luke and Acts in the Period before Irenaeus* (WUNT, 2.169; Tübingen: Mohr Siebeck, 2003); Charles E. Hill, *The Johannine Corpus in the Early Church* (Oxford: Oxford University Press, 2004); Andrew Gregory and Christopher Tuckett, eds., *The Reception of the New Testament in the Apostolic Fathers* (Oxford: Oxford University Press, 2005); Stephen E. Young, *Jesus Tradition in the Apostolic Fathers: Their Explicit Appeals to the Words of Jesus in Light of Orality Studies* (WUNT 2.311; Tübingen: Mohr Siebeck, 2011). While these studies have stricter methodologies, they do not undercut the main point that the Gospel of Matthew was the most referenced Gospel in the early patristic period.

27. Schildgen, *Power*, 39–41.

28. E. P. Sanders and Margaret Davies, *Studying the Synoptic Gospels* (London: SCM, 1989), 14.

Two verses about the tax collector Matthew became the foundation on which the entire patristic edifice about the authorship of the so-called Gospel of Matthew was built. There may have been no intent to signal that Matthew was the author of this Gospel, or one of its sources, behind the evangelist's placement of Matthew at the tollbooth. No one may have construed these two verses as the evangelist's self-reference before Papias, the early second-century bishop of Hierapolis in Asia Minor. His tradition about the evangelist Matthew was also formulated in reaction to an older tradition about the evangelist Mark. Neither authorial traditions were suddenly embraced by every Christian across the Roman Empire, many of whom continued to read the Gospels as anonymous writings. Some time elapsed before the majority of them were persuaded that Matthew was a Gospel writer. The consensus about the names of all four evangelists was finally solidified at the same time when an authoritative canon or sacred collection of four Gospels was taking shape. Papias's notion that Matthew had composed his Gospel in his native language before it was translated into Greek had a significant impact on the reception of Matthew's Gospel as well. It even caused some fourth-century Christians to mistake another work known as the *Gospel According to the Hebrews* as either an earlier edition or a later corruption of the text of Matthew's Gospel. Deconstructing these authorial traditions about the evangelist Matthew may have theological ramifications. It may be naïve to think that there are no theological stakes involved in the decision to either uphold the traditional authorship of the Gospel or not. Ultimately, the identification of the human author of this historical account of the life of Jesus need not have any bearing on its scriptural authority for communities of faith.

❧ 1 ❧

THE APOSTLE AT THE TOLLBOOTH

THERE IS A stable core to the short story about the tax collector who quit his dishonest trade after encountering Jesus in the Gospels of Matthew, Mark, and Luke.[1] He was seated at his tollbooth when Jesus saw him and invited him to "follow me." Instantly, he rose out of his seat and followed Jesus. The scene is similar to the calling of the apostles Peter, Andrew, James, and John.[2] They were casting their fishing nets into the sea when Jesus beckoned them to participate in his mission of fishing for people. They dropped everything that they were doing; James and John even ditched their father Zebedee in their boat. They were drawn to Jesus's personal magnetism. Where the Gospels of Mark and Luke differ from the Gospel of Matthew is that they do not conflate the tax collector Levi with the apostle Matthew.[3]

This apparent discrepancy is crucial to the debate over the traditional authorship of the Gospel of Matthew. If Matthew was the evangelist, then he may have been drawing the readers' attention to his own participation in the story. If Matthew was one of the evangelist's informants, then the insertion of him into this episode may have functioned like a footnote acknowledging him as a notable source. Oppositely, Matthew may have had nothing to do with this Gospel at any stage of its composition. Whoever was responsible for composing it may have known an oral or written tradition that is no longer extant, which designated Matthew as a tax collector. The specifics about the circumstances of his employment had long been forgotten. This may be why the decision was reached to replace Levi with Matthew at the tollbooth.

---

1. See Matt 9:9//Mark 2:13–14//Luke 5:27–28.
2. See Matt 4:18–22//Mark 1:16–20. The scene is creatively rewritten in Luke 5:1–11. Peter, astonished by the miraculous catch of fish, knelt before Jesus and urged him to leave him because he is a sinful man. An alternate version of the miraculous catch of fish appears in John 21:1–14, though it is set in the post-Easter period.
3. Note that Matt 10:3 reinforces the point that it was the apostle Matthew at the tollbooth by appending the words "the tax collector" to Matthew's name in the list of the twelve apostles.

Did This Tax Collector
Have Two Names?

There have been valiant efforts to resolve the ostensible contradiction over whether the tax collector was Levi or Matthew. One could appeal to the individuals in the New Testament who had a Jewish name and a Greek or Latin cognomen.[4] A famous example is Saul of Tarsus. According to the book of Acts, Saul was transformed from a persecutor of the adherents of "the way" to a proclaimer of Jesus. On his way to Damascus to carry out his persecution campaign there, Saul was stopped in his tracks by the risen Jesus appearing in a bright light. The popular misconception that Saul was newly christened as Paul after his "Damascus Road" experience is belied by his retention of the name Saul after his baptism.[5] The Latin *Paulus* may have been picked as a suitable cognomen because of its sound-equivalence to his Hebrew name.[6] As an analogy for why Saul was called Paul, Origen offered the example of the tax collector who had two names in the Gospels in his *Commentary on Romans*.[7] Ironically, Origen insisted that Levi was not an apostle when answering Celsus's insult about the disreputable character of the apostles.[8] Evidently his mind was not made up about whether or not Levi and Matthew were the same person. The flaw in Origen's analogy is that it was exceedingly rare, if not unparalleled, for Second Temple Jewish parents to give their children two popular Semitic names.[9]

---

4. See France, *Matthew*, 69, 69n.54; Morris, *Matthew*, 219; Robert H. Gundry, *Matthew: A Commentary on his Handbook for a Mixed Church Under Persecution*, 2nd ed. (Grand Rapids: Eerdmans, 1994), 166; Donald A. Hagner, *Matthew 1–13* (Dallas: Word, 1993), 238; Carson, *Matthew*, 224; Ben Witherington III, *Matthew* (Macon: Smyth & Helywys, 2006), 197. For a complete list of Jewish characters in the New Testament with a Greek or Latin cognomen, see Richard Bauckham, "Paul and Other Jews with Latin Names in the New Testament" in *The Jewish World Around the New Testament: Collected Essays I* (ed. Richard Bauckham; WUNT 233; Tübingen: Mohr Siebeck, 2008), 371–72.

5. See Acts 9:22, 24; 11:25, 30; 12:25; 13:1, 2, 7, 9.

6. Bauckham, "Paul," 373–78.

7. See Origen, *Comm. Rom.* praef.10.

8. See Origen, *Cels.* 1.62.

9. For the most popular Palestinian Jewish names from 330 BCE to 200 CE, see Tal Ilan, *Lexicon of Jewish Names in Late Antiquity: Part I: Palestine 330 BCE–200 CE* (TSAJ 91; Tübingen: Mohr Siebeck, 2002). Based on the data she has compiled, Richard Bauckham (*Jesus and the Eyewitnesses: The Gospels as Eyewitness Testimony*

Levi may have been given a new name by Jesus, a name that was an abbreviation of Mattaniah or Mattithiah and meant "gift of Yahweh."[10] This is analogous to when Jesus hailed Simon as the "rock."[11] Simon's nickname in Aramaic was *Kepha* and *Petros* (i.e., Peter) in Greek. There is a wordplay between Peter and the "bedrock" (*petra*) on which Jesus would build his "assembly" (*ekklēsia*).[12] There is no record, though, of Jesus bestowing a new name on Levi. The Gospel writers never capitalize on the theological significance of the name Matthew. More importantly, the author of

---

[2nd ed.; Grand Rapids: Eerdmans, 2017], 108–9) noted that Matthew was the ninth most popular name and Levi the seventeenth most popular. Other scholars have also noted that it is unlikely that the same Jewish individual would have two Semitic names. See J. P. Meier, *The Vision of Matthew: Christ, Church and Morality in the First Gospel* (New York: Paulist, 1978), 24; Luz, *Matthew 8–20*, 32, 32n.14. William L. Lane (*The Gospel of Mark*, [NICNT; Grand Rapids: Eerdmans, 1974], 100–101n.29) presents three names from Nabatean inscriptions—Honainu the son of Aba, who is surnamed Abdallahi; Martai, who is surnamed Zabdath; and Malku, who is surnamed Bashamah—as corroborative evidence that Levi may have been surnamed Matthew. Bauckham (*Jesus*, 109n.54) protests that these Nabatean inscriptions do not shed light on Second Temple Jewish naming practices. He isolates five examples from Ilan's lexicon that may be more relevant *comparanda*: Simon had the additional name Benaiah, Joseph had the additional name Zaboud, Judah had the additional name Addan or Annan, Petahiah had the additional name Mordecai, and Tehina had the additional name Eleazar (p. 109, 109n.56, n.57, n.58, n.59). None of them, in his estimation, can withstand critical scrutiny (p. 110). Simon may have been given an epithet meaning "builder," Joseph may have been a resident of Nabatea who took on a secondary Nabatean name, Petahiah may have been a nickname, and the examples of Judah and Tehina come from "late and unreliable sources."

10. Gundry, *Matthew*, 166; Hagner, *Matthew*, 238; Witherington III, *Matthew*, 197.

11. See Matt 16:18; John 1:42. Since Simon was previously introduced as "the one who is called" (*ho legomenos*) Peter in Matt 4:18, Robert H. Gundry contests the standard interpretation of Matt 16:18 as the moment when Jesus bequeathed this nickname on Simon after his confession of Jesus's messianic status. For Gundry, "there is no indication [in Matt 16:18] of a name-*giving*, only of a name-*recognizing*." See Robert H. Gundry, *Peter: False Disciple and Apostate According to Saint Matthew: Second Edition with Responses to Reviews* (Eugene: Wipf & Stock, 2018), 7n.2 (emphasis original).

12. See Matt 16:18. Gundry (*Peter*, 15–26), unpersuasively in my view, downplays the positive characterization of Peter in Matt 16:16–19. He contends that Peter only discovered the truth of Jesus's Christological identity through a divine revelation, which is why he was "blessed," and that it is Jesus's teaching rather than the person of Peter that is the "bedrock" of the "assembly." Moreover, he equates the keys of the kingdom of heaven to Jesus's teaching as well, so it is no more meaningful that Jesus handed these keys over to Peter than that the scribes and Pharisees had inherited keys, which they used to lock the entrance to the kingdom (23:13).

Matthew's Gospel had a habit of employing *legomenos* ("being called") with proper names,[13] while putting the article before *legomenos* with surnames or epithets.[14] The evangelist follows this pattern in introducing Matthew as a proper name rather than a nickname.[15]

Another explanation is that the tax collector may have been a Levite, but someone mistranslated the tribal name as the personal name Levi when translating an Aramaic source.[16] The priests were descendants of the tribe of Levi. If there were too many Levites officiating at the Jerusalem Temple, Matthew may have had to seek out other means to support his livelihood. His knowledge of his ancestral traditions may have been comprehensive, but he may have become embittered against the religious establishment.[17] This imaginative scenario does not work if the Levite was named in the hypothetical Aramaic source. Otherwise, the tax collector's tribal affiliation would not have been mixed up by a translator as his name.[18] Additionally, none of the lists of the apostles in the Gospels or in Acts ever tag Matthew as a Levite.[19] This is unlike how Joseph, surnamed Barnabas or "son of encouragement" due to his generosity, was identified as a Levite in Acts.[20] Finally, it would be quite unexpected for a Levite to opt to collect customs revenue in Galilee.

These are clever attempts to evade an apparent contradiction between the Gospels. Alas, they are ultimately unconvincing. The remaining option is that someone deliberately altered the name of the tax collector. To discover

---

13. See Matt 2:23; 9:9; 26:36; 27:16, 33.
14. See Matt 1:16; 4:18; 10:2; 26:3, 14.
15. See Rudolf Pesch, "Levi-Matthäus (Mc 2.14/Mt 9.9; 10.3). Ein Beitrag zur Lösung eines alten Problems" *ZNW* 59 (1968): 47; Luz, *Matthew* 8–20, 32n.13, n.21.
16. See W. F. Albright and C. S. Mann, *Matthew* (AB; Doubleday: New York, 1971), CLXXVIII; cf. Gundry, *Old Testament*, 183; Gundry, *Matthew*, 166; Witherington III, *Matthew*, 197; Powers, *Progressive Publication*, 51.
17. Albright and Mann, *Matthew*, clxxviii–clxxxiv. Goodspeed (*Matthew*, 7–8) argues that Levi was Matthew's alternative name signifying his tribal identity. Much more problematically, he infers that none of the evangelists put the name Levi on their list of the Twelve because it was "too deeply saturated in Judaism" and that Matthew avoided the name Levi in his Gospel because it reminded him of the religious heritage that he repudiated.
18. France, *Matthew*, 70.
19. See Matt 10:3; Mark 3:18; Luke 6:15; Acts 1:13.
20. See Acts 4:36.

whether Levi or Matthew was in the earliest source, it is necessary to subject the Gospels to a source-critical analysis. This requires a detour through the so called Synoptic Problem.[21]

Was Levi or Matthew in the Earliest Gospel?

The story of the tax collector in the Gospels of Matthew, Mark, and Luke is a great case study for displaying the similarities and differences between them. Mark's Gospel has the most detailed setup to the scene. Jesus ventured out to the Sea of Galilee where a crowd flocked to him. After teaching them, he strolled alongside the lake when he came across Levi, the son of Alphaeus, at a tollbooth.[22] The Gospels of Matthew and Luke have fewer details about the setting and do not name the tollbooth operator's father, but some of their vocabulary echoes Mark's introduction to the scene.[23] In all three Gospels, Jesus saw an individual "sitting in the tollbooth" (*kathēmenon epi to telōnion*).[24] There is then a string of nine Greek words in the Gospels of Mark and Matthew that are identical to each other. The Greek line can be translated as follows: "and he says to him, 'Follow me!' And having gotten up, he followed him."[25] The wording of the parallel line in the Gospel of Luke is similar, but there is less verbatim agreement.[26] In all three Gospels, Jesus's invitation to the tax collector to "follow me" is preceded by his act of

---

21. The Synoptic Problem is relevant to the question of the authorship of Matthew's Gospel, despite the complaint of B. Ward Powers (*Progressive Publication*, 49) that "a view about Gospel sequence is not a valid reason for rejecting apostolic authorship." It matters whether Matthew was identified as the tax collector in the earliest source or was substituted for Levi at a secondary stage.
22. See Mark 2:13–14. The character is explicitly referred to as a tax collector (*telōnēs*) in Luke 5:27 and Matt 10:3.
23. There are verbal parallels with Mark 2:13–14. In Luke 5:27, Jesus "went out" (*exēlthen*) to see the tax collector. In Matt 9:9, Jesus was "passing by" (*paragōn*) when "he saw" (*eiden*) the tax collector.
24. See Matt 9:9; Mark 2:14; Luke 5:27.
25. See Mark 2:14; Matt 9:9. This is my wooden translation to show the verbatim agreement.
26. In Luke 5:27, the verb *eipen* ("he said") is in the aorist tense, not the present tense *legei* ("he says") that can be translated as a historic present. In Luke 5:28, the phrase "having left everything" (*katalipōn panta*) appears before "having gotten up" (*anastas*) and the verb *ēkolouthei* ("he was following") is in the imperfect tense.

healing a paralyzed man and followed by him fielding questions about the bad company that he dined with and his refusal to fast.[27]

The three evangelists were not independently rehashing their memories about what transpired on this day. If three students submitted essays that were as alike as these Gospels are to each other in their wording and structure, their professor would flag their essays for plagiarism.[28] The faithful preservation of the Jesus tradition in writing was a more pressing concern for the evangelists than signing their names and getting credit for their intellectual property. Their texts are grouped together as the "Synoptic" Gospels. The adjective "synoptic" is derived from the Greek *synoptikos,* meaning "seeing the whole together." There is extensive agreement in the wording and sequence of much of the "triple tradition" or the material common to the Gospels of Matthew, Mark, and Luke. At times the evangelists even have identical parenthetical asides. For example, the narrators in the Gospels of Mark and Matthew interrupt Jesus's apocalyptic speech on the Mount of Olives with the words "let the readers understand."[29] The "double tradition" consists of roughly 235 verses shared by the Gospels of Matthew and Luke that are not found in the Gospel of Mark. Lastly, each Synoptic Gospel has its own *Sondergut* or "special material" that is not paralleled in the other two Gospels.

The evangelists were either copying each other or common sources for their shared material. An academic consensus over the question of who was copying who remains as elusive as ever.[30] Most Christian intellectuals during

---

27. For the former miracle story, see Matt 9:1–8; Mark 2:1–12; Luke 5:17–26. For the latter scene, see Matt 9:10–17; Mark 2:15–22; Luke 5:29–39. There is extensive agreement in the order of the pericopes or textual units between Mark 1:21–3:19 and Luke 4:31–6:19. The sole exceptions are due to Luke relocating the call of the fishers (5:1–11; cf. Mark 1:16–20) and the summary about Jesus's healing activity (6:17–19; cf. Mark 3:7–12).
28. Mark Goodacre evokes the plagiarist's charter in his discussion on the literary relationship between the *Gospel of Thomas* and the Synoptic Gospels in his *Thomas and the Gospels: The Case for Thomas's Familiarity with the Synoptics* (Grand Rapids: Eerdmans, 2012), 54–56.
29. See Matt 24:15; Mark 13:14. Luke 21:20 omits the parenthetical aside and rewords the ambiguous oracle about a desecrating sacrilege to a clearer prediction about the Roman siege of Jerusalem.
30. The arguments in favor of different solutions to the Synoptic Problem are rehearsed in standard introductory textbooks on this topic. See, for instance, Sanders and Davies,

the patristic era were not so preoccupied with sorting out the precise lit-erary relationship between the Synoptic Gospels. What mattered to them was championing the apostolic origins of the Gospels. Augustine, the influ-ential fourth-century bishop of Hippo, underestimated Mark's contribution by demoting him to Matthew's epitomizer or abbreviator.[31] It was not an unbelievable proposition since over 90 percent of Mark's content is paralleled in the Gospel of Matthew. It is inconsistent, however, with the older patristic tradition that Mark got his information straight from the apostle Peter.[32]

By the eighteenth century, Augustine's hypothesis was displaced by the Two Gospel Hypothesis as the leading solution to the Synoptic Problem.[33] Mark's Gospel was deemed a later abridgement or conflation of the Gospels of Matthew and Luke. There may be precedent for this model in an excerpt quoted from a lost text entitled *Hypotyposes* or *Outlines* by Clement of Alexandria, a Christian philosopher who lived between 150 and 215 CE.[34]

Studying, 51–119; Robert Stein, *Studying the Synoptic Gospels: Origin and Interpretation* (2nd ed. Grand Rapids: Baker Academic, 2001), 49–172; Mark Goodacre, *The Synoptic Problem: A Way through the Maze* (London: T&T Clark, 2001).

31. See Augustine, *Con. Evan.* 1.2.4. For modern upholders of the Augustinian solution, see B. C. Butler, *The Originality of St Matthew: A Critique of the Two Document Hypoth-esis* (Cambridge: Cambridge University Press, 1951); Wenham, *Redating*, 11–115.

32. See Eusebius, *H.E.* 3.39.15. For reflection on the tension between the conflicting tradi-tions that Mark was Peter's interpreter or Matthew's abbreviator, see Schildgen, *Power*, 35–36; Michael J. Kok, *The Gospel of the Margins: The Reception of Mark in the Second Century* (Minneapolis: Fortress, 2015), 3.

33. The Two Gospel Hypothesis has also been called the Griesbach Hypothesis after the name of its formulator Johann Jakob Griesbach (1745–1854). See Bernard Orchard and Thomas R. W. Longstaff, *J. J. Griesbach: Synoptic and Text-Critical Studies 1776–1976* (Cambridge: Cambridge University Press, 1978), 74–135. Some proponents of the Two Gospel Hypothesis include William R. Farmer, *The Synoptic Problem: A Critical Analysis* (Dillsboro: Western North Carolina Press, 1976); Orchard and Riley, *The Order of the Synoptics*; William R. Farmer, *The Gospel of Jesus: The Pastoral Relevance of the Synoptic Problem* (Louisville: Westminster John Knox, 1994); David Laird Dungan, *A History of the Synoptic Problem: The Canon, the Text, the Composition, and the Interpretation of the Gospels* (New York: Doubleday, 1999); Allan J. McNichol, David L. Dungan, and David B. Peabody, *Beyond the Q Impasse: Luke's Use of Matthew: A Demonstration by the Research Team of the International Institute for Gospel Studies* (Philadelphia: Trinity Press International, 1996); Allan J. McNichol, David L. Dungan, and David B. Peabody, *One Gospel from Two: Mark's Use of Matthew and Luke: A Demonstration by the Research Team of the International Institute for Gospel Studies* (Philadelphia: Trinity Press Interna-tional, 2002); Powers, *Progressive Publication*.

34. See Eusebius, *H.E.* 6.14.5–7. Farmer, *The Synoptic Problem*, 226; Orchard and Riley, *The Order*, 164.

Clement may have held that the Gospels "to have been written first" (*pro-gegraphthai*) were the ones that started with the genealogies of Jesus's ancestors.[35] If the preposition *pro* in the compound word *prographō* is taken in a locative sense, Clement may have actually meant that the Gospels of Matthew and Luke were "written before the public" or "set forth publicly."[36] Mark, Clement alleged, produced a draft of Peter's preaching at the request of those who had listened to Peter in Rome. He did not anticipate that his rough draft would be publicly distributed beyond this intended audience.[37] Clement's learned successor, Origen, took it for granted that the Gospels were arranged in the New Testament in the chronological order in which they were published.[38]

Treating the Gospel of Mark as an abbreviated version of the Gospel of Matthew, or a conflated version of the Gospels of Matthew and Luke, does not do justice to the fact that its individual episodes are frequently more detailed than their Synoptic counterparts. After all, it is Mark's Gospel that has the longest introduction about Jesus strolling along the lake and educating the crowds in the triple tradition about the tax collector.[39] Mark's

---

35. See Matt 1:1–17; Luke 3:23–38.
36. See Stephen C. Carlson, "Clement of Alexandria on the 'Order' of the Gospels" *NTS* 47 (2001): 122–23. Francis Watson (*Gospel Writing: A Canonical Perspective* [Grand Rapids: Eerdmans, 2013], 432–34) reaffirms the temporal meaning of *prographō*, arguing that Clement dated the publication of the Gospels of Matthew and Luke before John got around to composing his Gospel "last" (*eschaton*) of all (*H.E.* 6.14.5, 7). Watson thinks that Eusebius interpolated an extended note about the origin of Mark's Gospel from Clement's commentary on 1 Peter into the eighth book of Clement's *Hypotyposes*, wrecking Clement's original comparison between the Gospels reporting "the bodily facts" (*ta sōmatika*) with John's "spiritual gospel" (*pneumatikon euangelion*). Eusebius, however, claims that the entire passage was derived from Clement's *Hypotyposes*. Carlson's translation has the merit of holding the whole passage together as an interconnected account.
37. Kok, *The Gospel*, 210–11. Margaret Mitchell ("Patristic Counter-Evidence to the Claim that "The Gospels Were Written for all Christians'" *NTS* 51 [2005], 50n.42, 51) classifies Clement's report of the circumstances that lead to the production of Mark's Gospel as an "audience request tradition."
38. See Eusebius, *H.E.* 6.25.4–6. Carlson, "Clement of Alexandria," 119–20.
39. Some Two Gospel theorists have pointed out that Mark 2:13–14 is filled with Markan vocabulary and may be a redactional addition to the earlier accounts in Matt 9:9 and Luke 5:27–28. See Farmer, *The Gospel*, 137–38; McNichol, Dungan, and Peabody, *One Gospel*, 103–4. However, it may be more likely that the authors of Matt 9:9 and

Gospel has lots of unparalleled, vivid details such as Jesus's emotional states[40] and Aramaic expressions.[41] It even specifies the color of the grass when Jesus multiplied food for a crowd exceeding five thousand people.[42] If it was the earliest rather than the latest Synoptic text, it is easy to see why these trivial details were omitted in the Gospels of Matthew and Luke. It is also easy to see why a few of Mark's stories were excluded from the other two Gospels altogether. Take Mark's account of the two-stage healing of a blind man.[43] After Jesus spat in his hands and touched the blind man's eyes, the man was not instantaneously healed. People looked to him like walking trees. Jesus touched his eyes a second time and his sight was fully restored. Mark's Gospel may have been making a profound point about the partial sight of Jesus's fallible followers, metaphorically speaking, but this moral was not comprehended by the latter two evangelists who left the story out of their Gospels.

Mark's Gospel was like an initial draft that was updated and refined by the evangelists behind the Gospels of Matthew and Luke. They reproduced most of its content, often in the same sequence, and improved its grammar. They edited out its excessive use of the phrase "and immediately." They supplemented its outline from the baptism of Jesus to the empty tomb with the material about Jesus's miraculous birth, ethical exhortations, and resurrection appearances.[44] If Mark's Gospel was the last Synoptic Gospel to be written, its exclusion of all of this valuable content from the Gospels of Matthew and Luke, along with its inclusion of enigmatic episodes such as the two-stage healing of a blind man, is hard to explain. Markan priority, the theory that the Gospel of Mark was the source for the Gospels of Matthew and Luke, is more feasible than either Matthean or Lukan priority.

Luke 5:27–28 were dependent on Mark 2:13–14, yet cut out the extraneous Markan details that were superfluous to the main point of the story.

40. See Mark 1:41; 3:5.
41. See Mark 3:17; 5:41; 7:11, 34; 14:36.
42. See Mark 6:39.
43. See Mark 8:22–25.
44. See the infancy narratives in Matt 1:1–2:23 and Luke 1:5–2:39, the Sermon on the Mount or Plains in Matt 5:1–7:29 and Luke 6:20–49, and the resurrection appearances in Matt 28:9–10, 16–20 and Luke 24:13–51.

The Synoptic Problem is pertinent to ascertaining why the names of select minor characters were changed from one Gospel to another.[45] Zeroing in on the triple tradition, the Gospels of Matthew and Luke agree against Mark's Gospel in omitting the names of Bartimaeus,[46] Alexander, Rufus,[47] and Salome.[48] The name Jairus is absent in Matthew's Gospel as well.[49] In addition to the disagreement about the tax collector's name, the Gospels of Mark and Matthew disagree about whether one character's name should be spelled Joses or Joseph.[50] A whole cast of characters is featured in Luke's special material, including Zechariah, Elizabeth, Simeon, Anna, Simon, Joanna, Susanna, Martha, Mary, Zacchaeus, and Cleopas.[51] In one instance, two unnamed characters in Mark's Gospel are identified as Peter and John in Luke's Gospel,[52] but this is not the same thing as introducing new characters.[53] How might different solutions to the Synoptic Problem handle this data? Augustine's deduction that Mark was Matthew's abbreviator does not square with Mark naming characters that Matthew kept anonymous. The Two Gospel Hypothesis may account for why Mark eliminated Luke's unparalleled named characters when conflating the Gospels of Matthew and Luke. It does not account for why Mark added more detail in naming nameless characters in triple tradition passages. On the supposition of Markan priority, there is an evident trajectory toward the elimination of names when moving from the earlier to the later Gospels in triple tradition passages. This does not discount the evidence that other sources were available to the author of Luke's Gospel that had named characters.[54]

Some characters in Mark's Gospel may have been omitted in the Gospels of Matthew and Luke because the authors or their readers were unacquainted with them.[55] Alexander and Rufus, the sons of Simon of Cyrene

---

45. The following data is brilliantly examined in Bauckham, *Jesus*, 39–66.
46. See Matt 9:27–31; Luke 18:35–42 (contra Mark 10:46).
47. See Matt 27:32; Luke 23:26 (contra Mark 15:21).
48. See Matt 27:56; 28:1; Luke 23:49; 24:10 (contra Mark 15:40; 16:1).
49. See Matt 9:18 (contra Mark 5:22; Luke 8:41).
50. Compare Mark 6:3 and 15:40 with Matt 13:55 and 27:56.
51. See Luke 1:5; 2:25, 36; 7:40, 43, 44; 8:3; 10:38, 39, 40, 41, 42; 19:2, 5, 8; 24:18.
52. See Mark 14:13; Luke 22:8.
53. Bauckham, *Jesus*, 42.
54. Bauckham, *Jesus*, 42, 43.
55. Bauckham, *Jesus*, 50; cf. Pesch, "Levi—Matthäus," 53.

who carried Jesus's cross, were left out on the cutting-room floor. Salome saw Jesus hanging on the cross from a distance and went to the tomb to anoint his corpse in Mark's Gospel.[56] She may have been relatively unknown by the time Matthew's Gospel was written, so she was swapped with the mother of James and John.[57] This was not the sole appearance of this mother in Matthew's Gospel. Earlier in it, she entreated Jesus to let her two sons sit at his right and left hands when he is enthroned as king.[58] In Mark's Gospel, it was the sons of Zebedee themselves who dared to make this audacious request.[59] The Gospel of Matthew subtly lifts the blame off the shoulders of the apostles James and John and loads it onto their mother. The key take-away is that there are two examples in Matthew's Gospel where one character is substituted for another in passages taken over from Mark's Gospel. Levi is swapped with Matthew at the tollbooth and Salome with the mother of James and John as one of the witnesses of Jesus's crucifixion.[60]

If Matthew's Gospel was the first one to be written, there would need to be some justification for why Levi was substituted for Matthew in the Gospels of Mark and Luke.[61] It might be understandable if there was some

---

56. See Mark 15:40; 16:1.

57. See Matt 27:56.

58. See Matt 20:20.

59. See Mark 10:35.

60. Pesch, "Levi-Matthäus," 54–55. Gundry (*Matthew*, 166) protests that Matt 20:20 is not an exact parallel to Matt 9:9 because, unlike the tax collector, the mother is kept anonymous.

61. Curiously, this is often not identified as a problem needing to be solved. When dealing with the passages, Butler (*The Originality*, 153) just turns to the use of *legomenos* ("being named") in Matt 9:9 as an example of an Aramaism. Farmer (*The Synoptic Problem*, 238; *The Gospel*, 136–38) notes that Mark 2:13–14 both expanded and conflated Matt 9:9 and Luke 5:27–28 without a clear preference for either passage, but this does not explicate why Mark 2:13–14 followed Luke 5:27 rather than Matt 9:9 in keeping the name Levi. In their source-critical analysis of Luke's Gospel from the perspective of the Two Gospel Hypothesis, McNichol, Dungan, and Peabody note that the tax collector Levi in Luke 5:27 is not conflated with the apostle Matthew in Luke 6:15. They comment that the author of Luke 5:27 replaced Matthew with Levi "to prevent confusion for his readers" (cf. McNichol, Dungan, and Peabody, *Beyond*, 97), but it would have been far less confusing if the author stuck with Matt 9:9 as his or her source by keeping Matthew at the tollbooth. In their second volume on Markan posterity (cf. McNichol, Dungan, and Peabody, *One Gospel*, 104), they add that the expansion of the name Levi with "son of Alphaeus" in Mark 2:14 is consistent with other supplementary details such as naming the blind man "Bartimaeus the son of Timaeus" (10:46) or noting that Simon of

embarrassment over the representation of an esteemed apostle as a collaborator with Herod Antipas in the oppression of his own people. Yet the Gospel of Mark does not hesitate to present the apostles in a bad light. It uniquely describes their hearts as hardened twice.[62] The Pharisaic opponents of Jesus are characterized as having this same heart condition.[63] Jesus rebukes Peter for his satanic resistance to his divinely-ordained mission of suffering.[64] James and John misapprehended Jesus's mission, too, when they longed to sit on thrones.[65] The twelve disciples wanted to have an exclusive monopoly on exorcizing evil spirits in Jesus's name.[66] One of the Twelve betrays Jesus, another denies him, and they all run away in his hour of greatest need.[67] The author of Mark's Gospel would not have been fazed by an apostle's crooked past.

Tax collectors are also not vilified in the Gospels of Mark and Luke to the same extent that they are in Matthew's Gospel. There are triple and double tradition passages about Jesus's fellowship with tax collectors. Jesus was compared to a physician caring for the sick and earned a scandalous reputation for his friendship with "tax collectors and sinners."[68] The religious elites are contrasted with tax collectors who heeded John's demand for repentance when he was baptizing sinners in the wilderness.[69] Tax collectors are positively portrayed in Luke's special material. Some approached John to be baptized.[70] A tax collector's prayer of contrition is extolled in a parable.[71] The tax collector Zacchaeus was willing to repay anyone he defrauded after

---

Cyrene was "the father of Alexander and Rufus" (15:21). These are observations about what the authors of the Gospels of Mark and Luke have done given the premises of the Two Gospel Hypothesis, but they are not explanations for why they did so. Harold Riley, another proponent of the Two Gospel Hypothesis, admits that "it is not clear why he [Luke] substitutes the name 'Levi' for Matthew" (cf. Orchard and Riley, *The Order*, 55).

62. See Mark 6:52; 8:17.
63. See Mark 3:5; 10:5.
64. See Mark 8:33.
65. See Mark 10:35–45.
66. See Mark 9:38.
67. See Mark 14:43–45, 50–52, 66–72.
68. See Matt 9:10–12//Mark 2:15–17//Luke 5:29–32; Matt 11:19//Luke 7:34.
69. See Matt 21:31–32//Luke 7:29–30.
70. See Luke 3:12–13.
71. See Luke 18:9–14.

Jesus announced his intention of visiting his home.[72] Mark and Luke would not have necessarily been embarrassed by the presence of a former tax collector among the twelve apostles. It is the special material in the Gospel of Matthew that is hostile toward tax collectors.[73] This includes a "church rule" advising Jesus's disciples to spurn an excommunicated member from their Jewish "assembly" like a tax collector or a non-Jew.[74] This coupling of tax collectors and non-Jews occurs earlier in the Matthean version of a double tradition saying; the parallel saying in Luke's Gospel just speaks about sinners in general.[75] In the saying in its Matthean form, Jesus reminds his audience that it is hardly impressive if they love those who reciprocate their affections, for even tax collectors are capable of loving those who love them in return. Likewise, Matthew's Gospel pairs tax collectors and prostitutes, a pairing missing from the parallel verses in Luke's Gospel.[76]

Given the greater likelihood that Mark's Gospel was the earliest Synoptic Gospel, it may seem shocking that it was in the Gospel of Matthew that the tax collector Levi was reidentified as the apostle Matthew. This seems to cut against the grain of the evangelist's editorial tendency to paint tax collectors as outsiders to the righteous assembly. This may be evidence that

---

72. See Luke 19:1–10.

73. For my analysis of the negative treatment of tax collectors in Matthew's Gospel, see Michael J. Kok, "Re-naming the Toll Collector in Matthew 9:9: A Review of the Options" *JGAR* 4 (2020): 30–31.

74. See Matt 18:16–17. Since Matt 18:15 is paralleled in Luke 17:3, it is possible that the entirety of Matt 18:15–17 was taken over from Q, the hypothetical source of the double tradition. See W. D. Davies and Dale C. Allison, *A Critical and Exegetical Commentary on The Gospel According to Saint Matthew. Volume II: Introduction and Commentary on Matthew VIII—XVII* (ICC; Edinburgh: T&T Clark, 1991), 781. Alternatively, Matt 18:16–17 could have been taken from an earlier church rule in M, the hypothetical source of the special material in Matthew's Gospel. See Luz, *Matthew 8–20*, 448–50. Finally, Matt 18:16–17 may be a redactional creation by the evangelist. See Gundry, *Matthew*, 367–68. Irrespective of whether the ruling in Matt 18:15–17 stemmed from an earlier source or not, the evangelist evidently endorsed this excommunication procedure.

75. See Matt 5:46–47//Luke 6:32–34. Davies and Allison (*Matthew I–VII*, 557–58) and Luz (*Matthew 1–7*, 345) judge that the pairing of "tax collectors" and "sinners" in Matt 5:46–47 preserves Q's wording, which was generalized as "sinners" in Luke 6:32. Conversely, Gundry (*Matthew*, 99) judges that "sinners" was original and that the insertion of "tax collectors" in Matt 5:46–47 is in line with the author's distinct interest in this group.

76. See Matt 21:31–32//Luke 7:29–30.

the evangelist had heard about Matthew's ignoble occupation and had to deal with it in some way.[77] It should not be overlooked that the evangelist retained Jesus's declaration that tax collectors and prostitutes were entering the kingdom ahead of the Judean religious aristocracy because they believed the Baptizer's dire threats of divine judgment.[78] The primary purpose of this saying was to shame Jesus's detractors by castigating them as worse than the persons ostracized from polite society. The secondary point is that outsiders can become insiders through repentance. This Gospel boldly proves this point by turning an illustrious apostle into a paradigmatic rehabilitated sinner.

Why Was the Name Changed?

The tax collector could have been renamed in the Gospel of Matthew for any number of reasons.[79] If the evangelist was Matthew, he may have been putting his own signature in the Gospel. This is the traditional position. If Matthew was not the author, he could have been a major source of some of the material contained in this Gospel or the founder of a community of Christ-believers in the evangelist's geographical locale.[80] In this case, the insertion of Matthew into a noteworthy scene was designed to shine a spotlight on him. If this Gospel was forged in Matthew's name as a pseudonym, these two verses could have been devised at the same time to reinforce this authorial fiction.[81] If Matthew had nothing to do with the composition of the Gospel or its sources, there may have been literary reasons for drawing the readers' attention to him as a character in the narrative. The non-apostolic

---

77. Kok, "Re-Naming," 30.
78. See Matt 21:31–32//Luke 7:29–30.
79. The theories recounted in this paragraph are summarized by Davies and Allison, *Matthew VIII—XVII*, 98–99.
80. See Pesch, "Levi—Matthäus," 56; Gundry, *The Use*, 184; David Hill, *The Gospel of Matthew* (Grand Rapids: Eerdmans, 1972), 53–54, 173; Davies and Allison, *Matthew VIII—XVIII*, 2.99; Hagner, *Matthew 1–13*, xlvi; Warren Carter, *Matthew: Storyteller, Interpreter, Evangelist* (Peabody: Hendrickson, 2004), 23; John Nolland, *The Gospel of Matthew*, NIGTC (Grand Rapids: Eerdmans, 2005), 3–4; Witherington III, *Matthew*, 5, 29; Keener, *The Gospel of Matthew*, 40; Bauckham, *Jesus*, 111. For objections against this theory, see Meier, *The Vision of Matthew*, 25n.26; Luz, *Matthew 8–20*, 32.
81. See George D. Kilpatrick, *The Origins of the Gospel according to St. Matthew* (Oxford: Clarendon, 1946),138–39.

Levi may have been swapped for the apostle Matthew if the group of disciples in Jesus's lifetime was deliberately restricted to the twelve apostles in this Gospel.[82] The evangelist may have relished the opportunity to make a pun between the name Matthew and the Greek noun *mathētēs* ("disciple").[83] Levi's call narrative may have been transferred over to Matthew because there was a vague recollection that the apostle used to be employed as a customs agent for the political authorities too.[84] The list of potential explanations could go on and on.

Each of these competing theories seeks to uncover the authorial intention behind the replacement of Levi with Matthew. What if it was not the evangelist but a scribal copyist, who changed the names? The following scenario for how Levi could have been altered to Matthew in the scribal transmission of the Gospel of Matthew can be tested.[85] Levi and the second James in the list of the twelve apostles were each designated as the "son of Alphaeus" in Mark's Gospel.[86] A scribe may have misjudged this to be an error and replaced Levi with James at the tollbooth in order to have a single son of Alphaeus.[87] Another copyist of the Gospel of Matthew may have then come across this variant reading in the Gospel of Mark. As a result, this scribe scribbled in "the tax collector" (*ho telōnēs*) as a note in the margins before the name of James, the son of Alphaeus, in the list of the twelve apostles in Matthew's Gospel. When this Gospel was subsequently recopied, this marginal note was mistaken as a reference to Matthew, the name immediately preceding James. Copyists of the Gospels of Mark or Luke would not have made the exact same mistake, for Thomas precedes James in their lists. Once a scribe got the wrong impression that Matthew

---

82. See Pesch, "Levi—Matthäus," 40–56.

83. See Mark Kiley, "Why 'Matthew' in Matt 9:9–13" *Biblica* 65.3 (1984): 347–51; Carter, *Matthew*, 23–24; Jean-Pierre Sonnet, "Matthieu, disciple (Maththaios, mathētēs) d'une langue à l'autre" *NRT* 143.4 (2021): 535–38.

84. See Luz, *Matthew 8–20*, 32; Bauckham, *Jesus*, 111; Kok, "Re-naming," 30–31.

85. The following reconstruction in this paragraph was developed by Benjamin Bacon, *Studies in Matthew* (New York: Henry Holt 1930), 39–40.

86. See Mark 2:14; 3:18. Goodspeed (*Matthew*, 6) surmises that Levi and James were brothers. On the other hand, Bauckham (*Jesus*, 87n.17) posits that there were two different men named Alphaeus.

87. See Mark 2:14 (D Θ f¹³ 565 it). Lindars ("Matthew," 222) explains that this textual variant arose out of "the scribe's desire for uniformity."

was marked as "the tax collector" in the list in the Gospel of Matthew, the next step was to rewrite the scene about Levi and put Matthew at the tollbooth in his place.[88] The Achilles' heel of this complex reconstruction is that there is no textual evidence for a manuscript of the Gospel of Matthew that had Levi at the tollbooth. Such a modification would need to have happened early enough for there to be no trace of it whatsoever in the textual tradition. For this hypothesis to work, the textual variant in a small handful of manuscripts that had James at the tollbooth in Mark's Gospel must be dated earlier still. However, this western reading does not surface in a manuscript until the copying of Codex Bezae, a fifth-century uncial manuscript of the New Testament.

It was the evangelist, not a scribal copyist, who situated Matthew at the tollbooth. The theory that Matthew was the evangelist and was making a self-reference in this chapter is hard to square with the standard solution to the Synoptic Problem, namely Markan priority. It seems incredible that Matthew, an apostle and eyewitness of Jesus, would have relied so heavily on a biography of his teacher penned by a non-apostle and a non-eyewitness. If the tradition that Mark was Peter's interpreter has any validity, then Matthew's dependence on Mark's Gospel may be explainable due to its preservation of the eyewitness recollections of Peter, the preeminent apostle.[89] It stretches credulity to believe that Matthew declined to share his own recollections about the time that he spent with Jesus and tried to pass off Levi's call narrative as his own. Apart from one reworked story obtained from the Gospel of Mark, Matthew has no more of a role in the Gospel of Matthew than the rest of the apostles. This makes it further unlikely that the anonymous author of this Gospel had any level of personal acquaintance with Matthew at all, much less had access to traditions that he handed down.[90] There might be a clue to the Syrian provenance of the Gospel in the summary statement that Jesus's fame spread throughout Syria.[91] Whether the apostle Matthew

---

88. Bacon, *Studies*, 39–40.
89. The origins of this tradition will be reviewed in chapter two. This argument is common among Markan prioritists who, nevertheless, defend the Patristic traditions about the authorship of the Gospels. See Goodspeed, *Matthew*, 15; France, *Matthew*, 73–74; Gundry, *Matthew*, 621–22; Carson, *Matthew*, 18.
90. Luz, *Matthew 8–20*, 32.
91. See Matt 4:24; contra Mark 1:28.

stepped foot in the Roman provenance of Syria or its capital in Antioch is unknowable.[92]

The title *Gospel According to Matthew* was almost certainly a secondary addition to an anonymous text. It is misleading, then, to brand this Gospel as a pseudonymous work.[93] A distinction must be made between conscious forgeries and the misattribution of anonymous works.[94] The *Gospel of Peter* may serve as a counterexample. Its utilization of the first-person pronoun gives the impression that one is reading about the events of the passion narrative through the perspective of Simon Peter.[95] There is an intriguing tidbit about a Christian congregation in Rhossus in Syria that was positively disposed toward the *Gospel of Peter*. Serapion, the bishop of Antioch (ca. 191–211 CE), initially gave them permission to study this Gospel.[96] Once Serapion had the opportunity to delve into the *Gospel of Peter* in more depth, he began to have serious reservations about its theology. He came to the decision that it must have been falsely ascribed to Peter, for the apostle, in Serapion's judgment, would not lead his flock astray into false teachings. Why this is relevant to the discussion about whether the Gospel of Matthew is a pseudonymous work or not is that Matthew as a character in the text never speaks in the first person. The reader does not get the impression that Matthew was narrating the events in the Gospel.

There is no explicit notice within the Gospel of Matthew that Matthew wrote anything about Jesus. Its silence about Matthew's status as an evangelist can be compared to the notice in the Johannine epilogue that an unnamed "disciple whom Jesus loved" was "the one who wrote these things" (*ho grapsas tauta*).[97] A straightforward interpretation of this verse is that the beloved disciple is credited as the author of a prior edition of the Gospel of John.[98] A group of editors probably affixed the epilogue

---

92. Meier, *The Vision*, 25n.26.
93. Contra Kilpatrick, *The Origins*, 138–39. See the survey about the origins of the Gospel titles in chapter four.
94. Bart D. Ehrman, *Forgery and Counterforgery: The Use of Literary Deceit in Early Christian Polemics* (Oxford: Oxford University Press, 2013), 43–67.
95. See *Gos Pet* 7:26–27; 14:59–60.
96. This anecdote is related in Eusebius, *H.E.* 6.12.1–6.
97. See John 21:24.
98. Analogously, John 19:19 states that Pilate "wrote" (*egrapsen*) the titulus posted on the cross when he really had his secretaries do this job for him. This would still mean that the beloved

at the end of this Gospel after its original conclusion.[99] They referred to themselves with the first-person plural pronoun "we" and verified the truthfulness of the beloved disciple's testimony in the previous chapters.[100] They dispelled a rumor that Jesus promised that the beloved disciple would live until he returned, likely because the beloved disciple had died by the time they attached the epilogue to the Gospel.[101] Unlike the Gospel of

---

disciple dictated to an amanuensis who penned the Gospel. See Bauckham, *Jesus*, 359–63. Chris Keith points to a parallel in Esth 8:8 LXX, where the Persian emperor Artaxerxes authorizes Esther and Mordecai to produce a draft of his edict and seal it with his ring. See Chris Keith, *The Gospel as Manuscript: An Early History of the Jesus Tradition as Material Artifact* (Oxford: Oxford University Press, 2020), 134n.15, 135.

99. See John 20:30–31. The best case that the epilogue is a secondary addition is in Armin Baum, "The Original Epilogue (John 20:30–31), the Secondary Appendix (21:1–23), and the Editorial Epilogues (21:24–25) of John's Gospel. Observations against the Background of Ancient Literary Conventions" in *Earliest Christian History: History, Literature, and Theology. Essays from the Tyndale Fellowship in Honor of Martin Hengel* (ed. Michael F. Bird and Jason Maston; WUNT 2.320; Tübingen: Mohr Siebeck, 2012), 227–70. In my book on the beloved disciple, I contend that this character was an elite Judean follower of Jesus who mingled with the aristocratic high priest (cf. John 18:15–16). He appears at key moments in the passion narrative to witness Jesus's prediction of Judas's betrayal (cf. 13:23–25), Peter's denials in the high priest's courtyard (cf. 18:15–16), Jesus's crucifixion (cf. 19:26–27, 35), and Peter's discovery of the empty tomb (cf. 20:2–10). Because the beloved disciple seemed to be distinct from the narrator who validated his testimony in John 19:35, I argued that the editors who added the epilogue were the first to pseudonymously credit the whole Gospel to the beloved disciple because he was the most important witness narrated in the text. See Michael J. Kok, *The Beloved Apostle? The Transformation of the Apostle John into the Fourth Evangelist* (Eugene: Cascade, 2017), 1–29, 30, 43–50. I am open to a second option. The fourth evangelist may have inserted himself into the scenes that he witnessed but, to maintain the account's anonymity, cryptically referred to himself in the third person as the "disciple whom Jesus loved." The later editors were less discreet in trumpeting the beloved disciple's status as the Gospel writer. Armin D. Baum argues that the references to the beloved disciple are autobiographical remarks in an otherwise anonymous work in "Autobiografische Wir- und Er-Stellen in den neutestamentlichen Geschichtsbüchern im Kontext der antiken Literaturgeschichte" *Biblica* 88 (2007): 493–94.

100. Baum, "The Original Epilogue," 258. Bauckham (*Jesus*, 370–81) counters that the beloved disciple was using the "we of authoritative testimony" in speaking about himself as the author of all twenty-one chapters of the Gospel. It would be grammatically awkward for the beloved disciple to refer to himself in both the third-person singular and the first-person plural in the same sentence in John 21:24. The "we" may be a genuine plural and the we-group who added the epilogue should be distinguished from the beloved disciple.

101. See John 21:22–23. For a list of commentators who argue that these verses signal that the beloved disciple had died, see Kok, *The Beloved Apostle*, 48n.71.

John in its final form and the *Gospel of Peter*, there are no authorial claims advanced in the Gospel of Matthew at all.

Literary explanations for Matthew's appearance at the tollbooth can also be explored. The author of the Gospel of Matthew may have restricted the disciples of Jesus during his ministry to the twelve apostles, necessitating that Levi could not have been one of his disciples.[102] The apostles as a collective group are distinctively called "the twelve disciples" in this Gospel.[103] The evangelist may have been motivated to upgrade the tax collector's rank to that of an apostle because his call to discipleship resembled the call of the first four apostles. Nonetheless, this theory may not be sustainable if there is at least one "disciple" in the Gospel of Matthew who was not a member of the Twelve. For instance, there was a potential "disciple" outside the circle of the Twelve who expressed his desire to bury his deceased father before he obeyed Jesus's summons to follow him.[104]

The best hypothesis needs to account for why Matthew, and not another random apostle, was chosen as a replacement for Levi.[105] It seems unsatisfactory to view the choice as a purely arbitrary decision.[106] Maybe Matthew was chosen because he had a Levitical-sounding name.[107] Mark's Gospel, however, does not accentuate the connection between the tax collector's name Levi and the eponymous ancestor of the Levites. Maybe Matthew was selected as a paradigmatic "learning disciple" because of the assonance between his name and the Greek noun *mathētēs* ("disciple"). When the Pharisees grilled Jesus about his table fellowship with the wrong crowd, his reply that they ought to "learn" (*mathete*) what the prophet Hosea taught about mercy is only found in the Gospel of Matthew.[108] The syllable *math* occurs

---

102. Pesch, "Levi-Matthäus," 50–53.
103. See Matt 10:1 (contra Mark 3:14; Luke 6:13); 11:1; 20:17 (contra Mark 10:32; Luke 18:31).
104. See Matt 8:21. Gundry, *Matthew*, 166; Carson, *Matthew*, 223–24; Luz, *Matthew 8–20*, 32n.16. Luke 9:59 just mentions "another one" (*heteros*) who was asking Jesus for permission to bury his father.
105. Pesch ("Levi-Matthäus," 56) resorts to the problematic theory that Matthew was the founder of a putative Matthean community to explain this choice.
106. Contra Meier, *The Vision*, 24–25.
107. See 1 Chr 9:31; 2 Chr 20:14. See Michael Goulder, *Midrash and Lection in Matthew* (London: SPCK, 1974), 325.
108. See Matt 9:13 (cf. Hos 6:6). See Kiley, "Why 'Matthew,'" 347–51; Sonnet, "Matthieu," 535–38.

at the beginning and end of the Gospel.[109] Matthan is Jesus's great-grandfather in his genealogy.[110] The Gospel closes with Jesus's command to his eleven apostles to "make disciples" (*mathēteusate*).[111] In the evangelist's self-estimate, he or she was one of the trained scribes "who was made a disciple" (*mathēteutheis*).[112] If this wordplay was intentional, it is not nearly as obvious as the pun between Simon's nickname Peter and the bedrock (*petra*) of the assembly that Jesus was building.[113] Similarly, the narrator explicitly deciphers the name Jesus as pertaining to Jesus's mission to save his people from their sins.[114] The evangelist never unpacks the theological symbolism inherent in the name Matthew.

The remaining theory for why Levi was exchanged with Matthew at the tollbooth is that the evangelist was informed by an oral or written source that is no longer extant that Matthew had worked in the same basic occupation as Levi. The highest bidders attained the rights to collect tolls. What kind of source may have been available to the evangelist? One option is that there were multiple lists of the twelve apostles floating around the early Christ congregations. This may be why there are minor variations in the ordering of the names, such as the order of Matthew and Thomas, and in the inclusion of either Thaddaeus or Judas the son of James in the different lists in the Synoptic Gospels and Acts.[115] Not all of these variations are explicable as redactional changes to the list in the Gospel of Mark. The author of the Gospel of Matthew might have known two lists, one from the Gospel of Mark and another from an unknown source that dubbed Matthew as "the tax collector." The evangelist may have had no prior knowledge about Matthew's former occupation before stumbling upon this note about him.

---

109. Sonnet, "Matthieu," 538–40.
110. See Matt 1:15.
111. See Matt 28:19.
112. Sonnet, "Matthieu," 542–44. See Matt 13:52.
113. Pesch, "Levi-Matthäus," 47; Luz, *Matthew 8–20*, 32n.13, n.21.
114. See Matt 1:21.
115. Thaddaeus is named in Matt 10:2–4 and Mark 3:16–19, while Judas the son of James is named in Luke 6:14–16 and Acts 1:13. Bauckham contends that the same individual bore the Semitic name Judas and the Greek name Thaddaeus (cf. *Jesus*, 100–101). If that is the case, there still may have been separate lists that included either his Semitic or his Greek name.

What Matthew once did for a living before he met Jesus may have been completely forgotten if the evangelist had not discovered some source that labeled him as "the tax collector." There are plenty of examples in Christian literature of epithets that are left unexplained because the writers who preserved them had no firsthand knowledge about why they were bestowed on certain figures in the first place. No other text besides the Gospel of Matthew clarifies why Simon was called the "rock." Mark offers no digression about why James and John were styled as the "sons of thunder."[116] Mary's sobriquet "the Magdalene" or "the Tower-ess" may signify her stature in the Jesus movement rather than the town of her origin,[117] but this is never elucidated in the Gospels. The conflicting rationales for why the evangelist Mark was remembered as "stump-fingered" —he had short fingers or amputated his fingers so that he would be disqualified from serving in the Jewish priesthood or the Christian episcopate—shows that everyone forgot the original meaning of this moniker.[118]

The evangelist may not have had firsthand knowledge about Matthew's backstory. Levi's backstory in the Gospel of Mark, however, could be adjusted to fit Matthew's prior situation.[119] It was an idealized scene that was shaped like a *chreia* or a short, pointed anecdote that drives home the message about the value of abandoning everything else for the sake of Jesus.[120] The setup to Jesus's climactic pronouncement to "follow me" is brief and stylized, so it was amenable to being reused as the backdrop for the call of another tax collector named Matthew.[121] The evangelist may not have needed to appropriate any more of Levi's backstory apart from the stereotypical features in the *chreia*. This might be why the Gospel of Matthew deletes the genitive pronoun *autou* ("his") after the words "in the house" (*en tē oikia*) in the very next verse taken over from the Gospel of Mark, for it was Levi, not Matthew, who owned a house in Capernaum.[122] Granted, the pronoun could have just

---

116. See Mark 3:17.
117. See Joan E. Taylor, "Missing Magdala and the Name of Mary Magdalene," *PEQ* 146.3 (2014): 205–23.
118. For further analysis, see J. L. North, "MARKOS HO KOLOBODAKTYLOS: Hippolytus, Elenchus, VII.30," *JTS* 29 (1977): 499–500; Kok, *The Gospel*, 221, 224–26.
119. Luz, *Matthew 8–20*, 32.
120. Sanders and Davies, *Studying*, 152–53.
121. Bauckham, *Jesus*, 111.
122. See Matt 9:10; contra Mark 2:15. See Bauckham, *Jesus*, 111.

been dropped because its antecedent was unclear, for it could be understood as referring back to either Levi or Jesus. In Luke's rewording, it is clearer that Levi is the subject who hosted a great feast at his house.[123] Still, it seems unlikely that Mark's readers did not take Levi to be the referent of the pronoun, for his homeownership was a sign of his relative wealth compared to a craftsman like Jesus. Regardless, the setting of the Markan *chreia* about the call of Levi was all that was needed for the author of the Gospel of Matthew to narrate the apostle Matthew's own call to discipleship.

The existence of a nonextant list of the twelve apostles that identified Matthew as a tax collector, or some other oral or written tradition about Matthew's occupation, is a hypothesis that merits further testing. If this conjecture is on the right track, there may be a genuinely historical memory about Matthew's past contained in the minimal descriptor "the tax collector." The evangelist made the most out of Matthew's dishonorable former way of life by turning him into a paradigm of the repentant sinner, borrowing Levi's call narrative from the Gospel of Mark to achieve this purpose. If this conjecture is found wanting, the mystery of why Levi was replaced with Matthew in the passage may remain unsolved. What the evangelist never says is that the apostle Matthew wrote this Gospel or any of its sources. The internal evidence within the text simply cannot be aligned with the external evidence concerning its authorship. It was not until the early second century that the Gospel came to be attributed to Matthew the tax collector.

---

123. See Luke 5:29. I came across this counterargument in Jason Engwer, "Richard Bauckham is Wrong about Matthew's Authorship" *Triablogue* (online at traiblogue.blogspot. com/2017/05/richard-bauckham-is-wrong-about.html). Accessed 13/11/2021.

2

THE CRITICISM OF MARK'S
UNORDERED NOTES

HISTORIANS SPECIALIZING IN the field of Christian origins bemoan how much ancient Christian literature has been lost to the dust of history. There are innumerable antique books that they might wish were recovered. The five-volume *Exposition of the Oracles of the Lord* by Papias, the bishop of Hierapolis in the early second century CE, may be near the top of the list. Papias was one of the few Christian authors in the crucial transitional period between the apostolic and post-apostolic eras. He was two or three steps removed from Jesus's disciples. He accumulated some interesting "facts" about them from the informants that he interviewed. He outlined his research methods in the prologue of his work as follows:

> *"But if anyone who had also followed the elders ever came along,*
> *I would examine the words of the elders—what did Andrew and*
> *what did Peter say, or what did Philip, or what did Thomas or*
> *James, or what did John or Matthew, or any other of the disciples*
> *of the Lord—and what Aristion and John the elder, disciples of the*
> *Lord, were saying."*[1]

Sadly, Papias's exposition only survives in fragmentary quotations from it or allusions to it in patristic and medieval literature.[2] The fourth-century

---

1. See Eusebius, *H.E.* 3.39.3. This translation is provided by Stephen Carlson, *Papias of Hierapolis Exposition of Dominical Oracles: The Fragments, Testimonia, and Reception of a Second Century Commentator* (Oxford: Oxford University Press, 2021), 141.
2. The most extensive collection of the alleged fragments from Papias's work and *testimonia* about his life can be found in Carlson, *Papias*, 111–337. Other collections lean either toward the maximalist or the minimalist end in what they count as fragments of Papias's work. See, for instance, William R. Schoedel, *The Apostolic Fathers, A New Translation and Commentary: Polycarp, Martyrdom of Polycarp, Fragments of Papias* (5 vol. ed. R. M. Grant; Camden: Thomas Nelson, 1967), 5.89–130; Josef Kürzinger, *Papias*

historian Eusebius of Caesarea extracted Papias's quotations about the evangelists Mark and Matthew from their original literary context(s) and placed them side by side in his *Ecclesiastical History*. The subject matter of Eusebius's magnum opus was the rise of the Christian movement from Christ to Constantine. He was keenly interested in the canonization of the Christian Scriptures, which is why he relayed Papias's knowledge of the Gospels of Mark and Matthew as well as two epistles ascribed to Peter and John.[3]

Eusebius credited one excerpt from Papias about Mark to the "elder" (*presbyteros*), most likely the second John in the quote above. The elder John asserted, "Mark, who had been Peter's interpreter, wrote what he remembered, yet not in order the things either said or done by the Lord."[4] This is supplemented by the concession that Mark had followed Peter, but not Jesus. In preserving Peter's public proclamations for posterity, Mark's singular concern was to neither omit nor falsify anything that he had heard from him. In other words, the issue was not about Mark's ability to memorize the "oracles" (*logia*) "of the Lord" (*kyriakōn*). The fundamental complaint concerned his literary arrangement of them. It is uncertain how much of this reflects the elder John's sentiments and how much of this was Papias's or Eusebius's clarifications.[5] After a brief interjection, Eusebius cited a second excerpt from Papias on Matthew. It begins with "so then" (*men oun*), so Eusebius must have skipped over the first part of Papias's quotation. The rest of the quotation is that "Matthew compiled the oracles in the Hebrew language, but each interpreted them as they could."[6]

---

von Hierapolis und die Evangelien des Neuen Testaments (Regensberg: Verlag Friedrich Pustet, 1983), 93–137; U. H. J. Körtner, *Papias von Hierapolis: Ein Beitrag zur Geschichte des frühen Christentums*, FRLANT 133 (Göttingen; Vandenhoeck & Ruprecht, 1983), 50–71; Bart D. Ehrman, *Apostolic Fathers: Epistle of Barnabas, Papias and Quadratus, Letter to Diognetus, The Shepherd of Hermas* (2 vol.; LCL Cambridge: Harvard University Press, 2003), 2.92–117; Enrico Norelli, *Papia di Hierapolis: Esposizione Degli Oracoli Del Signore I frammenti* (Figlie di San Paolo: Paoline, 2005), 174–499; Dennis MacDonald, *Two Shipwrecked Gospels: The Logoi of Jesus and Papias's Exposition of Logia about the Lord* (Atlanta: SBL, 2012), 3–42; Monte A. Shanks, *Papias and the New Testament* (Eugene: Pickwick, 2013), 105–260; Michael W. Holmes, *The Apostolic Fathers: Greek Texts and English Translations* (3rd ed.; Grand Rapids: Baker Academic, 2007), 722–67.

3. See Eusebius, *H.E.* 3.39.15–17.
4. See Eusebius, *H.E.* 3.39.15. This is a translation provided by Carlson, *Papias*, 145.
5. F. C. Grant, *The Gospels: Their Origins and Growth* (New York: Harper, 1957), 74; Joel Marcus, *Mark 1–8* (AB; New Haven: Yale University Press, 2000), 22.
6. See Eusebius, *H.E.* 3.39.16. This is a translation provided by Carlson, *Papias*, 145.

Any conclusions about the meaning of these fragments, mediated to modern scholars by a fourth-century reader of a lost second-century treatise, are provisional. They could be falsified if Papias's work were rediscovered. Respecting the limitations of the data, the fragmentary citations from the prologue seem to at least disclose that Papias inherited a tradition about the evangelist Mark from an elderly figure named John. The elder John's appraisal of Mark's text was that it was a loose, disjointed compilation of notes about the words and deeds of Jesus. The notes were based on the sermons that Peter delivered on various occasions and that Mark had translated into Greek. Although Mark was capable of accurately recalling what Peter had preached about Jesus, he was faulted for not organizing his notes into a sophisticated literary composition. The second fragment on Matthew's oracles is not credited to the elder John. Instead, Papias may have been the one to introduce the comparison between Mark's and Matthew's compilations of the oracles. Papias may have newly discovered that the Gospel of Matthew was a marked improvement over the presumed lack of "order" in the Gospel of Mark.

Who Was the Elder John?

The starting point for ascertaining the identity of the elder John is Papias's prologue. Its grammar and syntax are amenable to multiple interpretations. It could be taken as alternating between designating the same group of apostles as "disciples of the Lord" and as "elders" or "presbyters." Papias may have admired all of Jesus's disciples as his "elders" and was asking their followers about the words that they had spoken.[7] Or the "disciples of the Lord" and

---

7. Grammatically, this takes the interrogative pronoun *ti* ("what") in apposition to the "elders." Papias was inquiring about the "words" (*logoi*) of the seven elders Andrew, Peter, Philip, Thomas, James, John, and Matthew. See Joseph Barber Lightfoot, *Essays on the Work Entitled Supernatural Religion* (London: Macmillan, 1893), 145; Rupert Annand, "Papias and the Four Gospels" *SJT* 9 (1956): 47–48; Johannes Munck, "Presbyters and Disciples of the Lord in Papias: Exegetic Comments on Eusebius, Ecclesiastical History, III, 39" *HTR* 52.4 (1959): 236–37, 239; David G. Deeks, "Papias Revisited," *ExpTim* 88.11 (1977): 296–97; Orchard and Riley, *The Order*, 176, 177; Martin Hengel, *The Johannine Question* (trans. John Bowden; London: SCM, 1989), 27; Dungan, *A History*, 19; Christopher R. Matthews, *Philip: Apostle and Evangelist: Configurations of a Tradition* (Leiden: Brill, 2002), 20–21; Robert H. Gundry, "The Apostolically Johannine Pre-Papian Tradition Concerning the Gospels of Mark and

the "elders" could be taken as two separate groups. The words of the Lord's seven disciples were passed on to the "elders" and then to their pupils.[8] The Greek may not rule out that Papias met with the followers of the "elders" who visited Hierapolis and, on a separate occasion, with two of "the Lord's disciples."[9] A related issue is whether it is historically plausible that Papias's visitors in Hierapolis had socialized with the apostles, who may have mainly stayed in Judea and died decades earlier, or with elderly Christ-believers in Asia Minor.[10]

It may help to define the adjective *presbyteros*. For Papias, it may not have denoted an ecclesiastical office-holder (i.e., a "presbyter").[11] It applied to any believer in Christ who reached old age and was worthy of respect (i.e., an "elder").[12] The elders may have been the bearers of venerable traditions

---

Matthew" in *The Old is Better: New Testament Essays in Support of Traditional Interpretations* (edited by Robert H. Gundry; WUNT 178; Tübingen: Mohr Siebeck, 2005), 53–54; Shanks, *Papias*, 140–43; Kok, *The Beloved Apostle*, 67–69.

8. John Chapman, *John the Presbyter and the Fourth Gospel* (Oxford: Clarendon Press, 1911), 10–12; Schoedel, *The Apostolic Fathers*, 5.90, 98; Körtner, *Papias*, 114–22; William R. Schoedel, "Papias" in *Aufstieg und Niedergang der römischen Welt* 2.27.1 (ed. Wolfgang Haase; Berlin: de Gruyter, 1993), 251; R. Alan Culpepper, *John, The Son of Zebedee: The Life of a Legend* (Minneapolis: Fortress, 2000), 110; Charles E. Hill, "Papias of Hierapolis" *ExpTim* 117 (2006): 310n.4; David C. Sim, "The Gospel of Matthew, John the Elder and the Papias Tradition: A Response to R. H. Gundry" *HTS* 3 (2007): 292–93; Norelli, *Papia*, 42; Kok, *The Gospel*, 59, 62; Bauckham, *Jesus*, 16–18; Dean Furlong, *The Identity of John the Evangelist: Revision and Reinterpretation in Early Christian Sources* (Minneapolis: Lexington Books, 2020), 8–14. Gundry ("Pre-Papian Tradition," 53) and Shanks (*Papias*, 140–42) protest that the *ti* cannot be translated as an "accusative of general reference," or "the accusative of 'last resort,'" on grammatical grounds. Furlong (*The Identity*, 11, 16n.53) replies that this translation may not render the *ti* as an "accusative of general reference" but the direct object of the verb *anakrinō* ("inquire"). He uncovers parallel grammatical constructions where the verb *anakrinō* takes on a direct object, which is followed by interrogative pronouns introducing indirect questions that complement the verb. In the *Life of Crassus* 5.3, for example, Plutarch narrates how two slaves visited Marcus Licinius Crassus while he was in hiding and that "he was inquiring of them regarding what they wanted and who they were" (*anekrinon oun autas ti boulontai kai tines eisin*).

9. Chapman, *John*, 24–26.

10. Furlong (*The Identity*, 11) considers the latter option to be more historically probable.

11. Contra Bauckham, *Jesus*, 17; Shanks, *Papias*, 154n.52.

12. Lightfoot, *Essays*, 146; Chapman, *John*, 13; Schoedel, *The Apostolic Fathers*, 5.99–100; Munck, "Presbyters," 234–35; Deeks, "Papias Revisited," 296–97; Schoedel, "Papias," 251; Culpepper, *John*, 110; Hill, "Papias," 110.

in the Christ associations in Asia Minor.[13] Papias's usage of the term could be compared with contemporary writers.[14] In Acts, Jesus's brother James and the Jerusalem apostles were assisted by a larger body of elders or presbyters.[15] The implied author of the first Epistle of Peter was a "fellow-elder" (*sympresbyteros*) exhorting the older members of the Christ associations in Asia Minor to exercise oversight over the younger members.[16] The sender of the Johannine Epistles was an anonymous *presbyteros*, which may signify the author's age or ecclesiastical rank.[17] A late second-century bishop, Irenaeus, understood Papias's elders to be the contemporaries and disciples of the apostles.[18] He may have been influenced by the development of the monarchical episcopacy, as the hierarchical offices of bishops, presbyters, and deacons had become well-defined by his time.[19]

Papias's preface also contrasts what Andrew, Peter, Philip, Thomas, James, John, and Matthew "said" (*eipen*) with what Aristion and the elder John were "saying" (*legousin*). It is a safe bet that the individuals in the former group were no longer speaking when Papias was conducting his interviews because they were deceased.[20] What causes exegetical

---

13. Munck, "Presbyters," 233; cf. Azzan Yadin-Israel, "'For Mark was Peter's Tanna': Tradition and Transmission in Papias and the Early Rabbis" *JECS* 23.3 (2015): 344.

14. Some of the following New Testament texts could be read as suggesting that the terms "disciple," "apostle," or "elder" could be used interchangeably. See Gundry, "Pre-Papian Tradition," 53; Andreas Köstenberger and Stephen O. Snout, "'The Disciple Jesus Loved': Witness, Author, Apostle—A Response to Richard Bauckham's *Jesus and the Eyewitnesses*" *BBR* 18 (2008): 220; Shanks, *Papias*, 143, 143n.124. Others find a clear distinction between the "disciples" or "apostles" of Jesus and the "elders" or "presbyters" in these same texts. See Körtner, *Papias*, 116–21; Sim, "The Gospel of Matthew," 293–94.

15. See Acts 15:2, 4, 6, 22, 23; 16:4; 21:18.

16. See 1 Pet 5:1–4.

17. See 2 John 1:1; 3 John 1:1. Although the Johannine Epistles came to be attributed to the apostle John, some patristic writers argued that the latter two letters were written by the elder John due to the author's self-reference as a *presbyteros*. See Eusebius, *H.E.* 3.25.3; Jerome, *Vir. ill.* 9.

18. See Irenaeus, *Haer.* 2.22.5; 5.5.1; 30.1; 33.3; 36.2; *Dem.* 3. Irenaeus might have correctly understood Papias's distinction between Jesus's disciples and the "elders." See Chapman, *John*, 13–16; Furlong, *The Identity*, 12.

19. Shanks, *Papias*, 143.

20. Yadin-Israel ("Peter's Tanna," 345) is one of the few scholars who does not interpret the significance of the tense change in this way, arguing that it only implies that Papias listened to these two men speak in person.

difficulties is that both groups were praised by Papias as "the disciples of the Lord" (*hoi tou kyriou mathētai*). The phrase may denote the twelve apostles, a wider circle of Jesus's disciples outside the Twelve, or Christ followers in general.[21] As the reoccurrence of this phrase is missing from Rufinus's Latin translation of the Papian fragment in Eusebius's *Ecclesiastical History*, as well as the Syriac and Armenian translations, it could be omitted.[22] It could alternatively be amended to "the disciples" (*hoi mathētai*) or "the disciples of these ones" (*hoi toutōn mathētai*), meaning the disciples of the seven apostles.[23] It may be better to side with the Greek manuscripts in retaining the clumsy repetition of the whole phrase "the disciples of the Lord" as the *lectio difficilior* or the "harder reading."[24] Papias's repetition of the name John twice and the descriptor "the Lord's disciples" twice caused a great deal of confusion among his patristic interpreters. They especially disagreed over whether Papias was referring to one or two individuals named John.

If Papias mentioned the same John twice, it may be because he outlived the other six disciples of the Lord. He was an old man ministering alongside someone named Aristion, also identified as a disciple of the Lord.[25] Papias may have put an article before John's appellation *presbyteros* to signal that he was referring to "the aforementioned Elder John" a second time.[26] Then again, it seems redundant to repeat the same John twice in the same

---

21. See Munck, "Presbyters," 232. Munck favors the second option. The third option is defended in Kok, *The Gospel*, 63; Kok, *The Beloved Apostle*, 71.
22. Theodor Mommsen, "Papianisches" *ZNW* 3 (1902): 156–59; B. W. Bacon, "The Elder John, Papias, Irenaeus, Eusebius, and the Syriac Translator" *JBL* 27 (1908): 11, 19; Luise Abramowski, "The 'Memoirs of the Apostles' in Justin" in *The Gospel and the Gospels* (ed. Peter Stuhlmacher; Grand Rapids: Eerdmans, 1991), 329–30n.28; Culpepper, *John*, 111.
23. B. W. Bacon, "The Elder John, Papias, Irenaeus, Eusebius, and the Syriac Translator" *JBL* 27 (1908): 11, 19.
24. Chapman, *John*, 20–21; Munck, "Presbyters, 230. See also Jerome, *Vir il.* 18.
25. Gundry, "Pre-Papian Tradition," 55; Köstenberger and Snout, "The Disciple," 219; Shanks, *Papias*, 133. Furlong (*The Identity*, 9–10) traces the origins of the theory of a single John back to a book published in 1831, but, if the arguments below have any validity, it may date back to the end of the second century.
26. Köstenberger and Snout, "The Disciple," 219; Shanks, *Papias*, 19–21, 155–56. This takes the article before *presbyteros* as anaphoric. However, as Furlong (*The Identity*, 10) notes, Papias should have singled out a single elder if he meant for the article to be taken as anaphoric.

sentence.[27] The article may instead signal the titular nature of "the Elder." He was "the Elder" *par excellence*.[28] The title may have functioned to differentiate the second John from the first one due to his advanced age.[29] The second John was set apart with Aristion from the seven disciples who accompanied Jesus during his ministry. Aristion was not one of the twelve apostles. It cannot be verified that he was a disciple of Jesus who was not a member of the Twelve as he is unmentioned in the Gospels.[30] *Presbyteros* would have been a fitting label for Aristion too if he was one of the few remaining eyewitnesses of Jesus alive at the end of the first century, for the adjective can be translated as an elderly person. It was not an exclusive title for the apostles.[31] Since Aristion did not qualify to be an "elder," unlike his older contemporary John, it is doubtful that he was old enough to have been one of Jesus's acquaintances. "Disciples of the Lord," therefore, was a generic label for eminent followers of Jesus, irrespective of whether they committed their allegiance to him before or after Easter. The elder John and Aristion were not grouped with the seven disciples of the historical Jesus. They were second-generation disciples of the risen Lord residing in Asia Minor.

The elder John may have been at the height of his fame after the lifetimes of the first seven disciples of the Lord. Some of the apostle John's hagiographers would dispute this conclusion, however, as they posited that he lived until the third year of Trajan's reign, the Roman Emperor from 98 to 117 CE, and was peacefully laid to rest in Ephesus, the capital of Asia Minor.[32] If the apostle John lived until his eighties or nineties, he definitely

---

27. Munck, "Presbyters," 238; cf. Schoedel, *The Apostolic Fathers*, 5.99.
28. For Chapman (*John*, 39), the title is equivalent to "the Grand Old Man."
29. Deeks, "Papias Revisited," 297; Hengel, *The Johannine Question*, 27–28; Kok, *The Beloved Apostle*, 69.
30. Körtner, *Papias*, 125–26; Sim, "The Gospel of Matthew," 292, 294; Kok, *The Gospel*, 63; Kok, *The Beloved Apostle*, 71. There have been attempts to place Aristion among the larger group of seventy-two disciples commissioned by Jesus in Luke 10:1 or among the seven disciples fishing at the Sea of Galilee in John 21:2. See A. C. Perumalil, "Are Not Papias and Irenaeus Competent to Report on the Gospels?" *ExpTim* 91 (1980): 334; Bauckham, *Jesus*, 415.
31. Contra Gundry, "Pre-Papian Tradition," 55; Shanks, *Papias*, 153–54, 156–57; Köstenberger and Snout "The Disciple," 219.
32. See Irenaeus, *Haer.* 2.22.5; 3.3.4; Eusebius, *Chron.* A.M. 2114; *H.E.* 3.23.3–4; Jerome, *Vir. il.* 9.

fit Papias's definition of an "elder."[33] Such lengthy lifespans were rare, but not completely unparalleled, in antiquity. It was reported that Pothinus served as the bishop of Lugdunum, in modern-day Lyon in France, until he was ninety years old.[34] There may be an alternative stream of tradition, on the other hand, that the apostle John was slain.

The attribution of the defamatory accusation that John "the theologian" and his brother James were killed by the Jews to Papias's second volume is found in one of the De Boor fragments named after the scholar who rediscovered them.[35] The fragments contain lost material from ante-Nicene writers interpolated into a seventh-century Byzantine epitome of ecclesiastical histories, beginning with Eusebius's work and its continuation by Gelasius of Caesarea.[36] Seven interpolations into the section on Eusebius's work were initially attributed to the *Christian History* penned by the fifth-century historian Philip of Side,[37] but this attribution is questionable.[38] If Philip was not the epitomist, there is no need to get sidetracked

---

33. Köstenberger and Snout, "The Disciple," 219.

34. See Eusebius, *H.E.* 5.1.29. Shanks, *Papias*, 101. For skepticism about the lengthy age spans of some Christian luminaries reported in patristic literature, see Kok, *The Beloved Apostle*, 70.

35. For a sample of scholars who accept the accuracy of this attribution to Papias's exposition, see Hengel, *The Johannine Question*, 21, 158–59n.121; Norelli, *Papia*, 364–83, 434–41; MacDonald, *Two Shipwrecked Gospels*, 23–24, 59; Kok, *The Beloved Apostle*, 72–73; Bauckham, *Jesus*, 458–62; Furlong, *The Identity*, 23–25; Luke J. Stevens, "Did Eusebius Read Papias?" *JTS* 70 (2019): 166–68.

36. See C. de Boor, *Neue Fragmente des Papias, Hegesippus und Pierius: In bisher unbekannten Excerpten aus der Kirchengeschichte des Philippus Sidetes*, *TU* 5.2 (Leipzig: Hinrichs, 1888), 165–84; Pierre Nautin, "Théodore Lecteur et sa 'réunion de différentes Histoires' de l'Église," *REB* 52 (1994): 218–22; Luke J. Stevens, "The Origins of the De Boor Fragments Ascribed to Philip of Side" *JECS* 26.4 (2018): 635–39. De Boor was familiar with two fragments, B (Oxford, Bodleian Barocci 142) and the abridged P (Paris, BnF gr. 1555A), and P. Nautin's critical edition is based on B, P, and V (Athos, Vatopedi 286). Stevens points out that scholars have neglected R (Oxford, Bodleian Auctarium E.4.18).

37. De Boor, "Neue Fragmente," 173–74.

38. Stevens, "The Origin," 639–40. Only in B is a passage before the historiographical writings of Theodore the Lector introduced under the heading "As Philip of Side says in his twenty-fourth book." Accepting that this passage was original to the epitome, De Boor deduced that the fragments derived from a single hand and were consistent with what we know about Philip's lost history. However, Stevens explains that "once the excerpts of fourth-century history appended after Eusebius's HE were identified as coming directly from the lost work of Gelasius of Caesarea,

by the questions over Philip's competence as a historian.[39] Whether Papias's words about the deaths of John and James have been accurately preserved in the De Boor fragments is also questionable.[40] The epitomist gave John the anachronistic title "the theologian" and could alter the sources in the process of paraphrasing them.[41] A fragment in Codex Coislianus 305, an eleventh-century manuscript of the *Chronicle* by the ninth-century monk George the "sinner," is a second witness to the claim that Papias wrote about the apostle John's martyrdom. It is called the Nolte fragment based on the name of its discoverer.[42] There may be a literary relationship between the Nolte and De Boor fragments as they both drop *Exposition* from the title of Papias's work, call Papias's second book an "account" (*logos*), and repeat the malicious false charge that the apostle John was killed by the Jews.[43]

---

little reason then remained to connect the DBFs [De Boor fragments] with the passage from Philip, when they lay on opposite sides of excerpts from another author. Furthermore, the epitomist obviously worked from a text giving Eusebius's HE practically verbatim and in full, which actually stands in contrast to what is known of Philip's work. Lastly, de Boor's assumption that the passage from Philip in B had stood in the original Epitome, though recently defended by Nautin, is almost certainly wrong" (p. 640).

39. Schoedel (*The Apostolic Fathers*, 5.120) is the most dismissive of Philip of Side, ruling that he was "a bungler and cannot be trusted." On the contrary, Shanks (*Papias*, 216–17) and Furlong (*The Identity*, 25) point out that Philip's critics faulted him for his verbosity and pedantry or for pontificating on too many subjects beyond his areas of expertise. See, for example, Photius, *Bib.* 1.20–21. He was not attacked as an unreliable historian. See also Norelli, *Papia*, 368; Carlson, *Papias*, 67.

40. For a sample of scholars who argue that the De Boor fragments are unreliable witnesses to Papias's lost text and discount the historicity of the tradition about John's martyrdom, see Schoedel, "Papias," 240–41; Culpepper, *John*, 171–74; Shanks, *Papias*, 219–25, 239–40; Carlson, *Papias*, 65–75.

41. See Carlson, *Papias*, 72.

42. Johann Heinrich Nolte, "Ein Excerpt aus dem zum größen Theil noch ungedruckten Chronikon des Georgius Hamartolus" *TQ* 44 (1862): 464–68. See George Hamartolos, *Chron.* 3.134.1.

43. See Norelli, *Papia*, 437–41, Carlson, *Papias*, 71. Stevens ("The Origin," 650–54), however, argues that they independently drew on a common source. The most significant difference between the two fragments is that the Nolte fragment explicitly links Papias's tradition to the fulfillment of Jesus's prophecy that John would undergo Jesus's baptism and drink his cup (cf. Mark 10:39) and cites the "most learned" Origen as a second witness to the tradition, despite George the monk's generally negative attitude toward Origen (e.g., *Chron.* 9.17). The Nolte fragment wrongly enlists Origen as a witness to the apostle John's martyrdom, since Origen related Jesus's prediction of John's suffering to his exile to the island of Patmos (cf. *Comm. in Mt.* 16.6).

Irenaeus and Eusebius, the two earliest extant witnesses to Papias's exposition, had no clue that the apostle John was memorialized as a martyr or else they could not have been so mistaken about the longevity of his life.[44] It may be unfair to impute dishonest motives to them by suspecting that they suppressed what Papias had written because it conflicted with their beliefs about how the apostle John's life ended.[45] Eusebius would have had to have been totally in the dark about what Papias may have written about the apostle John's death, which might be feasible if he only received a handful of extracts from Papias's work through an intermediary.[46] Eusebius gives the impression, on the contrary, that he had pored over Papias's exposition in its entirety in observing that Aristion and the elder John appear frequently by name in its pages.[47]

---

44. See, for example, Irenaeus, *Haer.* 2.22.5; 3.3.4; Eusebius, *Chron.* A.M. 2114; *H.E.* 3.23.3–4.

45. The suppression theory is argued in Hengel, *The Johannine Question*, 21; Norelli, *Papia*, 369–71; Kok, *The Beloved Apostle*, 72; Furlong, *The Identity*, 25; Bauckham, *Jesus*, 461.

46. This is argued in Stevens, "Did Eusebius Read," 163–83. His case is built on how often Eusebius betrays no knowledge of certain traditions assigned to Papias (pp. 166–73). For instance, Eusebius does not pass on any traditions from Papias about the apostle John's martyrdom or the authorship of the third and fourth New Testament Gospels and the book of Revelation. Eusebius insulted Papias's intelligence as a naïve biblical literalist and chialist (cf. *H.E.* 3.39.12), but this conflicts with Papias's allegorization of the week of creation in Genesis according to Anastasius of Sinai (cf. *Hex.* 1.6.1; cf. 7b.5.5). Carlson rebuts these points (*Papias*, 32, 32n.159, 35n.170, 57–59, 87–89). Papias may have just been silent about the origins of the Gospels of Luke and John and the book of Revelation. It was only when Papias's elder John was confused with the apostle John, believed by Irenaeus to be the author of the fourth Gospel, that the elder John was identified as the fourth evangelist. Papias may have had chiliastic expectations without taking them directly from Rev 20:1–6. The seventh-century Cappadocian bishop Andrew of Caesarea was the one who brought Papias's quotation about the flawed temporary arrangement where angels ruled the world into dialogue with a scene narrated in Rev 12:7–9 (cf. *Comm. Rev.* 34.12). The late seventh-century writer Anastasius of Sinai lumped Papias in with several ancient luminaries (e.g., Irenaeus, Pantaenus, Clement of Alexandria) as supporting a Christological, spiritualizing mode of exegesis. The problem is that each of the thinkers that he lumped together had very different theological outlooks. Papias's hermeneutics may have been materialistic rather than allegorical. Irenaeus implies that Papias corroborated what was said by the elders who had seen John, the disciple of the Lord, about the abundant fertility of the earth during the millennium (*Haer.* 5.33.4).

47. Carlson, *Papias*, 31. See Eusebius, *H.E.* 3.39.7.

The book of Acts notes that James, the son of Zebedee, was executed by Herod Agrippa in the early 40s CE.[48] James's brother John may have lost his life sometime after the timeline narrated in Acts, for the book closes with Paul under house arrest in Rome from 60 to 62 CE.[49] Perhaps Papias only went into detail about the death of James too. The epitomist may have been influenced by Jesus's prediction that both James and John would undergo the same baptism and drink the same cup that he did.[50]

The oldest evidence for John's martyrdom cannot be confined to a few contested fragments from Papias's work.[51] After all, the insinuation that both sons of Zebedee suffered the same fate as Jesus is found in two Synoptic Gospels.[52] Papias's prologue implies that the apostle John was among the seven disciples who were deceased, without detailing the circumstances of how each one died. One late second-century witness did not include the apostle John among the disciples of Jesus who escaped having to publicly confess their faith before the authorities who put them to death.[53] The legend that the apostle John was exiled to an island after he was plunged into a boiling jar of oil at the order of the Emperor Nero shows traces of conflating different Johns whose lives ended differently.[54] The tale that the apostle John was tortured along with the Christians in Rome who were scapegoated by Nero for the fire that ravaged the imperial capital in 64 CE may not be historical, but perhaps it fictionalized a real memory of him suffering a violent end at the hands of the political authorities. The apostle John was not the seer John

---

48. See Acts 12:2. Luke omits Jesus's prediction of the fates of James and John (cf. Mark 10:39//Matt 20:23).

49. Norelli, *Papia*, 375–76; MacDonald, *Two Shipwrecked Gospels*, 59; Shanks, *Papias*, 220; Kok, *The Beloved Apostle*, 72.

50. See Mark 10:39//Matt 20:23. Alternatively, Furlong (*The Identity* 29–31) argues that the epitomist confused James, the son of Alphaeus, with James, the son of Zebedee. His reasoning is that the sons of Zebedee tend to be put in the order of "James and John," including in Papias's preface.

51. For an overview of the traditions of the apostle John's martyrdom, see Furlong, *The Identity*, 20–28. Carlson (*Papias*, 71n.315) disputes one of Furlong's examples. He argues that Clement of Alexandria's use of the verb *teleiō* was not intended to signal that the era of the apostles' preaching was finished by the end of Paul's ministry but that it reached its perfection at this time (*Str.* 7.17).

52. See also the interpretations of this prophecy by Cyprian (*Rebapt.* 13), Aphrahat (*Dem.* 21.23), and John Chrysostom (*Hom. Mt.* 20.23).

53. See Heracleon, in Clement, *Str.* 4.9.

54. Furlong, *The Identity*, 110–11. See Tertullian, *Praescr.* 36; Jerome, *Jov.* 1.26.

whose visions are in the book of Revelation and who spent his last days on the island of Patmos.[55] He was not the elder John who died peacefully of old age in Ephesus. The conflation of these figures left a trail of inconsistencies.

When Was the Elder John Identified as an Apostle?

The reception of Papias's prologue sheds additional light on the elder John. Irenaeus is the earliest explicit witness to Papias's work. He succeeded Pothinus in the episcopal chair of Lugdunum after Pothinus died in prison in 177 CE. Pothinus was imprisoned during a local outbreak of persecution.[56] Irenaeus, then a presbyter in Lugdunum, had already established quite a reputation for himself and was entrusted with delivering a letter from the persecuted Christians there to the Roman bishop Eleutherus.[57] Irenaeus's magnum opus is entitled *On the Detection and Overthrow of Knowledge Falsely So-Called*. Its abbreviated title is *Against Heresies*. Within this text, there are roughly sixty mentions of John, the "disciple of the Lord" and the alleged author of the Johannine Gospel, Epistles, and Apocalypse.[58]

In a letter that Irenaeus sent to his former friend Florinus,[59] he reminisced about his childhood when they sat in the presence of Polycarp, the bishop of Smyrna. Polycarp regaled them with tales about John, the Lord's disciple, and the rest of the eyewitnesses of the Lord with whom he had conversed in Asia Minor during the time of Trajan.[60] One of Polycarp's

---

55. See Rev 1:9.
56. See Eusebius, *H.E.* 5.1.1–63.
57. See Eusebius, *H.E.* 5.4.1–2. For a few studies on Irenaeus's life and thought, see Dennis Minns, *Irenaeus: An Introduction* (New York: T&T Clark, 2010); Paul Foster and Sara Parvis, eds., *Irenaeus: Life, Scripture, Legacy* (Minneapolis: Fortress, 2012).
58. See Irenaeus, *Haer.* 1.8.5; 1.16.3; 2.2.5; 2.22.3; 3.1.1; 3.3.4; 3.11.1, 3; 3.16.5, 8; 3.22.2; 4.20.11; 4.30.4; 5.18.2; 5.26.1; 5.33.3; 5.35.2). See Bernhard Mutschler, "John and His Gospel in the Mirror of Irenaeus of Lyons: Perspectives of Recent Research" in *The Legacy of John: Second-Century Reception of the Fourth Gospel* (ed. Tuomas Rasimus; Leiden: Brill, 2010), 320.
59. See Eusebius, *H.E.* 5.20.4–8.
60. A. C. Perumalil ("Are Not Papias," 336) argues that Irenaeus could not have been younger than fifteen years old to travel from Gaul or Rome to study with Polycarp in Smyrna, but he does not factor in the possibility that Irenaeus grew up in Smyrna before he moved elsewhere. Shanks (*Papias*, 74–78) stresses that Irenaeus spent a considerable amount of time with Polycarp in his youth and had vivid memories of what he had

funnier yarns was about the day that the Lord's disciple John ran away from a public bathhouse in Ephesus. He had caught a glimpse of his archnemesis, the theologian Cerinthus, inside the facility and feared that the walls would be divinely struck down.[61]

Irenaeus respected Papias as an "ancient man" and a "hearer" of John.[62] In his understanding, Papias heard John in person; he was not a second-hand recipient of John's oral traditions.[63] It is not explicitly stated that the John whom Papias heard was the Lord's disciple or the author of one of the New Testament books that Irenaeus ascribed to this disciple.[64] In the wider literary context, though, Irenaeus hailed this John as the Lord's disciple and the visionary who foresaw the resurrection of the saints to become heirs to the millennial kingdom.[65] There is some ambiguity about whether he identified the John who was the preeminent "disciple of the Lord" in Asia Minor and the author of the Johannine corpus as the son of Zebedee. It should not be overlooked that Papias included the elder John among "the Lord's disciples."[66] Although Irenaeus never names Zebedee, there is no doubt that he was referring to Zebedee as the father who was abandoned by the apostles in his fishing boat.[67] It is equally obvious when Irenaeus was referencing Zebedee's son John as one of the three closest disciples to Jesus in the Synoptic Gospels or one of the two foremost leaders of the Christ community in Jerusalem in the early chapters in Acts.[68] Irenaeus unambiguously grouped Papias's informant John with the apostles, not with the elders.[69] He tended

---

learned from him. Moreover, Irenaeus risked being called out by Florinus if he wildly fabricated what Polycarp had told both of them (cf. Culpepper, *John*, 126; Bauckham, *Jesus*, 326; Mutschler, "Mirror," 326; Shanks, *Papias*, 76).

61. See Irenaeus, *Haer.* 2.22.5; 3.3.4.
62. See Irenaeus, *Haer.* 5.33.4; cf. Eusebius, *H.E.* 3.39.1.
63. Yadin-Israel, "Peter's Tanna," 340–42.
64. Perumalil, "Are Not Papias," 333–34.
65. See Irenaeus, *Haer.* 5.33.3; 36.3. See Kok, *The Beloved Apostle*, 63; Carlson, *Papias*, 33n.163.
66. Furlong, *The Identity*, 43.
67. See Irenaeus, *Haer.* 4.5.4.
68. See Irenaeus, *Haer.* 2.24.4; 3.12.3, 5, 15. See Bauckham, *Jesus*, 364; Lorne Zelyck, "Irenaeus and the Authorship of the Fourth Gospel" in *The Origins of the Fourth Gospel* (ed. Stanley Porter and Hughson T. Ong; Leiden: Brill, 2016), 241–42; Furlong, *The Identity*, 40.
69. See Irenaeus, *Haer.* 2.22.5; 3.3.4. Zelyck ("Irenaeus," 252) adds that Irenaeus could use the terms "disciples" and "apostles" interchangeably (cf. *Haer.* 1.25.2; 3.5.1).

to restrict the noun "apostle" to the Twelve or to Paul.[70] There are a couple of debatable passages where he may have widened his definition of the term. He may have thought that John the Baptizer and the seventy disciples sent by Jesus to evangelize throughout Galilee had apostolic vocations.[71] He associates Polycarp with plural apostles, but the chances are low that the bishop of Smyrna was acquainted with multiple members of the original twelve apostles.[72]

The clearest example of Irenaeus acclaiming John, the Lord's disciple, as an apostle was in his review of the commentator Ptolemy's eisegesis of the Johannine Prologue. In his eyes, Ptolemy, and Ptolemy's teacher Valentinus, were purveyors of esoteric "knowledge falsely so-called." The sole point that they agreed on was their joint recognition of the apostleship of the evangelist John.[73] Irenaeus's preference for christening this John as the Lord's disciple, rather than the Lord's apostle, may not have been influenced by Papias's terminology. It may have been due to the portrayal of the "disciple whom Jesus loved" in the Gospel of John.[74]

Irenaeus alluded to the beloved disciple's first cameo in the Gospel by noting that John reclined on the Lord's bosom at the Last Supper.[75] In this episode, Jesus alarmed his disciples by revealing that he was about to be betrayed by one of them at the table. At Peter's behest, the beloved disciple discreetly leaned back to Jesus and asked him to expose the betrayer. Taking the text of this Gospel on its own terms, the beloved disciple is almost exclusively situated in Jerusalem. He was present at Jesus's last meal where the traitor was exposed, the high priest's courtyard where Peter denied Jesus, the foot of the cross where Jesus delegated the care of his mother to him, and

---

70. Köstenberger and Snout, "The Disciple," 224–25; Watson, *Gospel Writing*, 464n.48; Zelyck, "Irenaeus," 248, 251; Kok, *The Beloved Apostle*, 94.

71. See Irenaeus, *Haer.* 2.21.1 (cf. Luke 10:1–24); 3.11.4 (cf. Matt 11:9; Luke 7:26). The question about whether these passages expand the group of apostles beyond the Twelve is debated in Bauckham, *Jesus*, 458–63; Zelyck, "Irenaeus," 248–51; Furlong, *The Identity*, 41–42.

72. See Eusebius, *H.E.* 5.24.16. Furlong, *The Identity*, 42.

73. See Irenaeus, *Haer.* 1.9.2–3; cf. 3.5.1; 3.11.9; 3.21.3. Bauckham (*Jesus*, 366; cf. Furlong, *The Identity*, 41) minimizes this point because Irenaeus may have borrowed the title "apostle" from the Valentinian commentator.

74. Mutschler, "Mirror," 321; Zelyck, "Irenaeus," 253.

75. See Irenaeus, *Haer.* 3.1.1 (cf. John 13:23).

the tomb where Jesus's grave clothes were left behind.[76] Irenaeus searched for clues outside of John's Gospel to uncover the identity of the beloved disciple. In the Synoptic Gospels, Jesus ate his final meal with the Twelve.[77] Peter, James, and John were Jesus's closest disciples among the Twelve.[78] The beloved disciple was not Peter. There was a misguided expectation that the beloved disciple would live until Jesus returned, which rules out James, the first apostle to be martyred.[79] Irenaeus may have settled on the apostle John as the candidate for the beloved disciple, like previous exegetes did, via the process of elimination.

Therefore, Irenaeus did not retain Papias's distinction between the apostle John and the elder John. It was easy enough to miss it, for the grammar of Papias's prologue is perplexing. Irenaeus mixed up the apostle John with the elder John who mentored Polycarp and Papias in his twilight years. He may have been mistaken in thinking that the apostle John was the beloved disciple and the seer on the island of Patmos.[80] The Johannine epistles could be attributed to the elder John because they were signed by an anonymous "elder."[81] In the end, Irenaeus trusted his fragile adolescent memories of what his teacher Polycarp told him about someone named John. By accidentally misidentifying Polycarp's (and Papias's) teacher as the apostle John, Irenaeus conveniently positioned himself in the line of apostolic succession.[82]

---

76. See John 13:23–25; 18:15–16; 19:26–27, 35; 20:2–10. There may be two exceptions. The beloved disciple may be among the followers of John the Baptizer in John 1:35–40, but it is not explicit that the anonymous disciple became the one "whom Jesus loved." The beloved disciple is also among the seven fishers on the sea of Galilee in John 21:7, 20–24, but the epilogue may be a secondary addition to the text. There is virtually no overlap between the Johannine scenes featuring the beloved disciple and the Synoptic scenes featuring John the son of Zebedee (cf. Mark 1:29–31; 5:37–43; 9:2–9; 13:3–4; 14:33), though John 21:1–14 may be a variant account of the scene in Luke 5:1–11. For my analysis of the beloved disciple, see Kok, *The Beloved Apostle*, 1–29.
77. See Matt 26:20; Mark 14:17; Luke 22:14.
78. See Mark 5:37//Luke 8:51; Mark 9:2//Matt 17:1//Luke 9:28; Mark 14:33//Matt 26:37.
79. See John 21:23; contra Acts 12:2.
80. Culpepper, *John*, 131; Köstenberger and Snout, "The Disciple," 224–25; Watson, *Gospel Writing*, 464–67; Zelyck, "Irenaeus," 248; Kok, *The Beloved Apostle*, 9, 94–97.
81. See 2 John 1:1; 3 John 1:1.
82. Watson, *Gospel Writing*, 464–67; Zelyck, "Irenaeus," 254–57; Kok, *The Beloved Apostle*, 95–96.

At first, Eusebius reaffirmed Irenaeus's commendation of Papias and Polycarp as the hearers of the apostle John.[83] Once he acquired Papias's exposition for himself, he changed his mind. He distanced Papias from the apostles due to his own elucidation of Papias's prologue.[84] He did not disallow that Papias was an "ear-witness" (*autēkoos*) of the elder John and Aristion.[85] This was not mere guesswork on Eusebius's part based on how frequently John and Aristion appear in Papias's exposition.[86] It was based on Irenaeus's description of John. What Eusebius disavowed was Irenaeus's identification of Papias's elder John as the apostle John. He accentuated the difference between the apostles and the elders, though he did not maintain his distinction between the two terms completely consistently. He slipped up when paraphrasing Papias's preface as indicating that Papias received the words of the apostles from their followers.[87]

Prior to Eusebius, a third-century Alexandrian scholar named Dionysius disproved the common authorship of the Johannine Gospel and Epistles on the one hand and the book of Revelation on the other on linguistic and stylistic grounds. Dionysius assented to the tradition about the apostolic authorship of John's Gospel and Epistles, so he reckoned that Revelation must have been written by some other holy person named John.[88] For additional proof, he pointed out that there were two Christian tombs for persons named John in Ephesus.[89] Eusebius was pleased with Dionysius's assessment of Revelation. It is no secret that Eusebius wanted to reclassify Revelation as a spurious work and abhorred its apocalyptic and millenarian imagery.[90] One might have a sneaking suspicion that Eusebius conjured up the existence of a second John from Papias's prologue in order to ascribe Revelation to him, thereby dispensing with the apostolic

83. See Eusebius, *Chron.* A.M. 2114. See Chapman, *John*, 34–35n.1; Norelli, *Papia*, 242n.3; Shanks, *Papias*, 263; Carlson, *Papias*, 33–34.
84. See Eusebius, *H.E.* 3.39.2, 5–7.
85. Chapman, *John*, 28–32; Gundry, "Pre-Papian Tradition," 57; Furlong, *The Identity*, 13.
86. Contra Sim, "The Gospel of Matthew," 295.
87. See Eusebius, *H.E.* 3.39.7. To be consistent, he should have noted that Papias received the words of the elders from their followers. Gundry ("Pre-Papian Tradition," 54) may exaggerate the significance of Eusebius unintentionally contradicting himself.
88. See Eusebius, *H.E.* 7.25.6–27.
89. See Eusebius, *H.E.* 3.39.6; 7.25.16.
90. See Eusebius, *H.E.* 3.25.4; 39.6, 12.

authority that some Christians imputed to it.[91] Such a hunch downplays how Eusebius's mind about Papias's reputed association with the apostle John was genuinely changed after carefully examining Papias's prologue. He did not misread it and fabricate a second John from it, but he did have an ulterior motive in extrapolating that Papias's elder John was the seer on the island of Patmos.[92]

The elder John's biography was transferred over to the apostle John due to the phenomenon of homonymity. This can be defined as the confusion of one person for another because they have the same name. Therefore, it was the elder John who was laid to rest in Ephesus in the early years of Trajan's reign.[93] There were either competing claims concerning where he was buried or two memorial sites that commemorated his life in Ephesus.[94] His fan club cherished their memories of him. Some were amused by his reaction to Cerinthus in a bathhouse. Others were emotionally moved by his compassion to a wayward pupil who had become a robber.[95] Most importantly of all, he was the one who imparted to Papias the earliest tradition about a named Gospel writer.

The Date of Papias's Exposition

If Papias really was a hearer of the elder John, then he must have crossed paths with him sometime before he died around 100 CE. There is no information

---

91. Orchard and Riley, *The Order*, 178–79; Gundry, "Pre-Papian Tradition," 54, 57–58; Shanks, *Papias*, 134, 167–68.
92. Schoedel, "Papias," 252. Contra Furlong (*The Identity*, 89–92), who holds that Eusebius was right that the elder John wrote Revelation and attempted to deminish his standing as an authoritative figure by treating him as just another second-generation elder in Asia Minor.
93. Benjamin Bacon is one of the few scholars who argued against the elder John's residence in Ephesus. Bacon ("Syriac Translator," 141) identified Papias's elder John as the seventh bishop of Jerusalem, who died around 117 CE (cf. Eusebius, *H.E.* 4.5.3), but his theory is predicated on the assumption that Papias only had contact with the elder's students in Hierapolis and did not meet the elder in person. On the contrary, Papias was an "ear-witness" of the elder John and more likely visited him in nearby Ephesus than in distant Jerusalem.
94. Gundry, "Pre-Papian Tradition," 57. Gundry, however, uses this argument to weaken Eusebius's case for the existence of the second John, since it partially depends on Dionysius's inference about the two tombs.
95. See Clement of Alexandria, *Quis div.* 42.1–15.

about the date of Papias's birth and a dubious datum about the date of his demise in the seventh-century *Easter Chronicle*. According to the chronicler, Polycarp and Papias were martyred 133 years after Jesus ascended to heaven. Papias was included among the martyrs in Pergamum during the reign of the Roman Emperor Marcus Aurelius (161–80 CE). If Papias died in 163 CE, then he was blessed with an extremely long life too. Against this, the chronicler may have accidentally mistook Papylus as Papias when copying a section from Eusebius's *Ecclesiastical History*.[96] The martyrdom of Papylus of Thyatira in Pergamum is commemorated in the *Acts of Carpus, Papylus, and Agathonicê*.

It could be objected that Papylus may not have been so obscure to a Medieval historian to warrant changing his name to Papias and that the chronicler had another lost source about Papias's death.[97] Without this notice, however, there is no evidence that Papias died in Pergamum rather than his hometown of Hierapolis.[98] Other references to Papias as a "martyr" are far too late.[99] The oldest one may be in a quotation of a sixth-century writer, Stephen Gobarus, by Photius, the ninth-century patriarch of Constantinople.[100] Yet Photius sent an epistle to the Patriarch of Aquileia that praised Methodius for winning the crown of martyrdom, seemingly in

---

96. The chronicler follows the order of Eusebius's overview of the martyrdoms of Polycarp, Papylus, and Justin (cf. *H.E.* 4.15.1–46, 48; 16.1). The first scholar to catch this error was Lightfoot, *Supernatural Religion*, 147–49; cf. Vernon Bartlet, "Papias's 'Exposition': Its Date and Contents," in *Amicitiae Corolla* (ed. H. G. Wood; London: University of London Press, 1933), 21; Körtner, *Papias*, 32; Robert W. Yarbrough, "The Date of Papias: A Reassessment" *JETS* 26 (1983): 182; Schoedel, "Papias," 237; Norelli, *Papia*, 48, 443n.2; Kok, *The Gospel*, 109; Furlong, *The Identity*, 6; Carlson, *Papias*, 83–86. Carlson is open to the option that the name was intentionally, not accidentally, changed due to the prior known association of Polycarp with Papias.

97. Shanks, *Papias*, 92–96.

98. Shanks (*Papias*, 98) imagines a scenario where Papias was charged with a capital crime in Hierapolis but was not transported to Ephesus, the nearby capital of Asia, for his sentence to be carried out because he appealed to be tried in Pergamum.

99. The notices about Papias's martyrdom are listed in Carlson, *Papias*, 86n.398. Shanks (*Papias*, 96) concedes that they "are relatively late and can no longer direct the reader to other surviving documents for confirmation of the manner and date of Papias's death."

100. See Photius, *Bib.* 5.77 (cf. Carlson, *Papias*, 82n.373, 183n.7). Shanks (*Papias*, 96) argues that the description of Papias as a "bishop and martyr" may be from Photius, who may have depended on the *Easter Chronicle*.

contrast to Papias and Irenaeus. Papias may have originally been described as a *martys* just in the sense of a "witness."[101]

Eusebius is the best source for dating Papias's bishopric. In his chronology, Evarestus was appointed bishop of Rome in 100 CE, the third year of Trajan's rule.[102] He opens his fourth book chronicling the episcopal successors in Alexandria and Rome in the twelfth year of Trajan's rule.[103] The episcopacies of Polycarp, Papias, and Ignatius in Smyrna, Hierapolis, and Antioch respectively are set between these two dates. Papias "became well known" at this time.[104] Papias's exposition should not be dated earlier. Enough time had to pass for two Gospels and the first Epistles of Peter and John to have been in general circulation.[105] While Eusebius could have been ideologically motivated to date Papias as early as possible to guarantee the accuracy of the traditions that he received,[106] the internal evidence in Papias's exposition supports Eusebius's dating of Papias's writing activity.[107]

When Papias was questioning the elders' followers traveling through Hierapolis, the apostles were dead. The imperfect tense of the verb *anekrinon* ("I was inquiring") signals that Papias was relating his past experiences visiting the elder John and Aristion and listening to what they were "saying" (*legousin*). The present tense of the latter verb could be translated as a historic present.[108] Hypothetically, Papias could have conducted his interviews over

---

101. Furlong, *The Identity*, 6, 14n.8.
102. See Eusebius, *H.E.* 3.34.1.
103. See Eusebius, *H.E.* 4.1.1–2.
104. See Eusebius, *H.E.* 3.36.1–2.
105. Contra Annand, "Papias," 46–62. Annand dates Papias's exposition to 80 CE because he equates the Lord's disciples with the elders and dates the publication of Papias's exposition before the composition of the Gospel of Luke.
106. See Eusebius, *H.E.* 3.39.13. See Sim, "The Gospel of Matthew," 286.
107. See Bartlet, "Papias's 'Exposition'," 16–22; Robert M. Grant, "Papias and the Gospels" *ATR* 25 (1943): 218; Schoedel, *The Apostolic Fathers*, 5.91–92; Perumalil, "Papias," 335; Körtner, *Papias*, 89–94; Yarbrough, "The Date," 186–91; Schoedel, "Papias," 261; Gundry, "Pre-Papian Tradition," 50–52; MacDonald, *Two Shipwrecked Gospels*, 47; Kok, *The Gospel*, 110–11; Shanks, *Papias*, 91–92; Kok, *The Beloved Apostle*, 61–62; Bauckham, *Jesus*, 13–14; Furlong, *The Identity*, 7; Stevens, "Did Eusebius Read," 163. For an overview of all the arguments for the date of Papias's exposition, see Norelli, *Papia*, 37–54.
108. Körtner, *Papias*, 225; Hill, *The Johannine Corpus*, 384; Norelli, *Papia*, 53; MacDonald, *Two Shipwrecked Gospels*, 47; Bauckham, *Jesus*, 18, 459; Furlong, *The Identity*, 8.

an extended period in the last quarter of the first century.[109] Yet if the elder John was still around to be interviewed at the start of Trajan's reign, Papias could have talked to him in the last few years of the first century and published the results of his research shortly thereafter.[110]

Papias also chatted with Philip's daughters when he "had been with them" (*kata tous autous . . . genomenos*). The masculine participle may entail that he spent time with Philip too.[111] At any rate, his life overlapped with Philip's life.[112] It was common to misidentify Philip the evangelist, a leader of the Hellenizing wing of the Jewish Christ followers in Jerusalem and the father of four prophetesses, with the apostle Philip in another case of homonymity.[113] Philip's daughters astounded Papias with their news about the

---

109. Bauckham, *Jesus*, 18, 459.
110. I previously noted that it is not explicit in Papias's exposition that Aristion and the elder John had died (cf. Kok, *The Beloved Apostle*, 70). If they were alive, I should have dated Papias's exposition around 100 CE to match up with the date of John's death in Eusebius's *Chronicle*.
111. Shanks, *Papias*, 170.
112. Norelli, *Papia*, 46; Furlong, *The Identity*, 7.
113. See Eusebius, *H.E.* 3.31.3; 39.9; 5.24.2 (cf. Acts 6:5; 8:5, 6, 12, 13; 21:8). Matthews (*Philip*, 18–19, 93) defends an alternate theory that second-century Christian sources preserved the memory of a single Philip. He argues that the author of Acts, confused by the inclusion of "Philip" in the lists of the Twelve (Luke 6:14; Acts 1:13) and the Seven (Acts 6:5), invented a second Philip. Chapman (*John*, 64–71), Shanks (*Papias*, 169, 293–98), and Furlong (*The Identity*, 7, 15n.17) defend a third theory. They argue that Papias met the apostle Philip, not the evangelist Philip, in Hierapolis. They note that the evangelist Philip had four unmarried daughters who prophesied in Acts 21:9, whereas Polycrates of Ephesus specifies that the apostle Philip had three daughters, two of whom were virgins (cf. Eusebius, *H.E.* 3.31.3; 5.24.2). Yet after quoting Polycrates, Eusebius next quotes Gaius of Rome's rebuttal against the Montanist Proclus's boast that the evangelist Philip and his four daughters were buried in Hierapolis (3.31.4). Chapman (*John*, 69–71) avers that Gaius confused the apostle Philip who settled in Hierapolis with the evangelist Philip who had four daughters. Alternatively, Shanks (*Papias*, 297–98) contends that both the apostle Philip and the evangelist Philip, along with their daughters, migrated to Hierapolis. The simplest solution is that the two Philips were conflated due to the phenomenon of homonymity and someone forgot how many daughters the evangelist Philip had (cf. Schoedel, *The Apostolic Fathers*, 5.102; Körtner, *Papias*, 145–46; Kok, *The Beloved Apostle*, 96). Eusebius overlooked the contrast between the (apostle) Philip who had died before Papias began interviewing people and the (evangelist) Philip whom Papias may have met in Hierapolis (3.39.4, 9). Both Papias and the author of Acts independently attest to the charismatic authority of the evangelist Philip's daughters.

resurrection of a corpse and, perhaps, the miraculous survival of Justus Barsabbas after consuming deadly poison.[114]

Papias trusted his sources. They were not charlatans who "say many things" or impart "strange commands."[115] Papias's language was polemical, but the targets of his polemic are unidentifiable. There were second-century theologians such as Basilides, Marcion, and Valentinus, who famously divided the supremely transcendent spiritual deity from the demiurge, or "craftsman," who fashioned the material universe. Papias does not seem to be polemicizing against demiurgical cosmologies.[116] The followers of Basilides may have instead responded to Papias's claims about Mark by identifying their teacher as a disciple of Glaucius, the true interpreter of Peter.[117] There is the so-called "Anti-Marcionite Prologue" to John's Gospel, a Latin prologue dating to the fourth or fifth century, that pits the evangelist John and his amanuensis Papias against Marcion. The Latin text is garbled. It misspells the title of Papias's treatise, mistakes the elder John for the evangelist John, misunderstands Papias's role as John's hearer as meaning that he was the evangelist John's scribe, and misdates Marcion's ministry to the lifetime of the apostle John.[118] Papias's writing activity predated the rise of the demiurgical theologians.

---

114. See Eusebius, *H.E.* 3.39.9.
115. Eusebius, *H.E.* 3.39.4.
116. See Bartlet, "Papias's 'Exposition'," 21, 33; Munck, "Presbyters," 230; Schoedel, *The Apostolic Fathers*, 5.91, 97, 100–101, 104; Körtner, *Papias*, 167–72; Yarbrough, "The Date," 183, 187; Schoedel, "Papias," 270; Norelli, *Papia*, 95–105; Kok, *The Gospel*, 239–41. The efforts to find a critique of "Gnostic" theologies in Papias's wording are unconvincing (contra Lightfoot, *Supernatural Religion*, 147–49; Helmut Koester, *Ancient Christian Gospels: Their History and Development* [London: SCM, 1990], 34).
117. See Clement, *Str.* 7.106.4. See Martin Hengel, *The Four Gospels and the One Gospel of Jesus Christ* (trans. J. Bowden; London: SCM, 2000), 58. Hill ("Papias," 312–13) and Marcus (*Mark 1–8*, 22–23) reverse the direction of influence. Since Basilides produces twenty-four books commenting on the gospel (cf. Eusebius, *H.E.* 4.7.7), Hill reasons that Papias may have been complaining about Basilides' voluminous writings. Yet the vague charge about saying too much could be applied to any number of Christian writers in the period.
118. The evidence that Papias was polemicizing against Marcion is weak. Contra Markus Vincent, *Christ's Resurrection in Early Christianity and the Making of the New Testament* (Farnham: Ashgate, 2011), 96–98; Vincent, *Marcion and the Dating of the Synoptic Gospels* (Studia Patristica Supplements 2; Leuven: Peeters, 2014), 12–26. See the convincing analysis of this garbled Latin prologue in Carlson, *Papias*, 74–80.

There is also no basis in the De Boor fragments for dating Papias's exposition later in the second century. Isolating the interpolations added to Eusebius's *Ecclesiastical History* in a Byzantine epitome, the editor of the De Boor fragments printed some fragments that were adjacent to each other as one continuous fragment from Papias. This gave the misleading impression that Papias testified that there were individuals whom Christ raised from the dead living in the time of Hadrian, the Roman Emperor from 117 to 138 CE.[119] In Eusebius's *Ecclesiastical History*, it was Quadratus who directed an apology for the Christian faith to Hadrian and declared that there were resurrected persons who lived until his own day.[120] By double-checking the manuscript witnesses to the epitome, it was discovered that Papias was not credited as the source for the lengthy lifespans of the resurrected ones.[121] In *Codex Baroccianus* 142, one of the manuscript witnesses, the section on the persons resuscitated by Jesus stands apart from the preceding material about Papias in book three of Eusebius's *Ecclesiastical History*. In *Codex Vatopedi*, another manuscript witness, there is a heading about the opening of Eusebius's fourth book. The fourth book covers the apologies of Quadratus and Aristides.[122] Papias's writing activity should not be dated to Hadrian's reign.

Before the elder John died in the third year of Trajan's reign, Papias had a meeting with him. During the course of their conversation, Papias learned about the elder John's opinion about the origins of Mark's Gospel. This enables scholars to pinpoint when and where the tradition about the

---

119. See Bacon, "Syriac Translator," 17–18; Deeks, "Papias Revisited," 324; Martin Hengel, *Studies in the Gospel of Mark* (trans. John Bowden; London: SCM, 1985), 47, 149n.54; Hengel, *The Johannine Question*, 16, 97–98n.97; Hengel, *The Four Gospels*, 65, 252n.273; Culpepper, *John*, 109. Even if it is a genuine Papian fragment, Norelli (*Papia*, 52) does not date the publication of Papias's text beyond 125 CE. Shanks (*Papias*, 53–54; 216–19, 226) accepts the genuineness of the fragment but dates Papias's exposition around 110 CE. He reads the fragment as referring to Hadrian's whole life rather than just his tenure as emperor.

120. See Eusebius, *H.E.* 4.3.2. See Chapman, *John*, 97–98; Bartlet, "Papias's 'Exposition'," 22; Schoedel, *Fragments of Papias*, Körtner, *Papias*, 91; Yarbrough, "The Date," 185; Schoedel, "Papias," 236; Gundry, "Pre-Papian Tradition," 51–52; MacDonald, *Two Shipwrecked Gospels*, 46, 46n.5. Shanks (*Papias*, 53–54) counters that Quadratus may have taken this tradition from Papias.

121. Stevens, "The Origin," 636, 636n.26; Carlson, *Papias*, 67.

122. See Eusebius, *H.E.* 4.3.1–3.

evangelist Mark first emerged. It is a tradition that has shaped how Christians have read the Gospel of Mark for almost two millennia.

Who Was the Evangelist Mark?

The elder John could have been more specific about the Mark he had in mind. The Latin name *Marcus* may have been common in the Roman Empire,[123] but the list of candidates for the elder John's Mark can be narrowed down.[124] He may have been a non-Roman citizen. A Roman citizen would not be known by the praenomen *Marcus* alone (e.g., Marcus Tullius Cicero). He was a Jewish Christ-follower of some renown who needed no introduction. The best candidate may be a character in Acts known as John and surnamed Mark. Strangely, there are some late patristic and medieval authors who mixed up John Mark with the evangelist John behind the fourth Gospel. Both men were depicted as having a father named Aristobulus, possessing Levitical credentials, wearing the high priest's sacerdotal plate, owning the house where Jesus ate the Last Supper, upholding a Johannine Christology, or residing in Ephesus.[125] This is yet another illustration of how the phenomenon of homonymity works.

In Acts, John Mark's mother hosted a Christ assembly at her house in Jerusalem. Peter paid them a visit after he escaped from prison.[126] Next, John Mark traveled with the missionaries Paul and Barnabas, but Paul refused

---

123. This is noted, for example, by C. Clifton Black, *Mark: Images of an Apostolic Interpreter* (2nd ed.; Minneapolis: Fortress, 2001), 4, 17n.20; Maurice Casey, *Jesus of Nazareth: An Independent Historian's Account of His Life and Teaching* (London: T&T Clark International, 2010), 67.

124. For the following points, see Richard Bauckham, "The Gospel of Mark: Origins and Eyewitnesses" in *Earliest Christian History*, 159–61.

125. The parallels are surveyed by Dean Furlong, *The John also called Mark: Reception and Transformation in Christian Tradition* (Tübingen: Mohr Siebeck, 2020), 87–196. Furlong concludes that "while some of these correlations could be coincidental, the extent of the correlations for John and Mark is untypical for separate figures and is perhaps otherwise unattested" (p. 185). Even so, Black (*Mark*, 174n.29) is probably right in chalking this up to an accidental confusion of John Mark with the apostle John. Furlong's thesis that John Mark really was the fourth evangelist downplays the connection between Papias's tradition that the evangelist Mark assisted Peter and the association of (John) Mark with Peter in Acts 12:12 and 1 Pet 5:13.

126. See Acts 12:12.

to forgive him for deserting him in Pamphylia.[127] Mark is listed as one of Paul's coworkers in the undisputed and disputed letters of Paul.[128] The letter to the Colossians falls into the latter category due to the debates surrounding its authorship, but it has information about how Mark was Barnabas's cousin and one of Paul's coworkers "from the circumcision."[129] Paul had reprimanded Barnabas for hypocrisy for withdrawing from table fellowship with non-Jewish Christ followers at Antioch, which may be around the same time that Barnabas and John Mark parted ways with Paul.[130] Whatever tensions existed between Paul and Barnabas were smoothed over by the time the letter to the Colossians was penned. Finally, Peter, Silvanus, and Mark were toiling together in "Babylon" and Mark is praised as Peter's metaphorical son in 1 Peter.[131] A single person seems to be underlying every reference to (John) Mark in the New Testament.[132]

Nevertheless, Mark seems to have been increasingly attached to Peter in the later sources.[133] The earliest reference to Mark is in Paul's undisputed letter to Philemon. He is simply listed as one of Paul's coworkers. The letter to the Colossians adds biographical snippets about Mark's Jewish ethnicity

---

127. See Acts 12:25; 13:5, 13; 15:37–39.
128. See Phlm 1:24; Col 4:10; 2 Tim 4:11.
129. See Col 4:10.
130. Compare Gal 2:11–14 with Acts 15:37–39.
131. See 1 Pet 5:12–13.
132. This is contested by a few scholars. See Black, *Mark*, 25–43; Furlong, *The John*, 8–12. For Black, John Mark may have been the coworker of Paul and Barnabas, but he was also the failed missionary who did not get on board with expanding the Christ movement into non-Jewish territory. He was not the Mark who was Barnabas's "cousin" and Paul's loyal colleague in Black's view. However, Paul and John Mark may have reconciled at a later point, in the same way that Paul and Barnabas patched up their differences (cf. 1 Cor 9:6; Col 4:10). Furlong differentiates Paul's coworker John Mark in Acts and the Pauline Epistles from Peter's "son" Mark in 1 Pet 5:13, but Mark is always associated with Paul or a Pauline colleague like Barnabas or Silas/Silvanus in all the New Testament writings. This makes it more likely that the New Testament writers are referring to the same person. On this point, see Kok, *The Gospel*, 155.
133. My hypothesis that 1 Peter was the oldest text to associate Mark with Peter and its circulation in Asia Minor was the original impetus for the developing traditions about Mark in the region attested by the elder John and Acts was put forward in Kok, *The Gospel*, 121–60. For a critique of it, see Jonathan Bernier, *The Quest for the Historical Jesus after the Demise of Authenticity: Toward a Critical Realist Philosophy of History in Jesus Studies* (LNTS 540; London: T&T Clark, 2016), 131–33. I have revised some aspects of my reconstruction in light of Bernier's critique.

and familial bond with Barnabas. Like his cousin Barnabas, Mark may have acted as an intermediary between the Jerusalem apostles and Paul. Silvanus/Silas may have performed a similar role as someone who had been authorized as one of the delegates carrying a letter from the Jerusalem pillars to the Christ congregations in Antioch before voyaging around the Mediterranean with Paul.[134] The author of Acts had a penchant for supplying Semitic names for the characters in the narrative such as calling Paul Saul, Mark John, Silvanus Silas, or Justus Barsabbas Joseph,[135] but the details about John Mark's background are not at odds with the information supplied about him in the letter to the Colossians. Although he could have had ties with both the Jerusalem apostles and Paul, the three later sources that accentuate his relationship with Peter—1 Peter, Papias's exposition, and Acts—can all be isolated to Asia Minor.

Although it is signed by "Peter, an apostle of Jesus Christ,"[136] Peter may not have had an advanced education in literacy and rhetoric to pull off the composition of 1 Peter.[137] The expression "I wrote" (*egrapsa*) "through" (*dia*) Silvanus does not mean that Silvanus was Peter's secretary.[138] This idiomatic phrase presents Silvanus as the mail-carrier who delivered the letter to its recipients in the provinces of the Anatolian Peninsula in Asia Minor.[139] If Peter was one of the victims of Nero's pogrom against Christians in Rome,[140]

---

134. See Acts 15:22, 27, 32, 40; 16:19, 25, 29; 17:4, 10, 14, 15; 18:5; 2 Cor 1:19; 1 Thess 1:1; 2 Thess 1:1. Note that he is called Silas in the book of Acts and Silvanus in the letters.

135. MacDonald (*Two Shipwrecked Gospels*, 63) notes this Lukan tendency in arguing that the name Justus Barsabbas in Papias's exposition (cf. Eusebius, *H.E.* 3.39.9) is more primitive than the name in Acts 1:23.

136. See 1 Pet 1:1.

137. John H. Elliott, *1 Peter* (AB 37B; New Haven: Yale University Press, 2000), 3–7; Paul J. Achtemeier, *1 Peter* (Hermeneia; Minneapolis: Fortress, 1996), 44–68, 120.

138. See 1 Pet 5:12.

139. Elliott, *1 Peter*, 123–24; Achtemeier, *1 Peter*, 7–9. See Ignatius, *Smyrn.* 12:1; *Phil.* 11:2; *Magn.* 15:1; *Rom.* 10:1.

140. For the earliest references to Peter's death, see John 21:18–19; 2 Pet 1:14–15; *1 Clem* 5:4; Ignatius, *Rom.* 4.3; Dionysius of Corinth, in Eusebius, *H.E.* 2.25.8. For a case against the historicity of Peter's death in Rome, see Otto Zwierlein, *Petrus in Rom, die literarischen Zeugnisse: Mit einer kritischen Edition der Martyrien des Petrus und Paulus auf neuer handschriftlicher Grundlage. Untersuchungen zur antiken Literatur und Geschichte* (Bd. 96; Berlin: De Gruyter, 2009). Zwierlein reinterprets the cipher "Babylon" in 1 Pet 5:13 as a metaphor for living in exile rather than locating Peter in Rome specifically and dates *1 Clement* and the Ignatian Epistles quite late to 125 CE and 170 CE respectively.

he was no longer alive when 1 Peter was composed in the last quarter of the first century.[141] "Babylon" may be a cipher for Rome and may hint at the destruction of the Jerusalem temple in 70 CE.[142] It hearkens back to the national tragedy in the Hebrew Bible when the first temple was destroyed at the hands of the Babylonian Empire during a siege on Jerusalem in 587 BCE. The application of the identifying marker "Christian" to the implied audience of 1 Peter, marking out their collective identity in distinction from other Jewish and non-Jewish social identities, may be a late development as well.[143]

1 Peter may have originated among a school or circle in Rome founded by Peter and comprised of Silvanus, Mark, and the "elect lady."[144] The contents of the letter, however, do not seem to be particularly Petrine. Instead, the letter seems to construct an image of Peter as a figurehead legitimating a variety of liturgical and parenetic material stemming from multiple sources.[145] The setting in "Babylon" may be part of the transparent authorial fiction, enhancing the image of Peter constructed in the letter.[146] The audience of

---

His key contention is that the legends about Peter in Rome arose because Christian writers thought that Simon Magus had a following in the capital (cf. Justin, *1 Apol.* 26) and envisioned Peter moving there to confront his old nemesis (cf. Acts 8:18–24). I am not persuaded by his case against the historicity of Peter's death in Rome, though I accept that there may be hagiographical embellishment in the depiction of Peter's crucifixion. See Kok, *The Beloved Apostle*, 50–56.

141. See Elliott, *1 Peter*, 136–37; Achtemeier, *1 Peter*, 43–49.

142. See 1 Pet 5:13; cf. Rev 17:1–19:21.

143. See 1 Pet 4:15; cf. Acts 11:26; 26:28.

144. Elliott, *1 Peter*, 127–28, 888–89; cf. Achtemeier, *1 Peter*, 42; Chatelion Counet, "Pseudepigraphy and the Petrine School: Spirit and Tradition in 1 and 2 Peter and Jude," *HTS* 62.2 (2006): 404–10.

145. David G. Horrell, "The Product of a Petrine Circle? A Reassessment of the Origin and Character of 1 Peter," *JSNT* 86 (2002): 29–60; Kok, *The Gospel*, 138–39. For instance, there are parallels with the undisputed and disputed Pauline Epistles including the "grace and peace" formula in the salutation (1 Pet 1:2), the phrase "in Christ" (3:16; 5:10), and the terminology surrounding theological concepts such as the *charismata* or spiritual gifts (4:10–11). There are parallels with the letters of Paul and James in the parenetic sections, such as the ethic of nonviolence (3:9; cf. Rom 12:17; 1 Thess 5:15), the exhortation to submit to governing authorities (2:13–14; cf. Rom 13:1–17), the household codes (2:18–3:7; cf. Col 3:18–4:1; Eph 5:21–6:9), and the commands to be humble and resist the devil (5:5–10; Jas 4:6–10).

146. See Lutz Doering, "Apostle, Co-Elder, and Witness of Suffering: Author Construction and Peter Image in First Peter" in *Pseudepigraphie und Verfasserfiktion in frühchristlichen*

1 Peter would have known that Peter lost his life in Rome and was already participating in the glory that awaited them.[147] The addressees located on the Anatolian Peninsula may be as fictive as the letter's authorship.[148] However, the reception of the letter in the writings of early second-century bishops in Asia Minor substantiates that it circulated, and probably originated, somewhere in this region.[149] Christian unity is a central theme of the epistle.[150] This theme may have been reinforced by the inclusion of Mark and Silvanus in its final greetings. They were remembered as mediating between the Jerusalem apostles and Paul.[151]

An Ephesian provenance for Acts is defensible. The narrator steps into the action as a participant, using the first-person plural pronoun, in the chapters that are mostly set in the Aegean region. The exception is when the unidentified "we" sails with Paul to Italy.[152] Seventy verses, or 7 percent of the text, are located in Ephesus, and the author has an extensive familiarity with this locale.[153] Paul's speech to the Ephesian "presbyters" or "elders," urging them to guard the flock in their care as their "overseers" (*episkopoi*) from false teachers who would rise after Paul departed from this life, may mirror the author's own social context.[154] There are striking affinities with the pseudonymous letter of 1 Timothy. Timothy is instructed about the qualifications that ecclesiastical officeholders such as the "bishop" (*episkopos*) or the "presbyters" (*presbyteroi*) must possess and how to deal with rival teachers in Ephesus.[155] Finally, Ephesus was home to the elder John. Papias lived a mere

---

Briefen: Pseudepigraphy and Author Fiction in Early Christian Letters (ed. Jörg Frey et. al.; Tübingen: Mohr Siebeck, 2012), 647–62.

147. See 1 Pet 5:1.
148. See 1 Pet 1:1. See Will Robinson and Stephen R. Llewelyn, "The Fictitious Audience of 1 Peter" *Heythrop J.* 61.6 (2020) 939–50.
149. See Papias, in Eusebius, *H.E.* 2.15.2; 3.39.17; 4.14.9; Polycarp, *Phil.* 1:3; 2:1; 5:3; 7:2; 8:1, 2; 10:1.
150. See 1 Pet 2:4–10; 3:8; 4:8–11; 5:9.
151. Horrell, "The Product," 26; Doering, "Apostle," 666; Kok, *The Gospel*, 141–42.
152. See Acts 16:10–17; 20:5–15; 21:1–18; 27:1–28:16. Richard Pervo, "Acts in Ephesus (and Environs) 115" *Forum* 4.2 (2015): 128.
153. See Acts 18:19–21, 24–27a; 19:1–40; 20:16–38. See Pervo, "Acts," 128–29.
154. See Acts 20:17–37.
155. See 1 Tim 1:3–4; 3:1–7; 5:17–19. For a comparison between the social situations presupposed in Paul's speech to the Ephesian presbyters in Acts and in 1 Timothy, see Pervo, "Acts," 133–41.

93 miles or 150 kilometres away in Hierapolis. The Gospel of Luke, and its sequel Acts, provides independent multiple attestation for some traditions in Papias's exposition.[156]

Both Papias's exposition and Luke's Gospel begin with literary prologues.[157] They stress the necessity of discerning the right sources "to follow" (*parakolouthein*). Papias was satisfied that Mark "accurately" (*akribōs*) recalled Peter's teachings. Luke sought to follow everything documented about Jesus from the beginning "accurately" (*akribōs*). Where Mark allegedly failed in organizing the account in "order" (*taxis*) from the elder John's vantage point, Luke succeeded in arranging the narrative "in an orderly fashion" (*kathexēs*). There may be no direct literary relationship between their prologues if they utilized stock rhetorical terminology and tropes, but they both may presuppose an older critical evaluation of the Gospel of Mark.[158] There is no evidence from Papias's prologue, however, that he disparaged the "order" of Mark's Gospel by comparing it directly to Luke's Gospel.[159]

In both Papias's exposition and Luke's Gospel, Jesus has compassion for a woman reputed to be a transgressor. Papias has none of the details about how she washed Jesus's feet with her tears and anointed them with oil at the house of Simon the Pharisee.[160] One of the Armenian fragments that has been assigned to Papias has a quote from Luke's Gospel. In the Greek

---

156. Körtner, *Papias*, 173–76; Norelli, *Papia*, 105–12, 124; Kok, *The Gospel*, 151–53; Kok, *The Beloved Apostle*, 60–61; Michael J. Kok, "Justin Martyr and the Authorship of Luke's Gospel" *JGRChJ* 18 (2022): 20–22.

157. See Luke 1:1–4, Papias, in Eusebius, *H.E.* 3.39.3–4, 15–16.

158. For the scholars arguing that Papias was dependent on Luke's prologue, see Grant, "Papias," 219; Ralph P. Martin, *Mark: Evangelist and Theologian* (Grand Rapids: Zondervan, 1978), 81–83; Michael Goulder, *Luke: A New Paradigm* (Sheffield: JSOT, 1989), 1.200; Charles E. Hill, "What Papias Said about John (and Luke): A New 'Papian' Fragment" *JTS* 49 (1998): 625; Theo K. Heckel, *Vom Evangelium des Markus zum viergestaltigen Evangelium* (WUNT, 120; Tübingen: Mohr Siebeck, 1999), 262. Contrariwise, a few scholars argue that Luke depended on Papias's prologue. See Annand, "Papias," 50–53; MacDonald, *Two Shipwrecked Gospels*, 44–45, 53–58. I am not persuaded that there was any direct literary contact between their prologues.

159. Contra Martin, *Mark*, 81–83. Martin's theory is that Papias promoted Peter's Gospel in response to Marcion's advocacy for a Pauline Gospel. The flaw in his thesis, besides dating Papias's exposition to the time of Marcion, is that it would be counterproductive to admit that the Gospel of Mark lacked "order" if Papias wanted to set it on par with Marcion's Gospel. See Kok, *The Gospel*, 197.

160. See Luke 7:36–50; Papias, in Eusebius, *H.E.* 3.39.17.

text of the seventh-century Cappadocian bishop Andrew of Caesarea's *Commentary on Revelation*, Andrew was elucidating the chapter in Revelation about the war in heaven against the dragon.[161] He applied a quote from Papias about a short-lived arrangement in which the angels ruled the earth to this passage.[162] Two Vienna manuscripts of the Armenian translation of this section could be read as extending Papias's quotation to a line from Luke's Gospel about how Satan fell from heaven like lightning.[163] The quotation of this Lukan verse, however, was probably not original to Papias nor to Andrew but was added later as part of the supplementary commentary on Andrew's exegesis.[164]

Both Papias's exposition and Acts name-drop Justus Barsabbas and the daughters of Philip. Justus was almost elected as the twelfth apostle after lots were cast to pick Judas's replacement in Acts and was unharmed after drinking poison in the exposition.[165] Philip's daughters were located in Caesarea in Acts and Hierapolis in the exposition.[166] Both state that James, the son of Zebedee, was killed, but Acts blames Herod Agrippa for executing him.[167] Both had a tradition that Judas lived on after Easter.[168]

Sorting out the data about Judas's last days is complicated. An etymology for the "field of blood" is furnished in Matthew's Gospel and Acts by linking it to Judas's death. Judas hanged himself in Matthew's Gospel. The field that the chief priests bought with his blood money was known by its awful name "until this day" (*heōs tēs sēmeron*).[169] In Acts, Judas purchased the "field" (*chōrion*). There he fell face forwards, his body burst open, his intestines

---

161. See Rev 12:7–9.
162. See Andrew of Caesarea, *Comm. Rev.* 34.12.
163. See Luke 10:18. See Folker Siegert, "Unbeachtete Papiaszitate bei armenischen Schriftstellern" *NTS* 27 (1981): 606–7; cf. Lightfoot, *Supernatural Religion*, 186; Armin Daniel Baum, "Papias als Kommentator Evangelischer Aussprüche Jesu" *NovT* 38 (1996): 265, 265n.62; Hill, "What Papias Said," 625.
164. See Carlson, *Papias*, 91–93. Previous scholars just argued that the quotation from Papias did not extend to the citation of Luke 10:18. Körtner, *Papias*, 35–36; Schoedel, "Papias," 260; Norelli, *Papia*, 400–407.
165. See Acts 1:23–26; Papias, in Eusebius, *H.E.* 3.39.9.
166. See Acts 21:8; Papias, in Eusebius, *H.E.* 3.39.9.
167. See Acts 12:2.
168. See Acts 1:18–20; Apollinaris of Laodicea, *Comm. Matt.* 27.5; contra Matt 27:3–10.
169. See Matt 27:3–10.

spilled out, and his habitation became "desolate" (*erēmos*).[170] Whatever Papias wrote about Judas was extended by Apollinaris, the fourth-century bishop of Laodicea, in his lost *Commentary on Matthew*. There are two variant versions of Apollinaris's tradition in the catenae or collections of exegetical comments from Christian interpreters.[171] In both, Judas became a living illustration of the cost of impiety. His flesh became so bloated that he could not pass through an entrance that a wagon could pass through. His eyelids were so swollen that he could not see the light of day and his enlarged private parts emitted pus and worms. After much agony, he died in his "field" (*chōrion*).[172] It became "desolate" (*erēmos*) as the stench of his bodily discharges lingered there "until this day" (*mechri tēs sēmeron*). In the version that is likely secondary, the swelling of his body is repeated twice, he is crushed by "the wagon" (*hē hamaxa*), and his entrails poured out.[173]

The story in Acts may have been increasingly exaggerated by Papias, Apollinaris, and the catena compilers.[174] The direction of influence could also run from Papias to Acts.[175] Contrary to both views, the oral tradition

---

170. See Acts 1:18–20.
171. See Körtner, *Papias*, 26–30; Norelli, *Papia*, 336–50; Carlson, *Papias*, 42–47. See *Catena in Evangelium S. Matthaei* and the *Catena in Acta SS Apostolorum*. Carlson discovered a third form of the catena in an eighteenth-century Moscow manuscript published by Christian Fredrick Matthaei. It assigns the swelling of Judas's body solely to Apollinaris. Carlson also cites the twelfth-century chronicler Michael Glycas's refutation of Papias's claim that Judas continued to walk around as an example of ungodliness, without noting Apollinaris's details about Judas's medical condition or final demise (*Ep.* 56).
172. For Judas's medical symptoms and the cultural interpretation of them, see Candida Moss, "A note on the death of Judas in Papias" *NTS* 65.3 (2019): 388–97.
173. Carlson (*Papias*, 49) notes that the article before "wagon" presupposes a specific wagon, but the previous line was not speaking about a specific wagon. It was comparing the size of Judas's body to a hypothetical wagon. Judas also would not have been run over by a wagon while he was in a field. What Carlson suspects happened in the second form of the catena is that two citations from Apollinaris's commentary, one which had an interpolated note about Judas getting run over by "the wagon," were combined.
174. Shanks, *Papias*, 204–6.
175. MacDonald, *Two Shipwrecked Gospels*, 30–34, 59–63 76–78. MacDonald conjectures that Judas's suicide in Matt 27:3–10 was invented to show his remorse, thereby permitting a repentant Judas to sit on one of the twelve eschatological thrones (Matt 19:28// Luke 22:30). In his view, Papias rejected this story of Judas's contrition and devised an ignoble end for the traitor. Acts transformed Papias's account in picturing Judas falling "face down" (*prēnēs*) in a field like a coward fleeing from battle and getting struck down from behind. MacDonald's strongest argument is that the adjective *erēmos*

that Papias inherited may have been concocted independently from the accounts in Matthew's Gospel and Acts. Papias's tradition may have been limited to a rumor that Judas was divinely punished for his ungodliness when his body swelled up beyond the size of a wagon. Apollinaris may have expanded on Judas's physical ailment and death.[176] For instance, the putrefaction of Judas's genitals fits a condition known as Fournier gangrene. The Roman Emperor Galerius (ca. 305–11) contracted this disease.[177] If Papias reported that Judas was afflicted with these symptoms, Eusebius missed his chance to compare an infamous emperor who persecuted Christians to Jesus's betrayer.[178] The linguistic parallels with the accounts in Matthew's Gospel and Acts may, therefore, be attributable to Apollinaris. Apollinaris harmonized all three traditions by showing that Judas did not suffocate by hanging but contracted a medical condition that caused his death in the field.

Papias's oral tradents and the authors of Matthew's Gospel and Acts, on the other hand, just had Mark's narrative of Judas's betrayal before them. Mark did not divulge what happened to Judas after he betrayed Jesus, though there was another memory that a field was purchased in his name.

("desolate") in Acts 1:20 agrees with Apollinaris against the proof-text cited from Psalm 68:26 LXX that has the participle *ērēmōmenē* ("having become desolate"). Against this reconstruction, Matt 27:3–10 and Acts 1:18–20 may be independent accounts about Judas's death, since they only agree on the name of the field. MacDonald concedes that the author of Acts had independent information about this place when transliterating the Aramaic title given to it (p. 30). The linguistic parallels to Matt 27:3–10 and Acts 1:18–20 in Apollinaris's commentary may come from Apollinaris himself rather than from Papias. This may be why Apollinaris agrees with Acts in reusing the adjective *erēmos* ("desolate"). Papias may have had an independent and less embellished oral account about the swelling of Judas's body.

176. See Bartlet, "Papias's 'Exposition'," 36–39; Carlson, *Papias*, 50–56. As Carlson points out, Apollinaris switched to the vague "they say" (*phasi*) when communicating the gossip that was passed around about Judas's death in his own day. Papias, on the other hand, usually names his sources. Some of the textual evidence reviewed by Carlson, moreover, attributes some of the more gruesome details to Apollinaris rather than to Papias. Finally, no writer before Apollinaris notes that Papias wrote about Judas's agonizing death in his own field. Eusebius, for instance, simply mentions that Judas hanged himself (cf. *H.E.* 5.16.13). Carlson discovered a scholium attributed to Eusebius in which he harmonized Matt 27:3–10 and Acts 1:18–20 by claiming that Judas's rope broke and he died in his own bed two days later.

177. See Eusebius, *H.E.* 8.16.2–5; Lactantius, *On the Death of Persecuting Emperors* 33.6–8.

178. Carlson, *Papias*, 54–55.

In Matthew's Gospel, Judas's demise is conformed to how Ahithophel, the royal advisor who betrayed King David, hanged himself.[179] In Papias's oral tradition, Judas's body swelled up as a penalty for his greed.[180] The author of Acts might have been familiar with this oral tradition about Judas's swollen condition, which may be why Acts could picture Judas's body bursting open after his fateful fall in his field. Papias may have only come across Matthew's Gospel, and its alternate account of Judas's suicide, after he interviewed his various tradents in Asia Minor.

One last noteworthy parallel between Papias and Acts is that both writers link (John) Mark with Peter. John Mark is purposefully introduced in the company of Peter before he became Paul's and Barnabas's "assistant" (*hypēretēs*), likely to showcase the continuity between the ministries of Peter and Paul.[181] A *hypēretēs* may denote someone who handles texts, so he may have been involved in the catechetical training of the newly baptized.[182] He was less than an ideal character, deserting Paul on his first missionary journey.[183] His ambivalent characterization in Acts could be lined up with the lukewarm assessment of Mark's Gospel in the Lukan prologue.[184] Luke's sources went back to "the witnesses and assistants of the word from the beginning" (*hoi ap' archēs autoptai kai hypēretai genomenoi tou logou*).[185] Mark was a *hypēretēs* and Luke wanted to supplant his "narrative" (*diēgēsis*) with one that was "in order"

---

179. See 2 Sam 17:23. See MacDonald, *Two Shipwrecked Gospels*, 32; Gundry, *Peter*, 62.

180. Moss, "A Note," 365–67; Carlson, *Papias*, 56.

181. See Acts 12:12; 13:5.

182. B. T. Holmes, "Luke's Description of John Mark" *JBL* 54 (1935): 65–68; R. O. P. Taylor, "The Ministry of Mark," *ExpTim* 54 (1943): 136–38; Kok, *The Gospel*, 157.

183. See Acts 13:13.

184. For the possibility that this was an implicit critique of Mark's Gospel, see Adela Collins, *Mark: A Commentary* (Hermeneia; Minneapolis: Fortress, 2007), 5; Kok, *The Gospel*, 156–59.

185. See Luke 1:2–3. The wording of the Lukan prologue could be lined up with Papias's view that Peter was an eyewitness and Mark was his assistant. See MacDonald, *Two Shipwrecked Gospels*, 44–45. On the other hand, the Lukan prologue may be specifying a single group, bracketed by the article and the participle, whose job was to witness to and authenticate the foundational literary traditions of the Christian community. For this reading, see J. N. Collins, "Rethinking 'Eyewitnesses' in the Light of 'Servants of the Word' (Luke 1:2)" *ExpTim* 121 (2010): 451–52. Mark may have performed this service.

(*kathexēs*).[186] Luke may have known the elder John's tradition that Mark did not put Peter's eyewitness recollections in "order" (*taxis*).[187] On the other hand, the term *hypēretēs* may not specify the menial tasks that Mark performed for Paul and Barnabas. He may have organized their traveling arrangements, monitored their finances, or baptized their converts.[188] Whether or not the author of Acts knew what the elder John said about Mark may be inconclusive.

What can be concluded is that 1 Peter, Acts, and the elder John multiply attest an evolving tradition about Mark's affiliation with Peter in Asia Minor from the last quarter of the first century onwards. The circulation of 1 Peter in the region may have encouraged this development. Papias and the author of Acts may have been near contemporaries living in nearby locales, which may be why they share a handful of oral traditions, including one directly associating Mark with Peter. Mark was reconceived as Peter's son, colleague, and "interpreter" (*hermēneutēs*). The last description cannot be traced back before the elder John in Ephesus. Papias inherited two lines of tradition about Mark from the elder John and 1 Peter.[189] While the elder John's supposition about Peter's role in the composition history of Mark's Gospel has been contested by some modern scholars, his attribution of the Gospel to John Mark is generally accepted.[190] Nevertheless, it may have served the elder John's agenda to vouch for the accuracy of the text by linking it with an authoritative apostolic figure, while blaming its literary defects on Peter's less reputable assistant Mark.[191]

---

186. Luke's critical stance toward his predecessors is rightly stressed in Keith, *Gospel as Manuscript*, 125–29.
187. See Papias, in Eusebius, *H.E.* 3.39.15.
188. Black, *Mark*, 27; Furlong, *The John*, 9.
189. See Papias, in Eusebius, *H.E.* 2.15.2; 3.39.15.
190. Schoedel ("Papias," 258) points out that the attribution of the Gospel of Mark to John Mark "is the one element in the notice that receives broad scholarly support."
191. Kok, *The Gospel*, 108; cf. James G. Crossley, *The Date of Mark's Gospel: Insight from the Law in Earliest Christianity* (London: T&T Clark, 2004), 14. Dungan (*The Synoptic Problem*, 20–23) argues that the elder John had a competitive rivalry with Peter and was putting the blame on Peter for not providing Mark with a complete summary of Jesus's life. Yet it is unlikely that the elder John blamed Peter for Mark's daring decision to compile an entire biography of Jesus from Peter's occasional sermons that he transcribed.

What Did the Evangelist Mark
Do Wrong?

At a minimum, the elder John held that Mark was Peter's "interpreter," but did not put what Jesus "had said or done" in "order." Mark's role as the interpreter of Peter may have been to mediate the apostle's teachings to new audiences, explicating or expanding on what Peter said to them.[192] Peter may have had no need of a translator if he was somewhat conversant in Greek due to the Hellenization of Galilee.[193] Mark may have become Peter's "expositor" in reshaping Peter's teachings about Jesus for his Gospel.[194] Yet the emphasis of this fragment from Papias does not fall on Mark's creative exposition of Peter's teachings but on his accurate recollection and faithful transmission of them.[195] Mark was absolutely not a creative author in the eyes of the elder John; he was a textualizer of Peter's speeches.[196] It is not explicitly stated that Mark translated Peter's words from Aramaic to Greek when transmitting them in writing,[197] but it is likely that Papias took the elder John's description of Mark as a *hermēneutēs* in the sense of a "translator." Papias used the cognate verb *hermēneuō* when reporting that people "translated" (*hērmēneusen*) what Matthew had written in the Hebrew "language" (*dialektos*).[198] Peter could have had a limited facility in Greek as a second language but benefited from the services of a translator as he was not a native Greek speaker.

According to the elder John, Mark was Peter's translator. He may have thought that Peter left Mark with a written document in Aramaic for him to translate. Mark veered away from formally translating it word-for-word, adding "some things" (*enia*) to it based on his fuzzy memories about what he had heard Peter say.[199] It is far more likely that what the elder John had in

---

192. *Hermēneutēs* is translated as a "Mittelsmann" in Kürzinger, *Papias*, 16.

193. Gundry, "The Apostolically Johannine," 61.

194. Gundry, "The Apostolically Johannine," 62.

195. Candida Moss, "Fashioning Mark: Early Christian Discussions about the Scribe and Status of the Second Gospel" *NTS* 67.2 (2021): 187.

196. Matthew Larsen, *Gospels before the Book* (Oxford: Oxford University Press, 2018), 90.

197. Yadin-Israel, "Peter's Tanna," 347–48.

198. See Armin Daniel Baum, "Der Presbyter des Papias über einen 'Hermeneuten' des Petrus: Zu Eusebius, Hist. eccl. 3,39,15" *TZ* 56 (2000): 21–35; cf. Körtner, *Papias*, 205–6; Schoedel, "Papias," 258.

199. Terrence Y. Mullins, "Papias on Mark's Gospel," *VC* 14 (1960): 221–23.

mind was that Mark translated Peter's public speeches. Peter was a preacher, but he did not have formal training in literacy. *Enia* could be translated as a smaller portion of a larger text,[200] but it could also be a comment on the brevity of Mark's content as a whole.[201] It represented but a fraction of everything that Jesus did when he was on earth.[202] Mark translated Peter's spoken words about Jesus's sayings and deeds from Aramaic to Greek.[203] Unaccredited translation work was usually done by slaves or freed-persons who, even if paid for their labor, were treated as servile workers.[204] If the aorist participle *genomenos* ("having become") is taken as concurrent with the aorist verb *egrapsen* ("he wrote"), Mark may have been simultaneously translating and note-taking while Peter was dictating to him.[205] It may be more likely that Mark became Peter's interpreter before writing Peter's words down. That is, he offered his translation services for Peter whenever he communicated with Greek-speaking audiences. One day he transcribed "some things" as well as he could recall them from Peter's speeches.[206]

The elder John's frank assessment of the lack of "order" (*taxis*) in Mark's Gospel does not seem to accord with the literary artistry evident throughout it. It is conceivable that a scribe misheard *tachei* as *taxei* when copying an exemplar of Papias's exposition as it was read aloud to him or her. If so, the elder John's original point was that Mark's notes were not drafted up "in a hasty manner."[207] Appealing to hypothetical textual amendments should be the last resort when there is no supporting textual evidence. The Lukan prologue seems to concur with the elder John that the problem was with Mark's

---

200. Mullins, "Papias," 219–20. See 2 Macc 2:31; 1 Clem 44:6; 2 Clem 19:2; *Diog.* 5:3.

201. Bauckham, *Jesus*, 219. See Lucian, *Demon.* 12.

202. Carlson ("Papias," 39, 39n.191) has a different reading of this line. He argues that Mark only recorded a few scriptural oracles about Jesus in his Gospel, while Matthew produced a compilation of oracles from the Hebrew Bible in his native language. I will engage Carlson's reading in the next chapter on Matthew's "oracles."

203. Moss ("Fashioning Mark," 187) rightly explains that the elder John envisioned Mark as "acting as an oral linguistic interpreter who translated Peter's Aramaic into Greek . . . just as translators function in the Septuagint (Gen 42.23) and Pauline epistles (1 Cor 12.10; 14.23)."

204. Moss, "Fashioning Mark," 181–204.

205. Moss, "Fashioning Mark," 192; cf. Kürzinger, *Papias*, 45–46; Gundry, "Pre-Papian Tradition," 62; Bauckham, *Jesus*, 211–12.

206. Baum, "Der Presbyter," 22–23; Casey, *Jesus*, 67; Kok, *The Gospel*, 187.

207. Horace A. Rigg, "Papias on Mark" *NovT* 1 (1956): 171–72.

arrangement of the material. Scholars need to put themselves in the mindset of ancient thinkers who assessed the Gospels before the advent of modern literary criticism.

The elder John disapproved of Mark's "order" (*taxis*), which could be construed as a criticism of Mark's chronological outline.[208] Since Mark was not an eyewitness of Jesus and just had his memories of Peter's sermons to work with, it would be unfair to expect him to put every event that occurred during Jesus's ministry in the correct chronological order. The elder John may have been grappling with the issue of what to do when there are episodes about Jesus ordered in different sequences depending on the Gospel one reads. Any student who has studied the Synoptic Problem or compared the Synoptic and Johannine Gospels in any depth has faced this issue. Getting the chronology of certain events right mattered to some historians, but they tended to use the words *chronos* or *kairos* for sequential time.[209]

It is more likely that *taxis* denotes the literary or rhetorical arrangement of Mark's material.[210] In his analysis of the methodology of historiographers in *How to Write History*, the second-century satirist Lucian of Samosata outlines how a historian starts with a "rough draft" (*hypomnēma*) before putting his or her material in a proper "arrangement" (*taxis*) and improving its "style" (*lexis*).[211] The finished product has a suitable "beginning" (*archē*) and the proper "arrangement" (*taxis*) of the subject's deeds.[212] For an ancient rhetorical critic, Mark's Gospel seemed incomplete. It did not start with

208. Arthur Wright, "*Taxei* in Papias" *JTS* 14 (1913): 298–300; Körtner, *Papias*, 212; Hengel, *Studies*, 48–49; Hengel, *The Four Gospels*, 66; MacDonald, *Two Shipwrecked Gospels*, 13–14, 522–23; Casey, *Jesus*, 67; Bauckham, *Jesus*, 217–21.
209. Alistair Stewart-Sykes, "*Taxei* in Papias: Again" *JECS* 3 (1995): 489–90. See Thucydides, *Hist.* 1.97.2; Philostratus, *Vit. Apoll.* 1.2; Polybius, *Hist.* 5.33.
210. F. H. Colson, "Τάξει in Papias (The Gospels and the Rhetorical Schools)" *JTS* 14 (1912): 62–69; Schoedel, *The Apostolic Fathers*, 5.106; Kürzinger, *Papias*, 13–14; Schoedel, "Papias," 256; Alistair Stewart-Sykes, "*Taxei* in Papias: Again" *JECS* 3 (1995): 487–92; Gundry, "Pre-Papian Tradition," 63; Black, *Mark*, 91; Norelli, *Papia*, 301–7; Collins, *Mark*, 85; Kok, *The Gospel*, 188–90; Charles E. Hill, "The 'Orthodox Gospel': The Reception of John in the Great Church Prior to Irenaeus" in *The Legacy of John: Second-Century Reception of the Fourth Gospel* (ed. Tuomas Rasimus; Leiden: Brill, 2009), 291; Larsen, *Gospel*, 91–92 106–7; Furlong, *The Identity*, 144–46.
211. See Lucian, *Quom. Hist. conscr.* 48.
212. See Lucian, *Quom. Hist. conscr.* 6.

Jesus's ancestry and birth. It ended abruptly on a cliff-hanger with the women's discovery of the empty tomb. Apart from the tight chronological structure of Mark's Passion Narrative, Mark seems to narrate a bunch of episodes that are loosely tied together. Some sayings or stories are grouped together topically.[213] The strongest objection against taking *taxis* as a rhetorical term is that the elder John's excuse for Mark was not that he did not have an opportunity to be educated in rhetoric. It was that Mark did not witness the events that he recorded. Nevertheless, the connection between the admission that Mark followed Peter at a late stage and the lack of *taxis* in his Gospel is that the evangelist loosely strung some anecdotes together that he remembered from Peter's preaching. The resulting literary product lacked a proper beginning and ending and did not contain enough of Jesus's sayings and deeds nor arranged them in a rhetorically effective manner.

Mark's text could be categorized as a collection of *chreiai* or short, pithy sayings assigned to a particular person that unveils his or her character.[214] Not all of Mark's material conforms to the definition of a *chreia*.[215] This view depends on translating Papias's phrase *pros tas chreias* as Peter adapting his teachings "according to the style of *chreiai*."[216] It may be better to translate this line as Peter adapting his teachings according "to the needs" of his differing audiences who invited him to preach.[217] Another option is that the elder John was referring to Mark's preliminary notebook that lacked "order" before he shaped his notes into a publishable book.[218] However, it may be Mark's text itself that was appraised as a textualized *aide memoire*, like other unfinished "memorial writings" termed as *hypomnēmata* or *apomnēmoneumata* in Greek

---

213. For instance, see the controversy stories in Mark 2:1–3:6 or the parables in 4:1–34.
214. Stewart-Sykes, "*Taxei*," 490–92.
215. See Aelius Theon, *Prog.* 3.2–3.
216. See Kürzinger, *Papias*, 23; 52–56; cf. Schoedel, *The Apostolic Fathers*, 5.107; Gundry, "The Apostolically Johannine," 63–64; Bauckham, *Jesus*, 214–17; Shanks, *Papias*, 188–90.
217. Davies and Allison, *Matthew 1–7*, 16; Körtner, *Papias*, 158; Matthew Black, "The Use of Rhetorical Terminology in Papias on Mark and Matthew," *JSNT* 37 (1989): 34; Baum, "Der Presbyter," 24–25; Baum, "Ein aramäischer Urmatthäus im kleinasiatischen Gottesdienst. Das Papiaszeugnis zur Entstehung des Matthäusevangeliums," *ZNW* 92 (2001): 264.
218. George Kennedy, "Classical and Christian Source Criticism" in *The Relationship among the Gospels: An Interdisciplinary Dialogue* (ed. William O. Walker; San Antonio: Trinity University Press, 1978), 148.

and *commentarii* in Latin.[219] It could be objected that Papias employed the verb *apomnēmoneuō* for what Mark "remembered" (*apemnēmoneusen*), not the noun *apomnēmoneumata* to categorize the genre of Mark's Gospel.[220] Nevertheless, Mark's work was basically appraised as a rough draft that a highly trained writer would revise and polish by improving its order and style.[221]

The Gospels could be classified as *hypomnēmata* or *apomnēmoneumata* by the ancient Christian intelligentsia.[222] Clement of Alexandria interpreted Papias in this way in his lost *Hypotyposes*, which Eusebius paraphrased twice.[223] In both paraphrases, there is an "audience request tradition" from Peter's Roman listeners.[224] They urged Mark to draft up some *hypomnēma* for them to have a record of Peter's oral proclamations.[225] Unlike the Gospels with "the genealogies" that were "set forth publicly" (*prographō*),[226] Mark did not intend for this textualized *aide memoire* to be distributed beyond Peter's auditors in Rome.[227] When Peter learned what Mark had done, he responded with indifference, neither forbidding nor encouraging them to study Mark's notes.[228] Unable to fathom why Peter reacted to Mark's efforts so apathetically, Eusebius adjusted Clement's wording to read that Peter enthusiastically endorsed the dissemination of Mark's Gospel in the

---

219. For these terms as interchangeable, see Wally V. Cirafesi and Gregory P. Fewster, "Justin's Ἀπομνημονεύματα and Ancient Greco-Roman Memoirs" *EC* 7.2 (2016): 192–95. There is an excellent survey of *hypomnēmata* as unfinished textual objects in the Greco-Roman world in Larsen, *Gospels*, 11–36; Matthew D. C. Larsen and Mark Letteney, "Christians and the Codex: Generic Materiality and Early Gospel Traditions" *JECS* 27.3 (2019): 394–99.
220. Keith, *The Gospel*, 52–53; cf. Norelli, *Papia*, 79–80.
221. Larsen, *Gospels*, 93; cf. Kok, *The Gospel*, 192, 210–11.
222. See Justin Martyr, 1 *Apol.* 66.3; 67.3; *Dial.* 100.4; 101.3; 102.5; 103.6, 8; 104.1; 105.1, 5, 6; 106.1, 3, 4; 107.1; Clement, in Eusebius, *H.E.* 2.15.1 (cf. 3.24.5); Origen, *Cels.* 2.13.
223. See Clement, in Eusebius, *H.E.* 2.15.1–2; 6.14.5–7. For analyses of the similarities and differences between these two paraphrases, see Black, *Mark*, 143; Kok, *Margins*, 206–13.
224. See Clement, in Eusebius, *Hist. eccl.* 2.15.1; 6.14.6. Mitchell, "Patristic Counter-Evidence," 50n.42, 51.
225. The text is identified as Mark's *hypomnēma* in Eusebius, *H.E.* 2.15.1; Kok, *The Gospel*, 210–11; Larsen, *Gospels*, 97–98.
226. Carlson, "Clement of Alexandria," 122–23; cf. Kok, *Margins*, 210–11.
227. See Clement, in Eusebius, *H.E.* 6.14.5–6.
228. See Clement, in Eusebius, *H.E.* 6.14.6.

churches.[229] Clement differentiated the writings of Mark, Matthew, and Luke on the basis of whether they were intended for private use or wider public consumption. This is not to say that some of the evangelists did not consider their contributions to be more refined "books."[230] There is room to discuss whether the Synoptic Gospels were received as discrete and stable texts in antiquity,[231] but the elder John seems to have judged Mark's text to belong to the generic category of pre-literary *hypomnēmata*.

The elder John may have compared Mark's and Matthew's compilations of the *logia* ("oracles") to the detriment of the former. Peter and Matthew required translators because their native tongue was Aramaic. Mark was Peter's "translator" (*hermēneutēs*) and unidentified servile workers "translated" (*hērmēneusen*) Matthew's work. In contrast to Mark's inability to put Jesus's sayings and deeds in "order" (*taxis*) and make a suitable "arrangement" (*syntaxis*) of the "oracles" (*logia*) "of the Lord" (*kyriakōn*), Matthew carefully "arranged" (*synetaxato*) the "oracles" (*logia*). By removing Eusebius's editorial interruption separating the two excerpts in *Ecclesiastical History*, the conjunction *oun* ("so then") at the start of the line about Matthew could refer to the previous line about Mark.[232] This would be remarkably early support for the theory of Markan priority if Matthew arranged the "oracles" to compensate for Mark's failure to do so.[233] There may have even been some recognition that Matthew actually

---

229. See Clement, in Eusebius, *H.E.* 2.15.2.

230. Keith, *The Gospel*, 55. See Matt 1:1; John 20:30; 21:25. In contrast to Keith, Papias's contrast between the living voice and books should be excluded from this list (in Eusebius, *H.E.* 3.39.4). Papias was repeating a proverbial expression about why it is better to consult living witnesses rather than written texts. His literary assessment of the Gospels of Mark and Matthew is restricted to *H.E.* 3.39.15–16.

231. Larsen (*Gospels*, 1–9) critiques scholars for importing modern, anachronistic conceptions of book production onto the ancient data. Broadhead (*Landscape*, 50) conceives what we call the Gospel of Matthew as a "variable, viable work in process and that this process is an essential component of its identity and function." For a critique of Larsen's arguments, see Keith, *The Gospel*, 49–60.

232. See Eusebius, *H.E.* 3.39.15–16. Kürzinger, *Papias*, 10–11; Gundry, "Pre-Papian Tradition," 55–56; Watson, *Gospel Writing*, 126; Shanks, *Papias*, 193.

233. Kürzinger, *Papias*, 10–11; Gundry, "Pre-Papian Tradition," 55–56; Watson, *Gospel Writing*, 126; Larsen, *Gospels*, 92.

rearranged Mark's own *logia* ("oracles") in reproducing the bulk of Mark's content.[234]

The unmistakable parallelism between these two lines does not prove that the elder John originated the tradition about Matthew. Only the words about Mark are credited to "the elder" by Eusebius. The elder John need not have had a more polished Gospel at his disposal to issue his verdict about what he saw as a lack of literary artistry in Mark's work. The disorderly state of Mark's notes was at least proof that he stayed true to Peter's "living voice" by not reordering the oral traditions that he received from him.[235] His sentence may not have continued with an account about the Gospel of Matthew; Eusebius may have juxtaposed two separate sentences about Mark and Matthew from Papias's prologue together so that they stood side by side.[236] What preceded the conjunction *oun* at the start of the line about Matthew in Papias's prologue is now a mystery. Although the author of Acts seems to provide multiple attestation for the developing tradition about Mark and Peter, no significance is accorded to Matthew in the Gospel of Luke or in Acts.

Papias may have gotten a hold of Matthew's Gospel at a late stage. This may be why the oral traditions that he received from his informants in Asia Minor have little contact with the text of Matthew and one of them seems incompatible with Matthew's account of Judas's suicide. We cannot know how Papias may have harmonized these two notices, such as whether he reasoned like Apollinaris that Judas survived his suicide attempt. Once Matthew's Gospel came into Papias's possession, he may have relied on the elder John's evaluation of Mark's work as a template for assessing what looked to him like a new and improved biographical account of Jesus. He described the contents of both their works as "oracles" (*logia*). Just as the elder John indirectly attributed a Gospel to the apostle Peter, Papias directly attributed a Gospel to the apostle Matthew. Just as the elder John assumed that Peter's Aramaic speech had to be translated, Papias assumed that Matthew's

---

234. Larsen, *Gospels*, 92.

235. Black, *Mark*, 92–93.

236. Black, "The Use of Rhetorical Terminology," 32; Black, *Mark*, 92; Pier Franco Beatrice, "The 'Gospel according to the Hebrews' in the Apostolic Fathers" *NovT* 48.2 (2006): 177; Bauckham, *Jesus*, 222.

compilation of the oracles "in the Hebrew language" (*Hebraidi dialektō*) had to be translated. Incidentally, Papias did not regard Matthew's oracles to be the same as Mark's. Matthew wrote down his eyewitness recollections in his own language; he did not need to rely on Peter's recollections that Mark had already translated in Greek. All of this shows that Papias was not a modern student of the Synoptic Problem. Even so, it was obvious to him that Matthew's arrangement of the material about Jesus was superior to Mark's.

To reiterate the elder John's contribution about the origins of the Gospel of Mark, he put forward the idea that Mark was recruited as Peter's translator. The apostle's first language was Aramaic and he was not fluent in Greek. Mark took the initiative of transcribing Peter's public lectures in his unrefined notes. While the rough draft that Mark produced was accurate on the fundamentals of Peter's "proclamation" (*kērygma*) about the person and work of Jesus, it would not have been classified by the ancients as a work of literature. While Mark had been previously associated with Peter in Asia Minor, the elder John was the first one to speak about Mark as an evangelist and assess the quality of his work. Papias learned about the elder John's tradition about the evangelist Mark when he had a conversation with him in Ephesus sometime in the last few years of the first century. The bishop of Hierapolis may have been the one to introduce the comparison between the Gospels of Mark and Matthew.

3

THE ORACLES THAT MATTHEW
COMPILED IN THE HEBREW LANGUAGE

THE VERACITY OF Papias's testimony about the evangelists is the subject of ongoing scholarly inquiry. The elder John may not have been in the position to relay accurate information about the authorship of the Gospel of Mark, and his valuation of its literary merits was undeservedly negative. His central contention was that Mark was indebted to Peter for his information. Peter is an important minor character in Mark's narrative world.[1] He is named twenty-five times in Mark's Gospel, twenty-five times in Matthew's Gospel, and thirty-three times in Luke's Gospel. He appears with the most frequency in Mark's Gospel if the lengths of each Synoptic text are factored into the ratios. He is the first and last-named apostle in the Gospel, which may form a rhetorical inclusio.[2] It is doubtful, however, that Peter would be a fan of the portrayal of himself in this Gospel.[3] He is likened to Satan when he resisted Jesus's plan to be crucified. A nonsensical suggestion to set up tents for Jesus, Moses, and Elijah is put on his lips when he was terrified by the sight of these three figures appearing in radiant glory on a mountain. He slept when Jesus pleaded with him to stay awake in Gethsemane. He bitterly wept after denying Jesus three times in the high priest's courtyard. Although Peter may not have concealed his past failings, Mark's readers did not get to read about his rehabilitation, though his reunion with the risen Jesus in

---

1. For the following arguments about the frequency of Peter's appearances in Mark's Gospel and the Petrine inclusio, see Hengel, *Studies*, 50–52; Hengel, *The Four Gospels*, 83–84; Bauckham, *Jesus*, 132–45.
2. See Mark 1:16; 16:7. If this inclusio was intended, it could have been made more apparent by finding a way to introduce Peter's name right at the start of the Gospel before John the Baptizer and Jesus were introduced. Peter may not have singled out in Mark 16:7 to close a rhetorical inclusio but to affirm the primitive *kērygma* that singled out Peter as a key eyewitness of the resurrected Jesus (cf. 1 Cor 15:5; Luke 24:34).
3. For the following episodes, see Mark 8:32–33; 9:5–6; 14:37, 66–72.

Galilee is foreshadowed.[4] Peter, and the Twelve in general, are no better or worse than any fallible follower of Jesus. Their supposed insider status is nullified and they had no legitimate authority to lord over others.[5] Peter's leadership position does not seem to be validated by this Gospel.[6]

It is also not easy to reconcile Papias's own contribution that "Matthew compiled the oracles in the Hebrew language" and "each interpreted them as they could"[7] with the extant Greek text that had the title "according to Matthew" attached to it. The apostle Matthew is named in two verses in the text. While this is double the times that he is named in the other two Synoptic Gospels, one of those verses is a nearly verbatim duplicate of a verse in Mark's Gospel. Furthermore, the tax collector was Levi in the original story. The Gospel of Matthew was also not translated from a Hebrew or Aramaic original. It was written in Greek from the outset and its primary source was the Greek text of Mark's Gospel.[8] In fact, it edits out Mark's transliterated Aramaic terms.[9] Even some of Papias's contemporary defenders are willing to concede that he was wrong about the original language of Matthew's Gospel.[10]

The arguments that Papias did not actually have the canonical Gospels of Mark and Matthew in mind may be a last-ditch effort to salvage his reputation as a reliable fount of knowledge about Jesus's earliest biographers.[11] There are alternate proposals for what may have been the referent behind Matthew's Hebrew oracles. Theoretically, Papias could have had the hypothetical Sayings Gospel Q, a testimony book, or the *Gospel According to the Hebrews*

---

4. See Mark 16:7.
5. See Mark 9:33–40; 10:42–45.
6. Marcus, *Mark 1–8*, 23–24; Kok, *The Gospel*, 83–84.
7. See Eusebius, *H.E.* 3.39.16. This is a translation provided by Carlson, *Papias*, 145.
8. The few scholarly proponents of the thesis that there was an original Semitic edition of Matthew's Gospel tend to reject the theory of Markan priority. See Theodor Zahn, *Einleitung in das Neue Testament: Zweiter Band* (Leizpig: Deichert, 1897), 2.322–34; Butler, *The Originality*, 165–66; Albright and Mann, *Matthew*, XXXVI–XLVIII; Powers, *The Progressive Publication*, 47–49.
9. See Mark 3:17; 5:41; 7:11, 34; 14:36.
10. For instance, see France, *Evangelist and Teacher*, 64–66; Morris, *Matthew*, 14; Carson, *Matthew*, 13.
11. See Deeks, "Papias Revisited," 327–28; Beatrice, "The Gospel," 150–53. The most problematic thesis is Beatrice's proposal that Papias attributed an apocryphal Petrine text to Mark, which went under many names in the patristic period, such as the *Teaching of Peter*, the *Preaching of Peter*, and the *Gospel of Peter-Mark*.

in his scope. None of these options have any advantages over the traditional consensus that Papias was referring to the canonical text of Matthew, even if he was mistaken about its origins. His incorrect extrapolation that it was translated into Greek was rooted in nothing more than his judgment that Matthew, the Galilean tax collector turned apostle, was its author. It was the Greek Gospel of Matthew that raised the bar for Papias for what an orderly account about Jesus should look like.

What Did Papias Mean by Matthew's Oracles?

It would have been helpful if the fragments from Papias had a definition of the term *logion*.[12] There are plenty of surveys of the lexical data in Greco-Roman,[13] Second Temple Jewish,[14] and Christian literature.[15] Based

---

12. For lexical studies on *logion*, see Friedrich Schleiermacher, "Über die Zeugnisse des Papias von unsern beiden ersten Evangelien," *TSK* 5 (1832): 736–38; Lightfoot, *Supernatural Religion*, 170–77; Bacon, *Studies*, 443–51; T. W. Manson, *Studies in the Gospels and Epistles* (Manchester: Manchester University Press, 1962), 69–75; Körtner, *Papias*, 154–59; John S. Kloppenborg, *The Formation of Q: Trajectories in Ancient Wisdom Collections* (Studies in Antiquity and Christianity; Philadelphia: Fortress, 1987), 53n.40; Black, "The Use," 32; Dieter Lührmann, "Sayings of Jesus or Logia" in *The Gospel Behind the Gospels: Current Studies on Q* (ed. Ronald A. Piper; New York: Brill, 1995), 106–8; Baum, "Papias als Kommentator," 257–67; James M. Robinson, Paul Hoffmann, and John S. Kloppenborg, *The Sayings Gospel Q in Greek and English with Parallels from the Gospels of Mark and Thomas* (BBET 30; Leuven: Peeters, 2002), xxii–xxvi; Norelli, *Papia*, 59–80; B. Zuiddam, F. J. Van Rensburg, and P. J. Jordaan, "Λόγιον in Biblical Literature and Its Implications for Christian Scholarship" *APB* 19 (2008): 379–94; James R. Edwards, *The Hebrew Gospel and the Development of the Synoptic Tradition* (Grand Rapids: Eerdmans, 2009), 3–5; Shanks, *Papias*, 125–31, 193–95; Travis B. Williams, "Delivering Oracles from God: The Nature of Christian Communication in 1 Peter 4:11a" *HTR* 113.3 (2020): 335–40.

13. For example, see Herodotus, *Hist.* 1.64.2; 4.178.1; 4.203.1; 8.62.2; 8.141.1; Thucydides, *Hist.* 28.2; Polybius, *Hist.* 3.112.6; 8.28.7, 8; Strabo, *Geogr.* 1.3.7; 3.5.5; 6.1.5; 13.1.53; 14.1.27; 16.4.19; 17.1.17; Diodorus Siculus, *Bib. Hist.* 2.14.3; 2.26.9; 4.65.3; 4.73.6; Dionysius of Halicarnassus, *Ant. rom.* 19.2.1; Plutarch, *Rom.* 14.1; *Thes.* 26.4; *Lys.* 22.5, 6; *Fab.* 4.4; *Marc.* 3.4; *Aris.* 9.2; Cassius Dio, *Hist. rom.* 57.18.4–5.

14. For example, the term is used in the Septuagint in Num 24:4, 16; Deut 33:9; Ps 11:7; 17:31; 18:15; 104:19; 106:11; 118:11, 38, 41, 50, 58, 67, 76, 82, 103, 116, 123, 133, 140, 148, 158, 162, 169, 170, 172; 137:2; 147:4; Isa 28:13; 30:27; Wis 16:11.

15. For example, see the use of the term in the New Testament and the Apostolic Fathers in Acts 7:38; Rom 3:2; Heb 5:12; 1 Pet 4:11; *1 Clem* 13:4; 19:1; 53:1; 62:3; Polycarp, *Phil* 7:1; *2 Clem* 13:3.

on this data, a *logion* was normally defined as an "oracle" uttered by divine beings, sometimes through their delegated human spokesperson(s).[16] The first occurrence of the term in Papias's volumes is right in the title. By transliterating the plural form of the noun in the title *Exposition of the Logia of the Lord*, one could bypass the entire discussion about whether Papias defined a *logion* in the usual sense or assigned an idiosyncratic meaning to the term.[17] In the fourth century, Apollinaris of Laodicea reworded *logiōn* ("of the oracles") in Papias's title to *logōn* ("of the words"), while the title was translated into Latin by Jerome as *Explanatio Sermonum Domini* ("Exposition of the Discourses of the Lord") and Rufinus as *Verborum Dominicorum Explanatio* ("Exposition of the Words of the Lord"). The differing translations of Papias's title reveal the uncertainty that his translators had over how to best encapsulate the subject matter of his exposition.[18] Nevertheless, Papias could refer to the "sayings" (*logoi*) of the Lord compiled by Aristion or of the elders that were committed to their pupils' memories.[19] There must be a reason for why he shifted to the term "oracle."

Papias may have elevated Jesus's sayings to the status of "dominical oracles" (*kyriaka logia*) like his contemporary Polycarp did.[20] His title may convey his preoccupation with ascertaining the correct order and interpretation of the sayings of Jesus that were set within the narrative frameworks of the Gospels.[21] Matthew has five well-crafted discourses in his Gospel, so it may have been treasured as the compendium of the Lord's sayings *par excellence*.[22] Jesus's oracles could have alternatively been drawn from a sayings source

---

16. The translations of Schoedel (*The Apostolic Fathers*, 5.110), Holmes (*The Apostolic Fathers*, 740–41), and Carlson (*Papias*, 145) should be preferred over the translation of Ehrman (*Apostolic Fathers*, 2.99) on this point. Shanks (*Papias*, 126) goes too far in casting aspersions about the theological motivations underlying the preference of some translators for a neutral, "secular" rendering of *logia* as "sayings."

17. Hill, "Papias," 310; Bauckham, *Jesus*, 12n.2

18. Lührmann, "Sayings," 106.

19. See Eusebius, *H.E.* 3.39.3; 14. Körtner, *Papias*, 156–57; Robinson, Hoffmann, and Kloppenborg, *The Sayings Gospel Q*, xxvi; Norelli, *Papia*, 62; Edwards, *The Hebrew Gospel*, 5.

20. See Polycarp, *Phil.* 7:1. For another near-contemporary example, see Justin, *Dial.* 18.1.

21. Baum, "Papias als Kommentator," 264–65, 273–75; cf. Bacon, *Studies*, 443–48; Lührmann, "Sayings," 108; MacDonald, *Two Shipwrecked Gospels*, 3–5; Furlong, *The Identity*, 6.

22. Bacon, *Studies*, 446.

before it was integrated into the larger narrative structure of Matthew's Gospel.[23] Some of the traditions of the elders recited by Papias could be correlated with certain sayings of Jesus. Jesus expected that he would drink the fruit of the vine when his kingdom was established, that the sons of Zebedee would partake in his cup of suffering, and that Judas would wish that he had never been born.[24] It is harder to correlate the miraculous survival of Justus Barsabbas and the resuscitation of a corpse with specific sayings of Jesus. These events happened after Easter and Papias received the news about them from the daughters of Philip.[25] The case of *kyriakōn* ("of the Lord") in Papias's title can be translated as either a subjective genitive (i.e., "the Lord's oracles")[26] or an objective genitive (i.e., "the oracles about the Lord").[27] It could be neutrally translated as "pertaining to the Lord," so the oracles could have been spoken either by Jesus or by his supporters about him.[28]

"The oracles pertaining to the Lord" may have been about Jesus. For Eusebius, "the divine oracles" (*ta theia logia*) were akin to the Scriptures, though his Christian canon encompassed the Old and New Testaments.[29] Irenaeus and Origen could designate the Gospels as oracles.[30] It may be anachronistic to imagine that the Gospel texts themselves were venerated as scriptural oracles in Papias's time.[31] There are texts from Christ-followers predating or contemporary with Papias that use the term oracles in reference to the Law of Moses or for the entirety of the Jewish Scriptures.[32] The oracles, then, could be biblical prophecies forecasting the arrival of

---

23. Schleiermacher, "Über die Zeugnisse," 746–52.
24. Baum, "Papias als Kommentator," 273–74. See respectively Mark 14:25//Matt 26:29// Luke 22:18; Mark 10:39//Matt 20:23; Mark 14:21//Matt 26:24//Luke 22:22.
25. See Eusebius, *H.E.* 3.39.9.
26. Black, "The Use," 32–33; Baum, "Papias als Kommentator," 262–63.
27. Körtner, *Papias*, 154–56.
28. Schoedel, *The Apostolic Fathers*, 5.97; Schoedel, "Papias," 245; Norelli, *Papia*, 72; Carlson, *Papias*, 36.
29. Carlson, *Papias*, 37. See also the collection of references to the *logia* in Eusebius's writings in J. Donovan, "Note on the Eusebian Use of 'Logia,'" *Biblica* 3 (1926): 303–8.
30. See, for example, Irenaeus, *Haer. praef.* 1; 1.8.1; Origen, *Comm. Matt.* 5.19; 19.13.
31. Carlson, *Papias*, 37. Contra Lightfoot, *Supernatural Religion*, 172–77; Hill, "Papias," 312; Edwards, *The Hebrew Gospel*, 4, 215.
32. See, for instance, Acts 7:38; Rom 3:2; *1 Clem.* 13:1; 19:1; 53:1.

the Messiah.[33] The best solution may be that the oracles were inspired oral proclamations about Jesus in Christ-believing circles. They may have been inspired to pontificate about his fulfillment of prophecy, his teachings, his miracles, or his followers' achievements. In the excerpt on Mark, the "oracles about the Lord" seem to be equivalent to the reports about "the things said or done by the Lord" (*ta hypo tou kyriou ē lechthenta ē prachthenta*).[34] Mark heard Peter preach the oracles before writing them down.[35] Papias bestowed a revelatory status on the oral testimonies about Jesus that were organized differently in the Gospels of Mark and Matthew. There was precedent in 1 Peter for regarding the abilities of Christian preachers as a "gift" (*charisma*) from heaven and their speech acts as imparting divine "oracles."[36]

The next puzzle is what Papias meant by *Hebrais dialektos*. Hebrew was the literary "language" (*dialektos*) of the Jewish Scriptures and Aramaic the vernacular of Palestinian Jews. If *dialektos* is translated as a rhetorical "style," Papias may have modified it with the adjective "Hebrew" to draw attention

---

33. See F. Crawford Burkitt, *The Gospel History and Its Transmission* (Edinburgh: T&T Clark, 1911), 127; Grant, *The Gospels*, 65, 144; Carlson, *Papias*, 39.
34. Lightfoot, *Supernatural Religion*, 175–76; Munck, "Presbyters," 228; Körtner, *Papias*, 155–56; Kürzinger, *Papias*, 50–51; Kloppenborg, *The Formation*, 54; France, *Evangelist and Teacher*, 58–60; Robinson, Hoffmann, and Kloppenborg, *The Sayings Gospel Q*, xxvi; Schoedel, "Papias," 245–46; Gundry, "Pre-Papian Tradition," 64–65; Beatrice, "The Gospel," 170; Norelli, *Papias*, 62–63, 68, 75; Edwards, The Hebrew Gospel, 4–5; Bauckham, *Jesus*, 214. Carlson (*Papias*, 39n.191) contests the equation of "the things said or done by the Lord" (*ta hypo tou kyriou ē lechthenta ē prachthenta*) with the "oracles pertaining to the Lord" (*logia kyriaka*). The acknowledgment that Papias was unable to arrange the Lord's sayings and deeds in "order" (*taxis*) may not be synonymous with the complaint that Mark only included a few "oracles pertaining to the Lord" or scriptural proof texts in his Gospel, especially if *syntaxis* is translated as a "composition" rather than an "ordered arrangement." However, if the "oracles" were equivalent to the reports about Jesus's sayings and deeds, the two complaints may have been that there was not enough material about Jesus in the Gospel of Mark and the few stories that were included in it were not arranged in a rhetorically effective manner. Papias granted the legitimacy of the second complaint but answered the first one by arguing that Mark recorded as much as he recalled from Peter's preaching. Matthew compensated for both defects in Mark's Gospel.
35. Burnett Hillman Streeter, *The Four Gospels: A Study of Origins, Treating of the Manuscript Tradition, Sources, Authorship, & Dates* (Rev. Ed.; Eugene, OR: Wipf & Stock, 2008), 20; Körtner, *Papias*, 156; Norelli, *Papia*, 68–69.
36. See 1 Pet 4:10–11. See Williams, "Delivering Oracles," 334–53.

to Matthew's exegetical and halakhic forms of argumentation.[37] The evangelist explicated the Jewish Scriptures through a Christological lens. It is better to translate *dialektos*, in Papias's usage, as a "language." It is modified by the name of an ethnic group, entailing that the language of the Hebrew people was in Papias's purview. Aramaic was the *lingua franca* of the Jewish people in Judea in the time of the apostles. Papias could have picked a different adjective to clarify that *dialektos* had a nonlinguistic meaning or more fitting rhetorical terminology to communicate a point about Matthew's literary style.[38] Too much has been made of the absence of an article before *dialektos*. When Paul heard a voice from heaven on the road to Damascus or delivered a speech to a crowd assembled in Jerusalem "in the Hebrew language" (*tē Hebraidi dialektō*), there is an article preceding the words "Hebrew language."[39] The lack of the article may not be determinative for whether or not *dialektos* should be rendered as a "language."[40] Irenaeus included the article in his restatement of Papias's claim that Matthew wrote to the Hebrews "in their same language" (*tē idia autōn dialektō*).[41] Papias's patristic interpreters

---

37. Kürzinger, *Papias*, 21–22; Gundry, *Matthew*, xxi–xxii, 619–20; Gundry, "Pre-Papian Tradition," 67–68; cf. Orchard and Riley, *The Order*, 198–99; Luz, *Matthew 1–7*, 80. Their reinterpretation of *Hebrais dialektos* has been, by and large, panned by most scholars. See Körtner, *Papias*, 203–6; Davies and Allison, *Matthew I–VII*, 16; Black, "The Use," 32–34, 38; France, *Evangelist and Teacher*, 57; Hagner, *Matthew 1–13*, xlv; Morris, *Matthew*, 13–14; Schoedel, "Papias," 257–59; Carson, *Matthew*, 13; Hengel, *Four Gospels*, 71; Baum, "Der Presbyter," 22–24; Nolland, *Matthew*, 3; Beatrice, "The Gospel," 170; Baum, "Ein aramäischer Urmatthäus," 262–64; Norelli, *Papia*, 328–29; Sim, "The Gospel of Matthew," 290; Shanks, *Papias*, 196; Michael J. Kok, "Did Papias of Hierapolis Use the *Gospel according to the Hebrews* as a Source?" *JECS* 25.1 (2017): 32; Bauckham, *Jesus*, 223.
38. Schoedel, "Papias," 259; Baum, "Ein aramäischer Urmatthäus," 263–64. See 4 Macc 12:7; 16:15; Acts 21:40; 22:2; 26:14; Josephus, *A.J.* 5.12.
39. See Acts 21:40; 22:2; 26:14. There is also an article when the name of the "field of blood" is transliterated in the Aramaic language (Acts 1:19) or when the Jews who had traveled to Jerusalem from all over the world for the festival of Pentecost heard the apostles proclaiming the good news about Jesus in their own languages (2:6, 8). Kürzinger, *Papias*, 22; Gundry, *Matthew*, 619; "Pre-Papian Tradition," xxi, 68; cf. Luz, *Matthew 1–7*, 80.
40. Beatrice, "The Gospel," 170, 170n.90; Baum, "Ein aramäischer Urmatthäus," 262. See Philo, *Mos.* 2.26; Eusebius, *H.E.* 6.14.2; Epiphanius, *Pan.* 29.7.4.
41. See Irenaeus, *Haer.* 3.1.1. Kürzinger (*Papias*, 24, 33–42), and at one time Gundry (*Matthew*, xxii) enlisted Irenaeus in support of his interpretation of Matthew's Hebrew *dialektos* as a "style" of argumentation. This contradicts their argument that the presence

were unanimous in comprehending Papias to be communicating that the Greek Gospel of Matthew was translated from a Semitic original.[42]

The excerpt on Matthew ends with how "each one" (*hekastos*) "interpreted" (*hērmēneusen*) his oracles as they were "able" (*dynatos*) to do so. A few scholars define the verb *hermēneuō* as the act of mediating, interpreting, or expositing the Jesus tradition.[43] Mark and Matthew could be the implied subjects. They were, in effect, interpreting the oracles through their editorial decisions about what to include, exclude, or rearrange in their Gospels.[44] However, if the line about Matthew was separated from the line about Mark in Papias's prologue, then the referents for "each one" were almost certainly the interpreters of Matthew's compilation of the oracles. Interpreters could be taken in the sense of exegetes. They may not have all had the same level of catechetical training before they undertook the task of exegeting Matthew's text.[45] Although *hermēneuō* could be defined in the rhetorical handbooks as how an author expresses his or her own thoughts in written words, this definition does not fit in this context when other people were working with what someone else wrote in another language.[46] The combination of *hermēneuō* and *Hebrais dialektos* supports the traditional reading that each person with the requisite skill set "translated" Matthew's Gospel from the "Hebrew language" (i.e., Aramaic) as far as they were capable of doing so. Correspondingly, Mark was Peter's "interpreter" when he translated his spoken Aramaic into Greek.

There are no more undisputed fragments from Papias's exposition that shed light on the referent behind Matthew's oracles. Yet there may be an unattributed excerpt from Papias about the compositional procedures of the four evangelists in an earlier section of Eusebius's *Ecclesiastical History*.[47] The first part of the section could be translated as follows:

---

of the article before *dialektos* in Acts is an indication that it should be translated as a "language."

42. Black, "The Use," 33–34.

43. Kürzinger, *Papias*, 15–16; Gundry, *Matthew*, 619; Gundry, "Pre-Papian Tradition," 61–62, 67.

44. Kürzinger, *Papias*, 18–19.

45. Gundry, *Matthew*, 619; Gundry, "Pre-Papian Tradition," 67.

46. Schoedel, *The Apostolic Fathers*, 5.107; Schoedel, "Papias," 257, 263; Bauckham, *Jesus*, 207–8.

47. For the debate over whether there is an unidentified Papian fragment in *H.E.* 3.24.5–13, see Hill, "What Papias Said," 582–628; Hill, *Johannine Corpus*, 387–94; Hill, "The

> *"Nevertheless then out of all of those who spent time with the Lord, Matthew and John alone have left behind memoirs for us, which a report holds that they came to the writing even out of compulsion. For Matthew having earlier preached to the Hebrews, as he was about to go to others, he delivered in his native language his Gospel in writing, and it was by this writing that he compensated for the lack of his presence to those he was sent from. But when Mark and Luke had made a publication of their Gospels, they say that John, having made use of an unwritten preaching throughout the whole time, came to his writing for this sake. When the three recorded earlier gospels were already distributed to everyone, even to John himself, they say he welcomed them, testified that they had the truth but only that they lacked an account of the actions done by Christ earlier and at the beginning of his preaching. And this report is true."*[48]

Eusebius specifies that he had a written "report" (*logos*) for this information.[49] One of its main emphases is that the evangelists felt compelled by necessity to leave behind their "memoirs" (*hypomnēmata*) of what they had seen. Other patristic writers who were arguably dependent on Papias divulge that the evangelists felt obliged to produce their Gospels for the benefit of others.[50] The Muratorian Canon, a late second-century Roman fragment rehearsing the Christian writings that were revered as authoritative, paints a picture of John's fellow disciples and elders exhorting him to

---

'Orthodox Gospel,'" 287–94; Hill, "Papias," 312; Dean Furlong, "Theodore of Mopsuestia: New Evidence for the Proposed Papian Fragment in *Hist. eccl.* 3.24.5–13," *JSNT* 39.2 (2016): 209–29; Furlong, *The Identity*, 139–53. For criticisms of Hill's hypothesis, see Norelli, *Papia*, 505–21; Kok, *The Gospel*, 196–97; T. Scott Manor, "Papias, Origen, and Eusebius: The Criticisms and Defense of the Gospel of John" *VC* 67.1 (2013): 1–21; Kok, *The Beloved Apostle*, 77–79; Bauckham, *Jesus*, 433–37; Kok, "Justin Martyr," 22–24.

48. See Eusebius, *H.E.* 3.24.5–8. This translation is provided in Carlson, *Papias*, 301.

49. See Hill, "What Papias Said," 589–92; cf. Manor, "Papias," 10–11; Kok, *The Beloved Apostle*, 177; Furlong, "Theodore of Mopsuestia," 212; Bauckham, *Jesus*, 433; Furlong, *The Identity*, 141.

50. The following references are noted in Hill, "What Papias Said," 585, 596–97. Furlong ("Theodore of Mopsuestia," 222; Furlong, *The Identity*, 159) adds the witness of Theodore of Mopsuestia to the list, since Theodore writes that there was a "request" (*paraklēsis*) from the believers in Asia for John to write his Gospel.

write a Gospel.[51] The tradition that John was urged to write is also attested by Clement of Alexandria and Victorinus, the late third-century bishop of Pettau.[52] Similarly, Clement devised a scenario where Peter's hearers in Rome implored Mark to supply them with a "draft" (*hypomnēma*) of what Peter had said.[53] According to Eusebius, Clement's information about Mark's circumstances was corroborated by Papias.[54] It was widely held by patristic writers that John's intent was to supplement the Synoptic Gospels. Clement extrapolated that John supplemented the "bodily facts" in the Synoptic Gospels with a "spiritual Gospel."[55] The Muratorian Canon certified that John arranged "all the wonders of the Lord" (*omnium mirabilium Domini*) "in order" (*per ordinem*).[56] Again, there is a chance that these patristic writers were indebted to Papias.

The section in *Ecclesiastical History* continues with how Matthew, after preaching "to the Hebrews," authored his "Gospel" (*euangelion*) "in his native tongue" (*patriō glōttē*). Afterwards, Mark and Luke followed suit in publishing their Gospels. While John approved of the three

---

51. See M. F. 10.
52. See Clement of Alexandria, in Eusebius, *H.E.* 6.14.7; Victorinus of Pettau, *in Apoc.* 11.1.
53. See Eusebius, *H.E.* 2.15.1–2; 6.14.6.
54. See Eusebius, *H.E.* 2.15.2. Hill, "What Papias Said," 585–86, 592–93; cf. Bauckham, *Jesus*, 433–34; Furlong, "Theodore of Mopsuestia," 214; Furlong, *The Identity*, 143.
55. See Clement of Alexandria, in Eusebius, *H.E.* 6.14.7; M.F. 9–33.
56. See M.F. 9–33. For the argument that the Muratorian Canon was dependent on Papias, see Hill, "What Papias Said," 586–87; cf. Furlong, "Theodore of Mopsuestia," 213; Furlong, *The Identity*, 142. Bauckham (*Jesus*, 431) also argues that the comments on the order of the Gospels and for the differentiation of John as "one of the disciples" from Andrew as "one of the apostles" in the Muratorian Canon (1.9, 14) built on what Papias may have written. For the arguments against detecting a Papian fragment about John in the Muratorian Canon, see Norelli, *Papia*, 507–8, 521–25; Kok, *The Beloved Disciple*, 77. First, if the terms "disciples" and "apostles" were used synonymously in the Muratorian Canon, then it does not preserve Papias's distinction between the apostle John and the elder John. Second, while the elder John faulted Mark's Gospel for its lack of "order," the Muratorian Canon sidesteps the concern over the discrepancies between the four Gospels by affirming their essential unity on the key saving events proclaimed in the *kērygma* (19–26). Third, it has not been sufficiently demonstrated that the Muratorian Canon reused vocabulary that was distinctive to Papias. For instance, Papias employed the Greek word *enia* to designate a smaller portion of a much larger number of stories about Jesus's sayings and deeds, but this is not paralleled by the use of *singula* in the Muratorian Canon for each single thing that John saw and heard.

evangelist's works, they overlooked what transpired at the "beginning" (*archē*) of Jesus's ministry. John filled in the gaps in their reporting. At this point, Eusebius departed from his source with his own observation about the chronology of the Synoptic Gospels.[57] His interjection can be translated as follows:

> *"In fact, it is possible to see at a glance that the three evangelists only wrote down the actions during one year after the confinement of John the Baptist in prison, and they indicate this at the beginning of their stories. In fact, after the fast for forty days and the temptation right after it, Matthew makes clear the time of his own writing by saying: 'But when he heard that John was handed over, he went away' from Judea 'into Galilee.' And Mark like this: 'But after John was handed over,' he says, 'Jesus went into Galilee,' and Luke too before he began the acts of Jesus, makes a similar observation, saying that Herod added to the evil deeds he did, 'he locked John up in custody.'"[58]*

Eusebius would factor his observation about the timing of the Baptizer's incarceration into his case that the chronologies of the Synoptic and Johannine Gospels are not in conflict with each other.[59] He prefaced the next few lines with "they say" (*phasi*). He may have resumed quoting his previous source.[60] On the other hand, he may have used this verb in introducing local hearsay or a written source citing oral tradition.[61] The last part of the section could be translated as follows:[62]

---

57. Hill, "What Papias Said," 593–94; Hill, "The 'Orthodox Gospel,'" 288; cf. Bauckham, *Jesus*, 433; Furlong, "Theodore of Mopsuestia," 213; Furlong, *The Identity*, 141, 143.
58. See Eusebius, *H.E.* 3.24.8–10. This translation is provided in Carlson, *Papias*, 301, 303.
59. John's imprisonment is noted in Matt 4:12, Mark 1:14, Luke 3:19–20, and John 3:24.
60. For Eusebius's use of *phasi* ("they say") to preface his sources, see *H.E.* 1.12.1, 3; 2.2.2; 2.15.2; 7.12. See Hill, "What Papias Said," 591n.25; Furlong, "Theodore of Mopsuestia," 212; Furlong, *The Identity*, 141.
61. Bauckham, *Jesus*, 345, 347; Manor, "Papias," 11. Hill ("The 'Orthodox Gospel,'" 289) counters that Papias himself may have been reciting oral traditions or what the elder John or the other elders in his region "say."
62. See Eusebius, *H.E.* 3.24.11–13.

> *"So they say that it was because of this that the apostle John was*
> *urged to relate in his own gospel the time omitted by the earlier*
> *gospels and the actions done by the savior at that time (these were*
> *those before the confinement of the Baptist), and he indicated the*
> *same, having said then, 'This first miracle Jesus did,' but then*
> *mentioning the Baptist in the midst of the acts of Jesus as he was*
> *still baptizing then in Aenon near Salem, and he clearly shows*
> *this by saying 'John had not yet been put in prison.' Accordingly*
> *John hands down in the writing of his Gospel the events done with*
> *Christ when the Baptist was not yet put in prison, but the other*
> *three evangelists mention those after the confinement of the Baptist*
> *in prison, about which there should no longer be an opinion that*
> *the gospels disagree with each other, in that John's contains the*
> *first acts of Jesus while the rest contain the story done by him at*
> *the end of that time. It is reasonable then that John maintained*
> *silence about the genealogy of the flesh of our savior which Matthew*
> *and Luke published, but led off with the divine account that was*
> *safeguarded to him who was superior with such things of the divine*
> *Spirit."*[63]

It is reiterated that John was exhorted to cover what the previous evangelists ignored. For example, Jesus's first miraculous "sign" (*sēmeion*) was transforming water to wine at the wedding in Cana before John the Baptizer was imprisoned.[64] It now becomes clear why Eusebius made such a big deal about the Synoptic Gospels covering the events of Jesus's life after the Baptizer was thrown into prison. They did not contradict John's Gospel, Eusebius avers, in narrating Jesus's trials in the wilderness but not his first "miracle" (*paradoxos*) at a wedding that took place after his baptism and before John was locked away in prison.[65] Eusebius admitted that John skipped over Jesus's genealogy, presumably because it was common knowledge, and commenced

---

63. See Eusebius, *H.E.* 3.24.11–13. This translation is provided in Carlson, *Papias*, 303.
64. See John 2:1–11; 3:23–24.
65. Jesus's wilderness experience is in Mark 1:12–13, Matt 4:1–11, and Luke 4:1–13. His first "sign" (*semeion*) at the wedding in Cana occurs soon after the Baptizer's vision of the spirit descending on Jesus in John 2:1–11.

his Gospel with a prologue about Jesus's divinity.[66] The section as a whole espouses five key points: the evangelists were so humble that they had to be pressured to undertake the project of writing about Jesus and their Gospels sum up the apostles' message, contain the apostles' memories, narrate the apostolic traditions in dissimilar ways, and were endorsed by different apostles.[67] Theodore, the fourth-century bishop of Mopsuestia, had the same basic tradition that Eusebius had, yet remarks on how John improved the "order" (*taxis*) of the Synoptic Gospels by filling in the gaps at the "beginning" (*archē*) of their narratives.[68]

Eusebius surely had a source for the first part of the section, but the source may have been Clement of Alexandria rather than Papias.[69] Papias's agreement with Clement may have been restricted to Mark's bond with Peter and the independent confirmation of this relationship in 1 Peter. Aside from these points, Clement created new traditions about the four evangelists in the eighth book of his lost *Hypotyposes*.[70] Eusebius twice paraphrased Clement's tradition that Peter's auditors in Rome requested that Mark hand over his *hypomnēma* or his *aide-mémoire* to them.[71] Clement may have devised similar scenarios for how Matthew and John were prompted by others to pen their *hypomnēmata* in the same book. He may have subscribed to the then-standard view that the Gospels were published first by Matthew, second by Mark, third by Luke, and fourth by John. The Gospels of Matthew and Luke were not "written before" (*prographō*) the Gospel of Mark, but were "set forth publicly," whereas Mark's intent was to distribute his notes privately.[72] Clement may have valued the literary "arrangement" (*taxis*) of

---

66. See John 1:1–18.

67. Hill, *The Johannine Corpus*, 389–90; Hill, "Papias," 312.

68. Furlong enlists Theodore of Mopsuestia's commentary on John's Gospel as an independent witness to the tradition from Papias because he differed from Eusebius in some of the vocabulary that he used and did not reproduce Eusebius's interjections in *H.E.* 2.25.8–10, 13. See Furlong, "Theodore of Mopsuestia," 219–23; Furlong, *The Identity*, 156–59.

69. Hengel, *Four Gospels*, 238n.192; Kok, *The Gospel*, 196–97; Kok, *Beloved Apostle*, 78–79; Carlson, *Papias*, 79n.354.

70. Norelli, *Papia*, 210–20; Kok, *The Gospel*, 196–97; Kok, *Beloved Apostle*, 78–79; Carlson, *Papias*, 69.

71. See Eusebius, *H.E.* 2.15.1–2; 6.14.6.

72. See Eusebius, *H.E.* 6.14.5–6. For this reading, see Carlson, "Clement of Alexandria," 122–23; Kok, *The Gospel*, 432–34.

John's Gospel over the Synoptic Gospels because it opened with a profound discourse about Jesus's heavenly pre-existence as the divine *logos* ("word") and revealed Jesus's first sign that displayed his glory.[73] This is why John's text was, for Clement, the "spiritual Gospel."

There may have been no other written source for the rest of Eusebius's section. The informal *phasi* ("they say") may have evoked the widespread "common sense" judgment in the fourth century that John supplemented the Synoptic Gospels.[74] This opinion had a long pre-history in the patristic period. Otherwise, it was Eusebius's ingenious premise that the tensions between the Synoptic and Johannine chronologies disappear once one dates certain events either before or after John the Baptizer was arrested. Origen had highlighted the disagreement over whether Jesus was tempted by the devil in the wilderness or was attending a wedding at Cana after his baptism as a case study for why the evangelists were not concerned with getting the historical record exactly right. Eusebius was refuting Origen's contention.[75] If Eusebius's argument about the timing of these events in relation to the Baptizer's incarceration predated Origen and went all the way back to Papias, Origen doubtlessly would have answered it.[76]

Eusebius was distressed by the prospect of discrepancies between the Gospels. Such worries were not on Papias's radar when he restated the elder John's blunt assessment of the lack of "order" (*taxis*) in Mark's Gospel.[77] One could argue that, if Eusebius's clarifications that the Gospels were not in conflict are removed from the section, then it could be read as an implicit criticism of the literary arrangements of the Synoptic Gospels. The beginnings of their narratives were unsatisfactory compared to John's fuller account.[78]

---

73. See John 1:1–18; 2:1–11; 3:23–24.
74. Manor, "Papias," 12.
75. See Origen, *Comm. Jo.* 10.2. Note that Eusebius defends the classification of the Gospels in the genre of a "historical record" (*historia*) in *H.E.* 3.24.8. See further Manor, "Papias," 13–15.
76. Manor, "Papias," 7.
77. See Eusebius, *H.E.* 3.39.15; Bauckham, *Jesus*, 435–36.
78. Hill brackets out Eusebius's interjections at *H.E.* 3.24.8–10 and 13 from the rest of the source. See Hill, "What Papias Said," 593–94; Hill, "The 'Orthodox Gospel,'" 288; cf. Bauckham, *Jesus*, 346; Furlong, "Theodore of Mopsuestia," 213, 215; *The Identity*, 141, 143. For the argument that a sense of literary completeness is essential to what it means for a Gospel to be in "order" (*taxis*), see Hill, "The 'Orthodox Gospel,'" 291; Furlong, "Theodore of Mopsuestia," 215–18; Furlong, *The Identity*, 144–47.

There is no hint in the undisputed fragment from Papias, however, that Matthew's Gospel was an incomplete narrative. It was Matthew that compensated for the lack of order in Mark's work. There is no subtle dig at the translators of Matthew's "oracles" in the admission that they performed their duties to the best of their abilities,[79] for the phrase "as far as possible" was a standard legal disclaimer.[80] Eusebius drew on Clement, Origen, local gossip, and his own ingenuity in this section, but not on Papias. In conclusion, historians are left with a single line from Papias about Matthew's arrangement of the oracles in the Hebrew language.

Matthew's Oracles as a Sayings Source?

Throughout most of Christian history, few dared to interrogate the ecclesiastical consensus about the authorship of the four Gospels. Even a learned textual critic who had proficiency in Greek and Hebrew like Origen had no reservations about assenting to the tradition that the Greek text of Matthew's Gospel was a translation from a Semitic language. Translations in the ancient world varied from formally equivalent ones to paraphrases.[81] As the Gospels came to be treated as amenable to the same source-critical analysis that was applied to any historical piece of writing in the eighteenth century, biblical scholars explored new interpretive avenues for what may have been the referent behind Matthew's Hebrew oracles. The reinterpretation of Papias's famous declaration about Matthew's oracles paved the way for the modern source-critical analysis of the Synoptic Gospels.[82]

Some eighteenth-century biblical scholars postulated that there was an Aramaic *Urevangelium* or "proto-Gospel" underlying all three Synoptic Gospels. In addition to Papias, they could appeal to the antique references to a text entitled the *Gospel According to the Hebrew* as evidence for a primitive

---

79. Contra Streeter, *The Four Gospels*, 416; Lührmann, "Sayings," 109; Bauckham, *Jesus*, 225.
80. Moss, "Fashioning Mark," 186–87n.23; cf. Watson, *Gospel Writing*, 126n.25.
81. Davies and Allison, *Matthew I–VII*, 1.12; cf. Körtner, *Papias*, 205.
82. For the history of research, see Farmer, *The Synoptic Problem*, 1–198; Lührman, "Sayings," 97–106; Robinson, Hoffmann, and Kloppenborg, *The Q Sayings Gospel*, xix–lxxi; Dungan, *The Synoptic Problem*, 302–41; Harry T. Fleddermann, *Q: A Reconstruction and Commentary* (Leuven: Peeters, 2005), 3–40; Watson, *Gospel Writing*, 99–113.

Aramaic Gospel.[83] A decisive step toward the Q hypothesis was taken when Matthew's oracles were equated with a lost collection of Jesus's inspired utterances behind Matthew's five discourses, three of which end with the formula about Jesus finishing his "sayings" (*logoi*).[84] This *logienquelle* ("*logia* source") is not quite like the modern reconstructions of the so-called "Sayings Gospel Q." Q is reconstructed by Two Source theorists from the Synoptic "double tradition" or the verses that are common to the Gospels of Matthew and Luke but are not found in Mark's Gospel.[85] The double tradition mostly consists of Jesus's sayings, but it has a few short stories such as how Jesus faced three temptations from the devil in the wilderness and healed a centurion's servant.[86]

The foundations of the Two Source Hypothesis were laid when the theory of a primitive *Ur-Markus* or "proto-Mark" and the theory of a *logienquelle* or "*logia* source" were combined. The first hypothetical text was conceptualized as the source of the triple tradition in the three Synoptic Gospels and the second as the source of the double tradition in the Gospels of Matthew and Luke.[87] One of the architects of the Two Source Hypothesis even used the Greek letter *lambda* (Λ) as an abbreviation for the second source.[88] When the Two Source Hypothesis was popularized among English-speaking scholars, "proto-Mark" was replaced with the canonical Gospel of Mark

---

83. Gotthold Ephraim Lessing, "New Hypothesis on the Evangelists as Merely Human Historians" in *Gotthold Ephraim Lessing: Philosophical and Theological Writings*, CTHP (trans. and ed. H. B. Nisbet; Cambridge: Cambridge University Press, 2005), 148–71; Johann Gottfried Eichhorn, "Über die drey ersten Evangelien. Einige Bermerkungen zu ihrer künftigen Behandlung" in *Allgemeine Bibliothek der biblischen Literatur* 5 (Leipzig: Weidmann, 1794), 761–996.

84. See Matt 7:28; 19:1; 26:1. For the discourses, see Matt 5:3–7:27; 10:5–42; 13:3–52; 18:1–35; 23:2–25:46. See Schleiermacher, "Über die Zeugnisse," 746–52.

85. Schleiermacher remained firmly committed to the Two Gospel Hypothesis, in which the canonical Gospel of Mark conflated the Gospels of Matthew and Luke. He did not equate Papias's Mark with the author of the canonical Gospel and reconstructed Matthew's oracles from the five discourses in the Gospel of Matthew alone. This important distinction is noted by Farmer, *The Synoptic Problem*, 15.

86. See Matt 4:1–11//Luke 4:1–13; Matt 8:5–13//Luke 7:1–10.

87. Christian Hermann Weisse, *Die evangelische Geschichte kritisch und philosophisch bearbeitet* (2 vols.; Leipzig: Breitkopf und Härtel, 1838); Heinrich Julius Holtzmann, Die synoptischen Evangelien. Ihr Ursprung und *geschichtlicher* Charakter (Leipzig: Wilhelm Engelmann, 1863).

88. Holtzmann, *Die synoptischen Evangelien*, 128.

as the source for the triple tradition, the abbreviation "Q" was employed for the source behind the double tradition, and "M" and "L" were adopted as abbreviations for the special traditions that were unique to the Gospels of Matthew or Luke.[89] Still, Papias's testimony about Mark's compilation of Jesus's sayings and deeds and Matthew's oracles was reaffirmed as backing the Two Source Hypothesis.[90]

Just as the siglum Q as a shorthand for the German word *quelle* or "source" came to be substituted for the siglum Λ,[91] the justifications for the existence of Q became untethered from Papias's ideas about the origins of the Gospels. Today, the justification for Q is that it is an unavoidable corollary of the critical judgments that the evangelists behind the Gospels of Matthew and Luke did not know each other's work, yet both had independent access to the Gospel of Mark as one of their sources. They share roughly 235 non-Markan verses that must have been derived from another shared source if they did not depend on each other's Gospels.[92] The literary independence of the Gospels of Matthew and Luke is the plank in the Two Source Hypothesis that is attacked by critics of the Q theory.[93] The cases for or against the literary independence of the Gospels of Matthew and Luke

---

89. Streeter, *Four Gospels*, 150–332. Because Streeter hypothesized two other sources in addition to the Gospel of Mark and Q, his solution to the Synoptic Problem has been labeled the Four Source Hypothesis.

90. As Streeter (*Four Gospels*, 22) puts it, Papias has been vindicated by "a critical comparison of the Synoptic Gospels, which suggests that the author of our First Gospel used Mark and at least one other source mainly consisting of discourse." He nuances this claim by admitting that Q may not have been entitled as "the oracles" (*ta logia*) and that Papias was primarily thinking of the prophetic utterances within Matthew's Gospel.

91. For the origins of the siglum Q, see F. Neirynck, "The Symbol Q (=Quelle)" *ETL* 54 (1978): 119–25; Lührmann, "Sayings," 101; Robinson, Hoffmann, and Kloppenborg, *The Sayings Gospel Q*, xxvi.

92. John Kloppenborg, "On Dispensing with Q? Goodacre on the Relation of Luke to Matthew" *NTS* 49 (2003): 211; Christopher M. Tuckett, *Q and the History of Early Christianity* (London: T&T Clark, 2004), 4.

93. For the Markan prioritists who argue that Luke was dependent on the Gospels of Mark and Matthew, see Michael D. Goulder, *Luke*; Mark Goodacre, *The Case against Q* (Harrisburg: Trinity, 2002); Watson, *Gospel Writing*, 117–216; John C. Poirier and Jeffrey Peterson, eds., *Marcan Priority without Q: Explorations in the Farrer Hypothesis* (London: Bloomsbury T&T Clark, 2015). For the argument that Matthew was dependent on the Gospels of Mark and Luke, see Robert K. MacEwan, *Matthean Posteriority: An Exploration of Matthew's Use of Mark and Luke as a Solution to the Synoptic Problem* (London: Bloomsbury T&T Clark, 2015).

are rehearsed in introductory textbooks on the Synoptic Problem.[94] Either the two evangelists independently drew on the sayings of Jesus in Q, contextualizing them in differing locations in their Gospels, or one of them meticulously extracted the non-Markan sayings in the other's Gospel and relocated them to new literary contexts. They either did not know each other's Christmas stories or one of them remained silent about the astrologers or the shepherds who visited the holy family in Bethlehem.[95] In editing Mark's baptism account, the Gospels of Matthew and Luke agree with each other in major and minor ways from the Baptizer's harsh warning to the broods of vipers to repent to his prediction that the coming one will baptize in the holy spirit "and fire."[96] On the other hand, John's ethical advice to those who came to him to be baptized is not reproduced in Matthew's Gospel and the conversation between John and Jesus over whether it is appropriate for Jesus to be baptized is not reproduced in Luke's Gospel.[97] Concerning the Lord's prayer, the shorter petition "your kingdom come" seems to be more primitive in Luke's Gospel, while the pairing of "debts" and those "indebted" to us seems to be more primitive in Matthew's Gospel.[98] This is a sample of the data in the double tradition that must be considered in determining the literary relationship between the Gospels of Matthew and Luke. The key

---

94. Sanders and Davies, *Studying*, 51–119; Stein, *Studying*, 97–142; Goodacre, *The Synoptic Problem*, 106–61. See also the specialist studies noted above for in-depth discussion on the following arguments for and against the literary independence of the Gospel of Luke from the Gospel of Matthew. Both Gospel writers often seem to have been ignorant of the other's editing of Mark's Gospel or the other's unique M or L traditions. The verses that they share in common that were not derived from Mark's Gospel often agree verbatim with each other and may be arranged in a similar order. Nevertheless, the verses are usually contextualized in dissimilar literary contexts. Occasionally Matthew seems to have a more primitive version of a double tradition verse and other times Luke seems to have the more primitive version. There are objections against all these points from the critics of the Two Source Hypothesis. The major and minor agreements between the Gospels of Matthew and Luke against their Markan source constitutes the most significant weakness to the Two Source Hypothesis. Two Source theorists may get around the problem of the major agreements by positing that there was overlapping material between Mark's Gospel and Q.

95. See Matt 2:1–12; Luke 2:8–20.

96. See Matt 3:7–10, 11; Luke 3:7–9, 16.

97. See Luke 3:10–14; Matt 3:14–15.

98. See Matt 6:9–13; Luke 11:2–4.

takeaway is that the debate over the existence of Q no longer revolves around Papias's ambiguous assertions.

If the Gospels of Matthew and Luke were written independently of each other, much of Q's wording and order may be reconstructable from the verbatim agreements and the similar sequencing of many of the verses in the double tradition. Even if the double tradition is extracted from the Gospels of Matthew and Luke, the material seems to display an internal coherence. Thus, Q has been theorized as a single document with a distinct theological profile.[99] It may have originated in Greek as its wording, at times, can be reconstructed and it references the Jewish Scriptures in Greek.[100] A competing model is that Q is merely a cipher for a variety of oral or written sources, in Aramaic and Greek, that Matthew and Luke had at their disposal. The variations in wording in some double tradition verses may be due to one of them mistranslating common Aramaic sources rather than both of them editing the same Greek text in divergent ways.[101] It is incorrect to say that Papias is never factored into the discussions about the existence and nature of Q.[102] Papias may support the latter model.[103] On the other hand, his supposition that Matthew's oracles were translated multiple times may have been his way of accounting for the dissimilarities between the Greek

---

99. Kloppenborg, *The Formation*, 41–88; Tuckett, *Q*, 1–41; Alan Kirk, *The Composition of the Sayings Source: Genre, Synchrony, & Wisdom Redaction in Q* (NovTSupp 91; Leiden: Brill, 1998); Fleddermann, *Q*, 41–68; Sarah E. Rollens, *Framing Social Criticism in the Jesus Movement: The Ideological Project in the Sayings Gospel Q* (Tübingen: Mohr Siebeck, 2014), 81–93.

100. Nigel Turner, "Q in Recent Thought" *ExpT* 80 (1968–69): 824–28; Kloppenborg, *The Formation*, 51–64; Tuckett, *Q*, 83–90; Fleddermann, *Q*, 155–57; Rollens, *Framing Social Criticism*, 91–93.

101. See, for instance, Matt 23:26//Luke 11:41 or Matt 23:23–24//Luke 11:42. This "chaotic model of Q" is championed in Maurice Casey, *An Aramaic Approach to Q: Sources for the Gospels of Matthew and Luke* (Cambridge: Cambridge University Press, 2002). For a critique of Casey's Aramaic reconstructions, see Peter M. Head and P. J. Williams, "Q Review" *TB* 54.1 (2003): 131–44; Fleddermann, *Q*, 156.

102. Lührmann ("Sayings," 101 [emphasis added]) exaggerates that "*Nobody* today argues for the existence of Q on the basis of the Papias quotation in Eusebius." On the contrary, see Manson, *Studies*, 77–87; Hill, *Matthew*, 24–27; Davies and Allison, *Matthew I–IV*, 1.17; Black, "The Use," 32–35; Hagner, *Matthew 1–13*; xlv-xlvi; Nolland, *Matthew*, 3; Carter, *Storyteller*, 16–17; Sim, "The Gospel of Matthew," 291; Casey, *Jesus*, 86, 87–88; MacDonald, *Two Shipwrecked Gospels*, 15.

103. Casey, *Jesus*, 86, 87–88.

documents of Matthew's Gospel and Q.[104] Papias may not need to be factored into this debate at all if he simply made an error about the original language of Matthew's Gospel.

A bigger problem with equating Matthew's oracles with Q is that the term *logion* is never used in the double tradition.[105] In one double tradition verse, the would-be disciple is encouraged to build his or her life on the bedrock of Jesus's "words" (*logoi*).[106] Another summary statement about Jesus finishing his "words" (*logoi*) is common to the Gospels of Matthew and Luke.[107] In the rest of the summary statements in Matthew's Gospel, Jesus finished his "words" (*logoi*) or "parables" or stopped teaching his disciples.[108] There is no evidence that the compilers of the Q material understood it as a collection of Jesus's *logia*.

If Papias concurred with the Elder John's negative evaluation of Mark's Gospel as an incomplete and disorganized narrative, it is difficult to see how Q, as reconstructed by Two Source theorists, was an improvement over it. Q has no infancy or passion stories and a minimalistic narrative framework for Jesus's sayings. It is also unlikely that Papias was denoting the unique material in Matthew's Gospel as the oracles.[109] What scholars label as "M" may be an amorphous grab bag of aphorisms,[110] parables,[111] and anecdotes[112] that were included in the Gospel of Matthew. Obviously, the equation of Matthew's oracles with Q or M hinges on the acceptance of a solution to the Synoptic Problem that does not command unanimous consent. Perhaps Matthew just let others consult his private collection of Jesus's sayings, which is no longer recoverable.[113] The oracles for Papias, on the contrary, may not have been Jesus's sayings. They were oral testimonies about the sayings and deeds of Jesus that were incorporated into the Gospels of Mark and Matthew.

---

104. MacDonald, *Two Shipwrecked Gospels*, 15.
105. Lührmann, "Sayings," 103; Robinson, Hoffmann, and Kloppenborg, *The Sayings Gospel Q*, xxiv.
106. See Matt 7:26//Luke 6:47, 49.
107. See Matt 7:28//Luke 7:1.
108. See Matt 11:1; 13:53; 19:1; 26:1.
109. Contra Witherington III, *Matthew*, 5, 19.
110. See, for example, Matt 10:16, 41–42; 11:28–30.
111. See, for example, Matt 13:24–30, 36–52; 18:23–35; 20:1–16; 21:28–32.
112. See, for example, Matt 1:1–2:23.
113. Goodspeed, *Matthew*, 17, 35, 88–89, 101, 108.

Matthew's Oracles as the Jewish Scriptures?

The Jewish Scriptures were cherished as divine oracles. Collections of biblical prooftexts in support of essential Christological doctrines may have been handy resources. It may not be an untenable inference that some New Testament and patristic writers consulted testimony books.[114] There is the recurrence of peculiar biblical passages, sometimes in the same order, in extant Christian testimony collections. Certain passages were ascribed to the wrong authors, so not everyone checked the actual biblical sources for their quotations. Similar introductory or explanatory comments were attached to the prooftexts featured in different Christian writings. Testimony books may have aided the Christ followers in their apologetical or polemical engagements with their interlocutors in an intra-Jewish context.

The most far-fetched case for a primitive testimony book centered on an extract of a sixteenth-century paper manuscript at the monastery of Iveron at Mount Athos. Its cataloger noted that the work was *anepigraphos*, meaning that it lacked a title and an introductory description.[115] It was assigned to Matthew the Monk due to six iambic verses prefixed to the codex about Matthew's confutation of the Jews in five books.[116] The cataloger knew about Matthew the Hieromonachus, the chancellor of the Byzantine emperor John VIII Palaeologus (ca. 1390–1448 CE), from Byzantine literature.[117] Two other manuscript copies of the work in the Bodleian Library identified this Matthew as the anti-Jewish polemicist.[118] The work was not mainly comprised of messianic prophecies; it contained biblical demonstrations of the Trinity and Jesus's divinity too.[119] A manuscript hunter argued that this work

---

114. J. Rendel Harris argues that a primitive testimony book predated the New Testament writings based on the following five arguments in *Testimonies: Part I* (Cambridge: Cambridge University Press, 1906), 8.

115. Harris, *Part I*, 101.

116. Harris, *Part I*, 109.

117. Harris, *Part I*, 101, 108, 109, 117; Harris, *Testimonies, Part II* (Cambridge: University Press, 1920), 2, 109.

118. Harris, *Part II*, 109–11. In the Selden codex, Matthew the Hieronomachus was the author of five tracts. In Harris's judgment, the writing style of the other tracts are inferior to the poetry in the anti-Jewish verses and, therefore, the works were not all by the same author (pp. 116–17).

119. Harris, *Part I*, 126, 130.

was the apostle Matthew's lost oracles and that Papias's five books were a commentary on it.[120] He judged its Christological titles and anti-Jewish polemic to be archaic, paralleling what one finds in the *adversus Judaeos* ("against the Jews") literature during the patristic era, and Matthew the Hieronomachus to be a fictional creation modeled on the apostle Matthew.[121] This hypothesis was too adventuresome for the tastes of most biblical scholars.[122] The manuscript evidence is quite late and the work is attributed to a Matthew who lived over thirteen centuries after the evangelist.[123]

If the oracles were messianic prophecies about Jesus, Papias was more likely pointing to the scriptural citations within Matthew's Gospel. Modern source critics are aware that these were not all drawn from one source. If the Two Source Hypothesis is right, some were copied from the Gospel of Mark[124] and others from Q.[125] In twelve instances, there is a formula about the fulfillment of the prophets that typically accompanies the unique biblical citations in the Gospel of Matthew.[126] They may have taken over from a collection of biblical prooftexts that had been compiled by the Apostle Matthew. This may be why the Gospel in which these prooftexts were embedded was named after Matthew.[127] Yet some of the prooftexts seem

---

120. Harris, *Part I*, 101–17; Harris, *Part II*, 2, 109–21.
121. Harris, *Part II*, 113–21.
122. Harris (*Part II*, 90) confesses that "it must be admitted that the argument was adventuresome, to the outside limits of a pioneer's audacity." This is his winsome reply to Benjamin Bacon's blistering criticism that "the romantic interest of Dr. Harris' interpretation of his data far outstrips its validity." See Benjamin Bacon, "The 'Five Books' of Matthew against the Jews" *Expositor* 15 (1918): 57.
123. Bacon gives the theory too much credence in allowing that the Matthew in the iambic verses was the evangelist and that the verses reflect a second-century apologist's summary of Matthew's Gospel. See Bacon, "The 'Five Books,'" 61–62; Bacon, *Studies*, xvi. However, Matthew's five discourses are not equivalent to five books and there is no evidence that Papias's five books were a commentary on Matthew's Gospel alone. For his part, Harris (*Part II*, 90) registered his surprise that Bacon "accepted the weakest part of my theory: he conceded the antiquity of the verses, the point I was myself most in doubt of; he admitted that Matthew was the actual Matthew of the New Testament but he denied that the *Testimonies* had anything to do with Papias."
124. See, for example, Mark 1:2–3//Matt 3:3; Mark 7:6–7//Matt 15:7–8; Mark 10:6–8// Matt 19:4–5.
125. See, for example, Matt 4:4, 6, 7//Luke 4:4, 10–11, 12.
126. See Matt 1:22–23; 2:15, 17–18, 23; 4:14–16; 8:17; 12:17–21; 13:14–15 (cf. Mark 4:12); 13:35; 21:4–5; 26:54, 56; 27:9–10.
127. Burkitt, *The Gospel History*, 127; Grant, *The Gospels*, 65, 144.

inseparable from their surrounding narrative context in this Gospel. For example, in its infancy narrative, Mary and Joseph fled to Egypt with their son to protect him from the massacre of the male children aged two years or under in the town of Bethlehem ordered by Herod the Great. Herod's goal was to eliminate potential competitors to his throne. The Gospel writer reapplies the prophet Hosea's words about the exodus of Israel, Yahweh's metaphorical son, to illuminate the return of Mary, Joseph, and Jesus to their homeland after departing from Egypt.[128] If this prooftext was applied to Jesus before it was inserted into Matthew's infancy account, it may have been interpreted typologically to present Jesus as the representative of the covenant people of Israel.[129] Papias may have recognized that there was a greater number of biblical prophecies about Jesus in the Gospel of Matthew than in the Gospel of Mark. He may have assumed that Matthew had amassed quite a collection of biblical prophecies in the Hebrew language.[130]

Then again, Papias did not have to be an expert in textual or source criticism to not miss the transparent citations of the Septuagint, the Greek translation of the Hebrew Bible, in the Gospel of Matthew. This may not be the case for every biblical citation,[131] but it is true for the very first one with the fulfillment formula. The prophet Isaiah promised Ahaz, the king of Judah, that a young woman would bear a son named Immanuel around 734 BCE. The child would be a symbol that the deity of the people of Judah was present among them, for the kingdoms of Aram and Israel that were threatening them to force them into a coalition against the Assyrian Empire

---

128. Burkitt, *The Gospel History*, 127. See Matt 2:15 (cf. Hos 11:1).
129. Harris, *Part I*, 126.
130. Carlson, *Papias*, 39.
131. In Gundry's analysis of the formal and allusive scriptural quotations in Matthew's Gospel and throughout the Synoptic tradition, his finding is that they tend to reflect a mixed text-type with the exception of the consistently Septuagintal character of the formal quotations in Mark's Gospel. See Gundry, *The Use*, 9–150. A recent analysis of the verses in the Gospel of Matthew printed as biblical quotations in NA27 or UBS4 comes to a different conclusion. M. J. J. Menken argues that the evangelist relied on an updated translation of the Septuagint that had been revised to coincide more closely with the Hebrew text for the biblical citations that were not inherited from other sources, such as the Gospel of Mark or Q. See M. J. J. Menken, *Matthew's Bible: The Old Testament Text of the Evangelist* (BETL CLXXIII; Leuven: Leuven University Press, 2004).

would be wiped out when the boy was still in his infancy.[132] The Greek translation of the passage identified the young woman as a "virgin" (*parthenos*). This enabled the Gospel of Matthew to link the sign of Immanuel, or "God with us," to another promised child who was born to the Virgin Mary.[133] In this instance, the evangelist relied on a verse that had already been translated into Greek.

Papias's five volumes on the "oracles pertaining to the Lord" do not seem to have primarily consisted of his scriptural exegesis in any case. It may be possible to read Papias's prologue as differentiating "the interpretations" (*hai hermēneiai*) of the Scriptures from the "words" (*logoi*) of the elders. In this case, Eusebius did not preserve any of Papias's exegesis of biblical passages, but only his miscellaneous traditions about Justus Barsabbas, the evangelists, and other Christian notables.[134] However, if the *logia* denoted inspired speech in general, it could encompass both inspired public expositions of Scripture and inspired oral traditions about Jesus and his followers. Papias compared how Mark and Matthew organized the latter oral traditions about Jesus's words and deeds in their Gospels.

Matthew's Oracles as the *Gospel According to the Hebrews*?

Immediately after the line about the translations of Matthew's oracles, Eusebius notes that Papias restated a story about "a woman who was accused of many sins before the Lord" that was found in "the gospel according to the Hebrews" (*to kath' Hebraious euangelion*).[135] Papias may have surmised that the Gospel of Matthew and the *Gospel According to the Hebrews* were varying translations of the oracles.[136] On the other hand, what if Matthew's oracles

---

132. See Isa 7:1–17.
133. See Matt 1:23 (cf. Isa 7:14 LXX).
134. Carlson, *Papias*, 38.
135. See Eusebius, *H.E.* 3.39.17.
136. France, *Evangelist and Teacher*, 64–66; Bauckham, *Jesus*, 224. Beatrice ("The Gospel," 180–81) boldly proposes that the *Gospel According to the Hebrews* was identical with Matthew's oracles, while the canonical Gospels were understood by Papias to be the subsequent translations of this text into Greek. Edwin K. Broadhead champions a third view, arguing that the living tradition ascribed to Matthew evolved along two trajectories, one that culminated in the Greek Gospel of Matthew in the fourth-century codices and the other in a Hebraic Gospel that circulated among the Jewish Christ associations

and the *Gospel According to the Hebrews* were Papias's alternating descriptions of a single text?[137] Papias may have ascribed the *Gospel According to the Hebrews* to Matthew, which may entail that the ascription of the New Testament Gospel to Matthew was a secondary development. The misascription of the latter text to Matthew may have been facilitated by the fact that both Gospels were produced in a Jewish sociocultural context.[138]

Papias's patristic interpreters, nonetheless, were convinced that he meant that the Gospel of Matthew was translated into Greek. They regularly brought up its alleged original language when summarizing the traditions about the four canonical Gospels.[139] Some of them wondered what happened to the lost Semitic edition of Matthew's Gospel. Pantaenus, who presided over the catechetical school in Alexandria starting in 181 CE,[140] believed that he had acquired a copy of it in India and returned to Alexandria with it. He was informed that the Apostle Bartholomew visited India and gifted this text to the Christ-followers living there.[141] Pantaenus may have obtained a translated version of Matthew's Gospel on his travels, but it was not the

---

during the patristic period. See Edwin K. Broadhead, *Jewish Ways of Following Jesus: Redrawing the Religious Map of Antiquity* (WUNT 266; Tübingen: Mohr Siebeck, 2010), 386–88; Broadhead, *The Gospel of Matthew*, 222–24, 302–3. Jeremiah Coogan is similarly convinced that there were varying recensions of the same Matthean text, but that patristic writers coined the titles of the *Gospel According to Matthew* and the *Gospel According to the Hebrews* in order to distance their "canonical" version of it from the Jewish "apocryphal" version of it. See Jeremiah Coogan, "The Ways that Parted in the Library: The Gospels according to Matthew and according to the Hebrews in Late Ancient Heresiology" *JEH* 73 (2022): 1–18.

137. This is argued by Beatrice, "The Gospel," 172; Edwards, *The Hebrew Gospel*, 2–10; David B. Sloan, "A Better Two-Document Hypothesis: Matthew's and Luke's Independent Use of Mark and the Gospel according to the Hebrews" Paper presented at the annual SBL Conference (San Diego, 2019).

138. Edwards, *The Hebrew Gospel*, 256.

139. See, for example, Irenaeus, *Haer.* 3.1.1; 11.9; Clement, in Eusebius, *H.E.* 3.24.6–7; Origen, in Eusebius, 6.25.4–6.

140. See Eusebius, *H.E.* 5.10.1, 4. For critical discussion on the existence and nature of this "school" (*didaskaleion*), see Annewies van den Hoek, "The 'Catechetical' School of Early Christian Alexandria and Its Philonic Heritage" *HTR* 90.1 (1997): 59–87; Willem H. Oliver, "The Catechetical School in Alexandria" *Verbum et Eccles* 36.1 (2015): 1–12.

141. See Eusebius, *H.E.* 5.10.3; Jerome, *Vir ill.* 36. Pantaenus is enlisted as a witness to the *Gospel according to the Hebrews* in Hans Josef Klauck, *Apocryphal Gospels: An Introduction* (trans. Brian McNeil; London: T&T Clark, 2003), 38; Beatrice, "Apostolic Fathers," 170–71; Edwards, *The Hebrew Gospel*, 12.

Gospel According to the Hebrews. His successor as the head of the catechetical school, Clement, did not attribute the *Gospel According to the Hebrews* to Matthew. In fact, the three earliest Alexandrian Christian scholars to quote the *Gospel According to the Hebrews* left the text unattributed.[142] It was not until the fourth century that anyone associated the *Gospel According to the Hebrews* with either a lost original edition of Matthew's Gospel or a later corrupted version of it.[143]

There are a handful of references to the *Gospel According to the Hebrews* in Eusebius's writings. He differentiated it from the Gospel of Matthew by categorizing it as a "spurious," albeit not heretical, work whose prime readership consisted of an unorthodox sect of Jewish Christ-followers.[144] Even so, he named Papias and Hegesippus as two orthodox interpreters of the text.[145] Hegesippus chronicled the history of the Christ movement and its sectarian offshoots in his five memoirs that he wrote in Rome during Eleutherus's pontificate from 174 to 189 CE.[146] Eusebius guessed that Hegesippus was ethnically Jewish because he cited extracts from the *Gospel According to the Hebrews*, a Syriac text, and other unwritten Jewish traditions in his memoirs.[147] There are a few references to a Gospel in the Hebrew language or in Hebrew letters in Eusebius's treatise on the incarnation in *On Divine Manifestation*.[148] This Gospel cannot be confidently identified as the *Gospel According to the Hebrews*, as Eusebius did not call it by this distinctive title.[149]

---

142. See Clement, *Str.* 2.9.45.5; Origen, *Comm. Jo.* 2.12.87; Didymus the Blind, *Comm. Ps.* 184.9–10.

143. See Epiphanius, *Pan.* 29.9.4; 30.3.7; 13.2; 14.3; Jerome, *Epist.* 20.5; *Vir. ill.* 3; *Tract. Ps.* 135; *Comm. Matt.* 12.13; *Comm. Is.* 11.1–3; *Pelag.* 3.2. See chapter 5 for further discussion about this development.

144. See Eusebius, *H.E.* 3.25.5; 27.4.

145. See Eusebius, *H.E.* 3.39.17; 4.22.8.

146. See Eusebius, *H.E.* 4.22.1–5.

147. See Eusebius, *H.E.* 4.22.8.

148. See Eusebius, *Theoph. fr.* 4.12, 22.

149. Andrew Gregory, *The Gospel according to the Hebrews and the Gospel of the Ebionites* (Oxford: Oxford University Press, 2017), 35–36, 141–42, 143–44. Most scholars have not been as cautious as Gregory on this point. For scholars who attribute both quotations to the *Gospel According to the Hebrews*, see Edwards, *The Hebrew Gospel*, 19, 63–65; Petri Luomanen, *Recovering Jewish-Christian Sects and Gospels* (Leiden: Brill, 2012), 128–35. For scholars who attribute the quotations to the *Gospel According to the Nazoreans*, see Philipp Vielhauer and Georg Strecker, "Jewish Christian Gospels" in *New Testament Apocrypha I: Gospels and Related Writings* (ed. Wilhelm

Papias might have read about a woman who was maligned in Jesus's presence in the *Gospel According to the Hebrews*. In the larger section where Papias's knowledge of the story is related, Eusebius summed up Papias's use of written texts, including a few Gospels and a few epistles.[150] The alternative is that Papias heard about this incident from one of his tradents and Eusebius misidentified his source as the *Gospel According to the Hebrews*.[151] The syntax of the sentence allows for either option.[152] Since Eusebius does not really betray any firsthand familiarity with the contents of the *Gospel According to the Hebrews* in his limited references to the text, it is not inconceivable that he was wrong in assigning the story of the allegedly sinful woman to this

---

Schneemelcher; trans. R. McL. Wilson; Louisville: Westminster John Knox, 1991), 139, 146, 152; A. F. J. Klijn, *Jewish Christian Gospel Tradition* (Leiden: Brill, 1992), 12–13, 31–32 Jörg Frey, "Die Fragmente judenchristlicher Evangelien," in *Antike christliche Apokryphen in deutscher Übersetzung. I. Band: Evangelien und Verwandtes. Teilband 1*, ed. Christoph Markschies and Jens Schröter (Tübingen: Mohr Siebeck 2012), 578; Frey, "Die Fragmente des Nazoräerevangeliums" in *Antike christliche Apokryphen*, 625, 630, 639–40. Klauck (*Apocryphal Gospels*, 43) is more hesitant about the limitations of our knowledge regarding which of these two Jewish Gospels Eusebius was referencing.

150. See Eusebius, *H.E.* 3.39.15–17. For this argument, see Luomanen, *Recovering*, 123–26. For other scholars who argue that Papias took this story from the *Gospel According to the Hebrews*, see Dieter Lührmann, "Die Geschichte von einer Sünderin und andere Apokryphe Jesusüberlieferungen bei Didymos von Alexandrien" *NT* 32 (1990): 311; Beatrice, "The Gospel," 165–66, 168; Edwards, *The Hebrew Gospel*, 7–10.

151. Bart D. Ehrman, "Jesus and the Adulteress" *NTS* 34 (1988): 29; Vielhauer and Strecker, "Jewish Christian Gospels," 138; A. F. J. Klijn and G. J. Reinink, *Patristic Evidence for Jewish-Christian Sects* (NovTSup 36; Leiden: Brill, 1973), 26–27; Körtner, *Papias*, 204–5; Klijn, *Jewish Christian Gospel Tradition*, 11, 119, 138; Klauck, *Apocryphal Gospels*, 40; Norelli, *Papia*, 331–32, 335; MacDonald, *Two Shipwrecked Gospels*, 14, 19–22, 246–53; Frey, "Die Fragmente judenchristlicher Evangelien," 571; Frey, "Die Fragmente des Hebräerevangeliums," in *Antike christliche Apokryphen*, 606; Kok, "Did Papias of Hierapolis," 47–52; Jennifer Knust and Tommy Wasserman, *To Cast the First Stone: The Transmission of a Gospel Story* (New Jersey: Princeton University Press, 2019), 62, 177; Dennis MacDonald, *From the Earliest Gospel (Q+) to the Gospel of Mark: Solving the Synoptic Problem with Mimesis Criticism* (Lanham: Lexington Press, 2020), 6.

152. Simon Claude Mimouni, *Early Judaeo-Christianity: Historical Essays* (trans. Robyn Fréchet; Leuven: Peeters, 2012), 186–87; Chris Keith, "Recent and Previous Research on the Pericope Adulterae (John 7.53–8.11)" *CBR* 6.3 (2008): 385; Keith, "The Initial Location of the Pericope Adulterae in Fourfold Tradition" *NovT* 51 (2009): 15; 186–87; Gregory, *The Gospel*, 34, 78.

text altogether.[153] It may be necessary to investigate other potential oral or written sources for the story.

The two closest parallels in the New Testament are in the Gospel of Luke and in a scribal interpolation to the Gospel of John. In Luke's Gospel, a woman from the city who was reputed to be a "sinner" entered the house of Simon the Pharisee, where Jesus was dining. She was crying when she knelt at Jesus's feet, washing them with her tears and anointing them with perfumed oil. Simon was offended by her extravagant gesture, so Jesus told a parable about a creditor who canceled a small and a large debt. The moral of the parable was that the woman acted more lovingly to Jesus than his host because she had the greater debt that was annulled. After telling this parable, Jesus forgave her sins.[154] Ironically, one of the most famous passages in the Gospel of John may not be original to it. The passage is known by the Latin title *pericope adulterae*, for a pericope is the technical term for a textual unit and Jesus's grace toward an adulteress is the subject matter. In the pericope,[155] the Pharisees and legal experts test Jesus by placing a woman convicted of adultery before him to see if he would enforce the capital sentence commanded by the Law of Moses. After stooping down to write on the ground, Jesus declared that no one who has sinned should throw the first stone. No one could measure up to this demand and the crowd dispersed. Since no one stayed behind to condemn her, Jesus pledged to her that he would not condemn her either and encouraged her to sin no longer. The pericope was inserted at the end of the seventh chapter of the Gospel of John in the vast majority of the manuscripts, though it could be relocated to other places in this Gospel or in the Gospel of Luke.[156] Eusebius's Latin translator, Rufinus, conformed his wording to the *pericope adulterae* by describing the person pardoned by Jesus as an "adulterous woman" (*mulier adultera*). If Papias's story looked identical to these two New Testament accounts, Eusebius would have assured his readers that Papias took it from a canonical rather

---

153. Klijn, *Gospel Tradition*, 11, 119; Frey, "Die Fragmente judenchristlicher Evangelien," 417; Frey, "Die Fragmente des Hebräerevangeliums," 606.
154. See Luke 7:36–50.
155. See John 7:53–8:11.
156. Keith ("The Initial Location," 5–6) calculates that 1,370 out of 1,428 Greek manuscripts containing the *pericope adulterae*, or 95.9 percent of them, attest to its insertion in John 7:53–8:11.

than an apocryphal Gospel.[157] Unlike the canonical parallels, the woman's innocence, rather than her guilt, may have been presumed by Papias. The verb *diaballō* in the passive voice may mean that she was accused maliciously or slandered.[158]

The best evidence that the *Gospel According to the Hebrews* had a passage in it like the *pericope adulterae* is in the commentary on Ecclesiastes by Didymus the Blind, a fourth-century Alexandrian scholar.[159] He discovered that the story about a woman who was condemned for a sin was "in certain Gospels" (*en tisin euangeliois*). Jesus intervened when she was about to be stoned in a place where it was customary for executions to occur. His powerful line that the only ones who should pick up stones to smite her were the ones who were conscious that they never sinned stopped the crowd from carrying out the sentence.[160] Didymus does not explicitly identify the *Gospel According to the Hebrews* as one of his sources,[161] but this text is a plausible candidate because it was the only Gospel outside of the New Testament canon that merited his approval.[162] Didymus put the admission in Ecclesiastes that everyone is guilty of cursing their enemies in their own hearts into dialogue with the story.[163] He then reapplied the story to a very different social situation. He chided hypocritical slaveowners who disciplined their slaves for their hostile attitudes toward them, when they themselves were guilty of ruminating on wicked thoughts. He decided that it was only permissible for them to punish their slaves for their disobedient actions, not for

---

157. Ehrman, "Jesus," 29; Lührmann, "Didymos," 305; Vielhauer and Strecker, "Jewish Christian Gospels," 138; Klijn, *Jewish-Christian Gospel Tradition*, 117; Klauck, *Apocryphal Gospels*, 40; Norelli, *Papia*, 333, 335; Frey, "Die Fragmente judenchristlicher Evangelien," 571–72; Kok, "Did Papias of Hierapolis," 34; Keith, "Recent," 385; Knust and Wasserman, *To Cast*, 62, 62n.43.

158. Knust and Wassermann, *To Cast*, 154, 158–59.

159. See Didymus the Blind, *Comm. Eccl.* 223.6–13.

160. For the English translation, see Ehrman, "Jesus," 25.

161. Klijn, *Gospel Tradition*, 576; Frey, "Die Fragmente judenchristlicher Evangelien," 576; Frey, "Die Fragmente des Nazoräerevangeliums," 596.

162. Ehrman, "Jesus," 29; Lührmann, "Didymos," 292, 307–8, 310; Keith, "Recent," 385; Knust and Wassermann, *To Cast*, 200–201. Didymus identified the tax collector Levi in Luke 5:27, not with Matthew in Matt 9:9 but with Matthias in Acts 1:23, 26 on the basis of something that was written in the *Gospel According to the Hebrews*. See Didymus, *Comm. Ps.* 184.9–10.

163. See Didymus, *Comm. Eccl.* 223.6–13 (cf. Eccl 7:22).

their internal dispositions. It is horrible that Didymus validated the institution of slavery at all and his application of the story seems unusual, since its principal character was accused of committing a capital offense rather than harboring a bad attitude. In the verses preceding the *pericope adulterae* in its usual location in the seventh chapter of John's Gospel, Jesus scolded the religious leaders for entertaining superficial thoughts about him. This may be evidence that Didymus also knew the story from John's Gospel.[164]

Conversely, Didymus may not have read this story in a manuscript of John's Gospel. His scene is set at an execution site rather than in the temple courts, the "Jews" rather than the Pharisees and teachers of the law were leading the proceedings, the charges against the woman were not specified, the situation was not devised as a test for Jesus, the activity of Jesus writing on the ground was not narrated, and the definitive pronouncement from Jesus was worded differently.[165] Didymus did not need the larger literary context in the Gospel of John to come up with the application that slaveowners ought to engage in a little self-scrutiny before beating their slaves. From the story itself, he discerned that the mob did not hurl any stones at the woman after engaging in some critical introspection.[166] Didymus would not have been so unspecific in referring to his sources as "certain Gospels" if he located the story in one of the canonical Gospels. He must have discovered this story in apocryphal Gospels, one of which was the *Gospel According to the Hebrews*.[167]

There is another version of the story that differs markedly from Didymus's account and from the *pericope adulterae* in a third-century instruction manual known as the *Didascalia Apostolorum* or the *Teaching of the Apostles*. In this version, the elders led a woman who had sinned to Jesus and then departed, expecting him to deliver a negative judgment against her. Noticing that they did not officially condemn her, Jesus refused to condemn her as well.[168] The time and place where this scene occurred is not disclosed. Against other anti-Jewish renditions of this story, the portrayal of the Jewish

---

164. Ehrman, "Jesus," 27. See John 7:24, 50–52.
165. Lührmann, "Didymos," 293–98; cf. Klauck, *Apocryphal Gospels*, 41; Norelli, *Papia*, 334; Knust and Wasserman, *To Cast*, 197.
166. Knust and Wasserman, *To Cast*, 201.
167. Knust and Wasserman, *To Cast*, 197–200; cf. Lührmann, "Didymos," 296.
168. See *Did. apost.* 7.

elders in the *Didascalia* is refreshingly positive in that they entrusted the Lord with the task of judging. Ecclesiastical leaders are advised to behave in the same manner in welcoming back the penitent into Christian fellowship.[169] The presumption that the woman was guilty of some sin does not prove that the author of the *Didascalia* depended on the conversation between Jesus and the woman at the end of the *pericope adulterae*.[170] The act of adultery is not specified and, in leaving the woman with Jesus, the elders were not stirring up a mob to stone her.

There may have been two separate stories, one known to Papias and the author of the *Didascalia* and the other to Didymus and the author of the *Gospel According to the Hebrews*, that were fused together in the *pericope adulterae*.[171] Conversely, the patristic authors could have been selectively rehearsing different details from the same story and Eusebius must have detected some lines of continuity between Papias's story and the one in the *Gospel According to the Hebrews*.[172] The most likely solution is that the version of the story in Papias's exposition and in the *Didascalia* was more primitive than the version in the *Gospel According to the Hebrews* and in the *pericope adulterae*. On form-critical grounds, it is a simple controversy dialogue. Jesus de-escalated a controversial situation with a witty one-liner.[173] There is no indication that the accusations against the woman amounted to a capital crime, let alone adultery, or that her accusers had any intention of stoning her. The setting in the temple courts in the *pericope adulterae* may be a remnant of this older version, for it is implausible that the woman was dragged to the temple courts to be stoned.[174] There are controversy dialogues set within the temple courts in the Synoptic Gospels. For example, Jesus was in the temple courts when the Pharisees tried to entrap him by asking him about the legitimacy of paying taxes to the Roman Emperor. His sharp retort was that if they possessed coins with Caesar's graven image on them, they

---

169. Knust and Wasserman, *To Cast*, 163–64.

170. Contra Lührmann, "Didymos," 301, 310–11; Knust and Wasserman, *To Cast*, 63, 163.

171. Ehrman, "Jesus," 34–38; Kyle R. Hughes, "The Lukan Special Material and the Tradition History of the *Pericope Adulterae*," *NovT* 55 (2013): 1–16.

172. Lührmann, "Didymos," 301; Norelli, *Papia*, 333–34; Keith, "Recent," 387.

173. Ehrman, "Jesus," 35–36; Hughes, "The Lukan Special Material," 12; Kok, "Did Papias of Hierapolis," 49.

174. Hughes, "The Lukan Special Material," 235–38.

should give them back to Caesar and give God God's due.[175] Eusebius must have heard that the *Gospel According to the Hebrews* had this story second-hand and did not know how much it had enlarged the simple controversy dialogue between Jesus, the woman, and the elders.

When the details about the stoning are removed from the *pericope adulterae*, it looks like one of Luke's controversy dialogues.[176] Just as Jesus spent his nights on the Mount of Olives and days teaching in the temple courts in Luke's Gospel,[177] so the *pericope adulterae* begins with Jesus on the Mount of Olives before "he arrived" (*paregeneto*) at the temple at "dawn" (*orthros*).[178] "After sitting down" (*kathisas*) and "teaching" (*edidasken*) "all the people" (*pas ho laos*) in the temple courts,[179] Jesus was confronted by the religious leaders who were searching for an excuse to level an accusation against him. The Gospel of Luke uses similar wording in unveiling the motivations of the Pharisees and the experts in the law.[180] While the words "sin no more" (*mēketi hamartane*) are paralleled in John's Gospel,[181] the addition "from now on" (*apo tou nun*) appears five times in Luke's Gospel.[182] One of Luke's characteristic themes is Jesus's kindness toward the marginalized, including women.[183] Although the scribe who penned the *pericope adulterae* could have imitated Luke's vocabulary and style,[184] these details may be remnants of the simpler oral story known to Papias and the author of the *Didascalia*. Given

---

175. See Matt 22:15–22; Mark 12:13–17; Luke 20:20–26.
176. For the following arguments, see Henry J. Cadbury, "A Possible Case of Lukan Authorship (John 7:53–8:11)," *HTR* 10 (1911): 237–44; Ehrman, "Jesus," 43n.60; Keith, "Recent," 380; Hughes, "The Lukan Special Material," 238–40.
177. See Luke 21:37–38.
178. See John 8:1–2. *Paraginomai* is used 28 times in Luke's Gospel, while *orthros* is otherwise only found in Luke 24:1 and Acts 5:21 in the New Testament.
179. See John 8:2. The phrase *pas ho laos* is found 15 times in Luke's Gospel and, out of the 142 occurrences of *laos* in the New Testament, the Gospel of Luke and Acts account for 84 of these occurrences.
180. In John 8:6, the Pharisees and the experts in the law tested Jesus "in order that they might have a basis to accuse him" (*hina echōsin katēgorein autou*). In Luke 6:7, the Pharisees and experts in the law were closely watching Jesus to see if he would heal a man with a withered hand on the Sabbath "in order that they might find a basis to accuse him" (*hina heurōsin katēgorein autou*).
181. Compare John 8:11b with John 5:14.
182. See Luke 1:48; 5:10; 12:52; 22:18; 22:69.
183. Hughes, "The Lukan Special Material," 241–47.
184. Keith, "Recent," 383; Keith, "The Initial Location," 211.

the literary independence of Papias's exposition from Luke's Gospel, his oral tradition may be pre-Lukan.

Papias's oral tradition about how the religious leaders hauled a woman accused of unspecified sins to Jesus while he was teaching in the temple courts was left out of Luke's Gospel.[185] There may be a slight trace of it in Luke's summary statement about Jesus teaching in the temple courts during the daytime and retiring to the Mount of Olives at night.[186] Luke narrates a different episode about Jesus's mercy toward a sinful woman, which also is a creative rewriting of Mark's story of the woman who anointed Jesus.[187] In Luke's story, the woman anoints Jesus with an alabaster jar of perfume at an earlier point in his Galilean ministry, instead of shortly before Jesus's last Passover. As in John's Gospel, it is Jesus's feet, not his head, that is anointed. The host who welcomed Jesus into his house is Simon the Pharisee rather than Simon the leper. Luke's contrast between the sinful woman and the Pharisee who disapproved of her may have also been influenced by the oral tradition known to Papias about a woman who was denounced by the religious elites.[188]

---

185. The *pericope adulterae* was not interpolated into Luke's Gospel after 21:38 before the family 13 manuscripts dating to the tenth or eleventh centuries. See Keith, "Recent," 378–79; Keith, "The Initial Location," 213.

186. Hughes, "The Lukan Special Material," 249, 249n.66. David Sloan reminded me of this parallel in personal correspondence.

187. Compare Mark 14:1–9 (cf. Matt 26:2–12; John 12:1–8) and Luke 7:36–50. See also MacDonald, *Two Shipwrecked Gospels*, 249–51; MacDonald, *From the Earliest Gospel (Q+)*, 5.

188. My theory that Luke 7:36–50 was based on a creative rewriting of Mark 14:1–9 and the pre-Lukan oral tradition about the sinful woman differs from the view that it was derived from a written source like Q (cf. MacDonald, *Shipwrecked Gospels*, 251; MacDonald, *From the Earliest Gospel*, 6). To make the case that these verses were derived from Q, MacDonald contends that the story was excluded from the Gospel of Matthew because it offended the evangelist's sensibilities. The woman's gesture of untying her hair and kissing Jesus's feet may have been provocative and Jesus forgave her sins without requiring her to repent. On the other hand, her unbound hair could be a symbol of mourning and Jesus interprets her actions as a display of her grateful devotion to him. See Charles H. Cosgrove, "A Woman's Unbound Hair in the Greco-Roman World, with Special Reference to the Story of the 'Sinful Woman' in Luke 7:36–50" *JBL* 124.4 (2005): 677–78, 682–84, 688, 690–91. Moreover, Jesus summons the tax collector Matthew to be his follower and has table fellowship with tax collectors and sinners before they repent in Matt 9:9–13. Indeed, Mark 2:17 (cf. Matt 9:13) is redacted in Luke 5:32 to make it clear that sinners were called "to repentance" (*eis metanoian*).

Papias's oral tradition about a woman reputed to be a transgressor was continually embellished through the many retellings of it over the centuries. By the time that it was incorporated into the *Gospel According to the Hebrews* and the Gospel of John, it had evolved into a story about Jesus rescuing a woman who was about to be stoned to death. Papias did not know this updated version of the story and, hence, did not know the *Gospel According to the Hebrews*. Therefore, he could not have identified Matthew as the author of this text. No patristic writer did before the fourth century.

Matthew's Oracles as the Canonical Gospel of Matthew?

The proposals that Papias considered Q, a testimony book, or the *Gospel According to the Hebrews* to be Matthew's oracles have been weighed and found wanting. The traditional position that he was referring to the canonical Gospel of Matthew may be right after all. Otherwise, Papias was utterly misunderstood by his earliest interpreters. By the time that titles were affixed to the Gospels, the patristic consensus about Matthew's authorship of the first canonical Gospel was firmly established. The title of the *Gospel According to Matthew* indicates that Matthew was remembered as the writer of the text, not one of the text's sources, just as the *Gospel According to Mark* was named after the one who wrote it (i.e., Mark) rather than its key source (i.e., Peter). This is paralleled in the title of the Septuagint, which is named after the "seventy" (or seventy-two) translators who penned the Greek translations of the Hebrew Scriptures.[189]

Once Papias got a hold of the Gospel of Matthew, he may have searched for clues within it to ascertain its authorship. As he diligently compared it with the Gospel of Mark, he may have narrowed in on the discrepancy between the two texts over whether the tax collector stationed at the tollbooth was Levi or Matthew. This was not a minor issue because this person was a noteworthy minor character whose call to discipleship echoed the calling of the first four apostles. His answer to this problem may have been that Matthew corrected Mark's "error" about the identity of the tax

---

189. Goodspeed, *Matthew*, 82, 84, 89, 106.

collector.[190] Mark was a mere secondhand reporter of what he remembered of Peter's preaching, but Matthew related his firsthand experience of the day when Jesus approached him at his tollbooth. Regrettably, Eusebius only preserved one quote about Matthew from Papias, so Papias's exact reasoning for attributing the Gospel to the tax collector cannot be verified. After identifying Matthew as the evangelist, Papias made the natural assumption that Matthew was not literate in any other language aside from his mother tongue, which was Aramaic. Now, Papias had two Greek Gospels, one of which had been ascribed to Peter's translator Mark. He deduced that Matthew's work was also translated into Greek. His erroneous assumption about the original language of Matthew's Gospel may have also been based on the deduction that it was originally intended for a Jewish audience.

Matthew's compilation of the oracles about the Lord had to have been similar enough to Mark's compilation to facilitate a comparison between them. What Papias wrote about the Gospel of Matthew was the mirror image of what the elder John said about the Gospel of Mark. Both texts were attributed, directly or indirectly, to apostles. Peter's speech and Matthew's written text were both translated from Aramaic to Greek. Mark did not arrange his material in order and Matthew did. The Gospel of Matthew was the ideal literary foil for the Gospel of Mark. Mark's Gospel seemed incomplete to ancient readers: it starts abruptly with John baptizing in the wilderness and wraps up before the women at the empty tomb let anyone else in on the news that Jesus was raised from the dead. Matthew's Gospel is more closely adapted to the genre of antique biographies in starting with the subject's ancestry and birth. Jesus's great commission to the eleven apostles on the mountain to make disciples of all nations and his promise to be with them until the end of the age brings the narrative to a satisfying close.[191] Its author skillfully organized the sayings of Jesus into five major discourses, which may have been invaluable in the education of catechumens.[192]

The other option, since Papias did not know Luke's Gospel, is that he depreciated Mark's Gospel for not measuring up to the "order" of John's

---

190. Sanders and Davies, *Studying*, 14.
191. See Matt 28:16–20.
192. See Matt 5:3–7:27; 10:5–42; 13:3–52; 18:1–35; 23:2–25:46.

Gospel.[193] Although the basic outlines of these two Gospels are alike in that both start with the Baptizer's immersion ritual in the Jordan River and conclude with Jesus's passion in Jerusalem, John's Gospel differs dramatically in narrating Jesus's extensive ministry in southern Judea, particularly during religious festivals. There are lengthy discourses about Jesus's divine identity and mission throughout the Gospel of John.[194] Some episodes in Mark's Gospel are relocated in John's Gospel. For example, Jesus drives out the money changers from the temple courts after his first miraculous sign at the wedding of Cana rather than after his triumphal entry into Jerusalem.[195] Papias's language in his prologue about receiving commandments (*entolas*) given "to the faith" (*tē pistei*) and coming "from" (*apo*) "the truth" (*tēs alētheias*) has a Johannine ring to it, as does his listing of the seven "disciples" rather than "apostles."[196] External witnesses, from Irenaeus to the so-called "Anti-Marcionite" Latin prologue, associate Papias with the evangelist John.

Against the postulation that Papias was contrasting the Gospels of Mark and John, Eusebius did not explicitly preserve a fragment from Papias informing his readers about the origins of John's Gospel, much less commending its orderly arrangement.[197] The efforts to explain away Eusebius's silence may not be compelling.[198] Papias was not associated

---

193. For all of the parallels between the Johannine writings and Papias, see Lightfoot, *Supernatural Religion*, 186–216; Deeks, "Papias Revisited," 325–36; Hengel, *The Johannine Question*, 17–23; Hill, "What Papias Said," 582; Hill, "'Orthodox' Gospel," 286; Shanks, *Papias*, 149, 260n.534, 260n.540; Furlong, *The Identity*, 123–71; Bauckham, *Jesus*, 226–33, 424.

194. See, for instance, John 13:31–16:33.

195. Compare John 2:13–21 to Mark 11:15–17.

196. See Eusebius, *H.E.* 3.39.3–4.

197. For scholars who doubt that Papias was comparing the Gospel of Mark to the Gospel of John, see Körtner, *Papias*, 173–76, 198–99; Koester, *Ancient Christian Gospels*, 246; Norelli, *Papia*, 114–23; MacDonald, *Two Shipwrecked Gospels*, 17n.26; Watson, *Gospel Writing*, 463; Kok, *The Gospel*, 198–99; Kok, *The Beloved Apostle*, 73–80; Carlson, *Papias*, 78–79, 79n.354, 79n.355.

198. For instance, Lightfoot (*Supernatural Religion*, 32–58) argues that Eusebius was silent about Papias's traditions about Luke and John because he was uninterested in repeating all of Papias's information about the four evangelists, for such questions had been settled in the fourth century. He was just passing along Papias's curious anecdotes about Mark and Matthew. Hengel (*The Johannine Question*, 21) and Bauckham (*Jesus*, 424) argue that Eusebius suppressed Papias's tradition that the elder John, rather than the apostle

with the fourth evangelist until the elder John was misidentified as the apostle John by Irenaeus. The evidence for Papias's knowledge of the Gospel of John from the undisputed fragments of his work is not unassailable. First John could have circulated independently from the Gospel of John. Papias could have known this letter and been influenced by its vocabulary. Papias's list of disciples replicates the first eight names from the list of the apostles in Matthew's Gospel in a different order, except that he skips over the relatively unknown Bartholomew.[199] It is implausible that Papias would have moved from the first three names in the opening chapter of the Gospel of John to Thomas in its eleventh chapter and to the unnamed sons of Zebedee in its epilogue in putting together his list of seven disciples.[200]

In conclusion, a sayings source and a testimony book may be too dissimilar to Mark's narrative to be suitable points of comparison. It would be more apt to compare Mark's Gospel to a narrative Gospel such as the Gospel of John or the *Gospel According to the Hebrews*, but it is uncertain whether Papias had come across these two texts. It is the literary arrangements of the Gospels of Mark and Matthew that are contrasted with each other in Papias's prologue. Papias seconded the elder John's verdict that the lack of "order" in the Gospel of Mark ought to be blamed on Peter's translator and secretary Mark. He was pleased to discover that, in contrast to the elder John's critical appraisal of Mark's Gospel, Matthew's Gospel set the gold standard for a properly ordered account. It also emphasized Matthew's call narrative, which was all the proof that Papias needed to advance his case that it was authored by the apostle himself. It may have taken some time for Papias's authorial tradition about Matthew's Gospel to gain a foothold over the popular Christian imagination.

John, was the author of the Gospel of John. Stevens ("Did Eusebius Read Papias," 168) argues that Eusebius was ignorant about the elder John's authorship of the fourth Gospel because he had not read Papias's work in its entirety.

199. See Matt 10:2–3.

200. See John 1:40–44; 11:16; 21:2. Note also that Matthew is absent from John's Gospel altogether. For the argument that Papias did not draw his list of seven disciples from John's Gospel, see MacDonald, *Two Shipwrecked Gospels*, 17n.26; Watson, *Gospel Writing*, 463.

4

THE PATRISTIC CONSENSUS
ABOUT THE EVANGELIST MATTHEW

OUT OF ALL the Christian writers in the first half of the second century, Papias stands alone in naming two Gospel writers. Others quote from or allude to the Gospels within this general time frame, but no one names a specific evangelist as the source of their quotations or allusions. Papias's speculations about the identities and compositional procedures of a few evangelists may not have instantly won over all Christians throughout the Roman Empire. Not all Christians rushed to assign named authors to the anonymous Gospels. At one point, the oral sources about Jesus may have been more highly regarded then the written ones.

Justin Martyr may have been one of the first Christian intellectuals to be persuaded by Papias.[1] Justin was born in the city of Flavia Neapolis in Samaria and moved to Ephesus.[2] His goal was to study the philosophies of Stoicism, Aristotelianism, Pythagoreanism, and Platonism. An elderly man pointed him to the best philosophers of all. These were the Hebrew prophets who foretold the advent of the Messiah.[3] He resolved to become a Christian philosopher. Trypho, a Jewish refugee after the Jews were expelled from their homeland in the aftermath of a failed messianic revolt against the Romans from 132 to 135 CE, approached Justin because he was donning the garb of a philosopher.[4] They spent two days dialoguing about the merits of Justin's philosophy and lifestyle. Justin then moved to Rome and set up

---

1. For a few studies on Justin's life and thought, see L. W. Barnard, *Justin Martyr: His Life and Thought* (Cambridge: Cambridge University Press, 1967); Eric Francis Osborn, Justin Martyr (BHT 47; Tübingen: Mohr Siebeck, 1973); Sara Parvis and Paul Foster, eds., *Justin Martyr and His Worlds* (Minneapolis: Fortress, 2007); Paul Parvis, "Justin Martyr" in *Early Christian Thinkers: The Lives and Legacies of Twelve Key Figures* (ed. Paul Foster; London: SPCK, 2010), 1–14.
2. See Justin, *1 Apol.* 1.
3. See Justin, *Dial.* 2.3–8.1.
4. See Justin, *Dial.* 1.3.

a philosophical school. He was executed at the order of the Urban Prefect Quintus Junius Rusticus, earning him the nickname "martyr."[5] There is a notable shift from Papias's fondness for the "living voice" to Justin's partiality toward the documented "memoirs of the apostles."[6]

Another major theologian who built on Papias's traditions about the Gospels of Mark and Matthew was Irenaeus, the famous bishop of Lyon and heresiologist. He placed these traditions alongside his traditions about the Gospels of Luke and John.[7] Indeed, he was the foremost defender of "the gospel in fourfold form" (*tetramorphon to euangelion*) and the authorial traditions attached to each Gospel. His logic was that there are four zones around the earth where people dwell, four principal winds, and four Gospels.[8] What these images evoke is that the choice of four authoritative Gospels was a "catholic" or universal decision of the global body of Christian believers.[9] He likened each Gospel to one of the four living creatures in the apocalyptic books of the Bible.[10] What may have happened is that, when the four Gospels were bound together in codices in the mid-second

---

5. See Tatian, *Orat.* 19; Eusebius, *H.E.* 4.16.7–9.

6. See Arthur J. Bellinzoni, *The Sayings of Jesus in the Writings of Justin Martyr* (NovTSup 17; Leiden: Brill, 1967), 4; Barnard, *Justin Martyr*, 53; Osborn, *Justin Martyr*, 124–25; Hagner, "The Sayings," 251; Koester, *Ancient Christian Gospels*, 40; Abramowski, "The Memoirs," 329–30; Graham Stanton, *Jesus and Gospel* (Cambridge: Cambridge University Press, 2004), 104; Oskar Skarsaune, "Justin and His Bible" in *Justin Martyr and His Worlds*, 73–74; Radka Fialová, "'Scripture' and the 'Memoirs of the Apostles': Justin Martyr and His Bible" in *The Process of Authority: The Dynamics in Transmission and Reception of Canonical Texts* (ed. Jan Dušek and Jan Roskovec; Berlin: De Gruyter, 2016), 171.

7. See Irenaeus, *Haer.* 3.1.1.

8. See Irenaeus, *Haer.* 3.11.8.

9. See Annette Yoshiko Reed, "ΕΥΑΓΓΕΛΙΟΝ: Orality, Textuality, and the Christian Truth in Irenaeus's *Adversus Haereses*" *VC* 56 (2002): 23n.40.

10. T. C. Skeat (Irenaeus and the Four-Gospel Canon" *NTS* 34 [1992]: 196–97; cf. Stanton, *Jesus*, 65–66) made an interesting observation about the comparison of the Gospels of Matthew, Mark, Luke, and John to the human, the eagle, the ox, and the lion respectively in the visions in the books of Ezekiel and Revelation in *Haer.* 3.11.8. The description of the four living creatures as four-faced cherubim corresponds with Ezek 1:10, but the order in which they are introduced corresponds with Rev 4:7. If Irenaeus's source for this tradition had followed the order in which Ezekiel introduced the four faces, it would correspond to the Western ordering of the Gospels. In the Western order, the Gospels of Matthew and John precede the Gospels of Mark and Luke. Reed ("ΕΥΑΓΓΕΛΙΟΝ, 39n.71, n.72) rejects Skeat's theory that Irenaeus's source followed the old Western order, arguing that it was Irenaeus's amalgamation of Ezekiel's and

century, titles were affixed to each one. The Gospel "according to" Matthew was distinguished from the ones "according to" Mark, Luke, and John. Irenaeus was partial toward the four-Gospel codices. Papias's conjectures about the origins of the Gospels of Mark and Matthew were broadly disseminated through these codices and emerged as the consensus position. Apostolicity, catholicity, antiquity, and orthodoxy were the four criteria for the inclusion of a book in the New Testament canon in the fourth century.[11] The ascription of the first canonical Gospel to Matthew satisfied the first criterion and it passed the rest of the tests with flying colors.

A Gospel as a Jesus Book

The singular noun *euangelion* may be translated as "gospel" or "good news." The verb *euangelizein* means "to proclaim good news."[12] When one searches for *euangelion* in the *Thesaurus Linguae Grecae*, it is striking how rare the

---

John's apocalyptic visions that led him to switch back and forth between them when comparing the Gospels to the four living creatures.

11. For research on the formation of the New Testament canon, see Hans von Campenhausen, *The Formation of the Christian Bible* (Philadelphia: Fortress, 1972); Henry Y. Gamble, *The New Testament Canon: Its Making and Meaning* (Minneapolis: Fortress, 1985); B. M. Metzger, *The Canon of the New Testament: Its Origin, Development and Significance* (Minneapolis: Fortress, 1985); Arthur G. Patzia, *The Making of the New Testament: Origin, Collection, Text & Canon* (Downers Grove: IVP, 1995); F. F. Bruce, *The Canon of Scripture* (Downers Grove: IVP, 1988); David Trobisch, *The First Edition of the New Testament* (Oxford: Oxford University Press, 2000); Lee Martin MacDonald, *The Biblical Canon: Its Origin, Transmission, and Authority* (Grand Rapids: Baker Academic, 2007); Michael J. Kruger, *The Question of Canon: Challenging the Status Quo in the New Testament Debate* (Nottingham: IVP, 2013).

12. For an overview about the development of gospel terminology, see Koester, *Ancient Christian Gospels*, 1–43; Robert Gundry, "ΕΤΑΓΓΕΛΙΟΝ: How Soon a Book?" *JBL* 115 (1996): 321–25; Hengel, *The Four Gospels*, 61–65, 131–35; Stanton, *Jesus*, 9–62; James A. Kelhoffer, "'How Soon a Book' Revisited: ΕΤΑΓΓΕΛΙΟΝ as a Reference to 'Gospel' Materials in the First Half of the Second Century" *ZNW* 95 (2004): 1–34; Silke Petersen, "Die Evangelienüberschriften und die Entstehung des neutestamentlichen Kanons" *ZNW* 97 (2006): 260–67; David E. Aune, "The Meaning of Εὐαγγέλιον in the *Inscriptiones* of the Canonical Gospels" in *Jesus, Gospel Tradition and Paul in the Context of Jewish and Greco-Roman Antiquity* (ed. David E. Aune; WUNT 303; Tübingen: Mohr Siebeck, 2013), 3–14; Petr Pokorny, *From the Gospel to the Gospels: History, Theology and Impact of the Biblical Term 'Euangelion'* (BZNW 195; Berlin: de Gruyter, 2013).

noun is in pre-Christian literature.[13] To defamiliarize the term, it could be translated as the "announcement."[14] The verb does appear in the book of Isaiah in the Septuagint.[15] The good news that was heralded was that the exile of the people of Judah in Babylon was coming to an end and Yahweh would reign over them. A spirit-empowered prophet would announce good news for the poor, healing for the broken-hearted, and liberty for the captives. The plural form of the noun was inscribed in a stone in the city of Priene in Asia Minor in 9 BCE. The Priene Calendar Inscription marked the commencement of a new calendar system starting with the birth of the god Augustus, the first Roman Emperor who inaugurated the *Pax Romana* or the "Roman Peace."

The announcement about the reign of Israel's deity was fundamental to Jesus's worldview.[16] Some of his devotees had their own announcement that Jesus had defeated the powers who crucified him through his resurrection and heavenly enthronement. The Greek noun *kērygma* is employed by scholars as a shorthand for the "proclamation" about the crucified and risen Christ. Despite the pride that Paul took in spreading "my gospel" or "our gospel" throughout the nations,[17] he was not the innovator who introduced the gospel terminology to Christ-believing circles.[18] He had his own slant on the social and theological implications of the gospel, but the term itself was embedded in creedal formula about the Son of God's royal descent from King David and exalted status after rising from the dead.[19] Over time, the definition of the gospel was expanded from the oral proclamation of the kingdom or its risen king to a genre of literature in which Jesus is the lead protagonist.

This development may have been underway by the time Mark penned his incipit "the beginning of the gospel of Jesus Christ [Son of God]."[20]

---

13. Steve Mason, *Josephus, Judaea, and Christian Origins: Methods and Categories* (Peabody: Hendrickson, 2009), 285–86.
14. Mason, *Josephus*, 287.
15. See LXX Isaiah 40:9; 52:7; 61:1.
16. See Mark 1:14–15; Matt 4:23; 9:35; 24:14.
17. See Rom 2:16; 2 Cor 4:3; 1 Thess 1:5; 2 Thess 2:14.
18. Contra Mason, *Josephus*, 285.
19. See 1 Thess 1:5, 9–10; Rom 1:1, 3–4; 1 Cor 15:1, 3–4; cf. 2 Tim 2:8.
20. See Mark 1:1. "Son of God" is placed in square brackets due to the text-critical debate about whether the words *huiou theou* were original to the text or interpolated into it by later scribes.

Mark's opening verse may have paved the way for a scribe to label his whole work as a Gospel.[21] Jesus's earthly life may have been regarded by Mark as the "beginning," or set the stage, for the Easter gospel about his exaltation as the risen Lord. This gospel would be proclaimed in the future from the vantage point of the narrative; its proclaimers would also notify their listeners about the generosity of the woman who anointed Jesus for his burial.[22] This is a possible reading of Mark's incipit, but it may also include the entire span of Jesus's ministry under the rubric of the gospel. Mark's Gospel was not as narrow in scope as Paul's Gospel, which concentrated on Jesus's vicarious death and resurrection. "Beginning" is the first word in the incipit because it alludes to the opening verse in Genesis.[23] A new beginning had dawned with the advent of the eschatological kingdom, which has been inaugurated but not yet consummated. Jesus's gospel, in Mark's text, mostly concerned the in-breaking of the reign of Israel's deity on the earth.[24] His followers needed to repent and surrender everything, including their very lives, to enter this divine kingdom and would promulgate the news about the kingdom all over the world until he returned.[25] The gospel message in the Gospel of Mark should not be taken in a strictly Pauline sense.

Euangelion is replaced with *biblos* ("book") in the incipit in the Gospel of Matthew. Its incipit reads "the book of the genesis of Jesus Christ, the son of David, the son of Abraham."[26] *Biblos geneseōs* could just be rendered as the "record of the genealogy" as the following verses cover Jesus's family tree. His genealogy is traced back to Abraham, the ancestor of the Jewish people, and David, the best ruler of the United Kingdom of Israel. Like the Markan incipit, however, it may have functioned as the title for the book as a whole and been patterned on the "book of Genesis" (*biblos geneseōs*).[27] Matthew's incipit may be evidence that a *euangelion* could be

---

21. Hengel, *The Four Gospels*, 90–97; cf. Pokorny, *From the Gospel*, 126.

22. Pokorny, *From the Gospel*, 122–23. See Matt 14:9.

23. Keith, *The Gospel*, 111.

24. See Mark 1:14–15; 8:35; 10:29; 13:10; 14:9.

25. See Mark 8:35; 10:29; 13:10; 14:9.

26. See Matt 1:1.

27. Pokorny, *From the Gospel*, 126; Keith, *The Gospel*, 115–18; Patrick Schreiner, *Matthew, Disciple and Scribe: The First Gospel and Its Portrait of Jesus* (Grand Rapids: Baker, 2019), 11. See Gen 2:4 LXX.

regarded as a *biblos*.[28] Contrariwise, Matthew may not have taken these two terms as interchangeable and may have avoided using *euangelion* in his incipit, judging it to be unsuitable as a label for a book about Jesus's life. Matthew restricted the *euangelion* to the message of "good news" about the kingdom. The omission of the term "gospel" in Matthew's parallel summary statement of Jesus's initial pronouncement of the nearness of the kingdom does not necessitate that there was a shift from the gospel being something that Jesus proclaimed to something that was proclaimed about him.[29] Three times the qualifier "of the kingdom" is appended to "the gospel" or "this gospel."[30] No theological weight should be placed on the editorial insertion of the demonstrative pronoun before "gospel" in two verses that Matthew copied from Mark's Gospel.[31] There is no wink to the readers that "this gospel" (*touto to euangelion*) was the text that they had in their possession.[32] The characters within Matthew's narrative could not have comprehended that the gospel was a book; it was the good news that they would "preach" (*kēryssō*) to the world.[33]

The noun "gospel" is absent in the Gospel of Luke, but the verb for preaching good news is present in it and in its sequel in Acts.[34] In Acts, the noun denotes the "good news" orally proclaimed by Peter and Paul.[35] Luke furnished Theophilus, the patron who may have sponsored his publication, with an orderly "account" (*diēgēsis*) reassuring him of the truthfulness of what he had been taught about the culmination of salvation history.[36] There is no evidence that Theophilus was inspired by Mark's incipit to entitle Luke's account as a Gospel when he disseminated it for a broader readership.[37] Mark was one of Luke's predecessors who were less than successful in putting out quality narratives about

---

28. Keith, *The Gospel*, 119.
29. Contra Pokorny, *From the Gospel*, 170. Compare Matt 4:17 to Mark 1:15.
30. See Matt 4:23; 9:35; 24:14 (contra Mark 13:10).
31. See Matt 24:14 (cf. Mark 13:10) and Matt 26:13 (cf. Mark 14:9).
32. Contra Stanton, *Jesus*, 56–58.
33. Gundry, "ΕΤΑΓΓΕΛΙΟΝ," 321. See Matt 26:13.
34. See Luke 1:19; 2:10; 3:18; 4:18, 43; 7:22; 8:1; 9:6; 16:16; 20:1; Acts 5:42; 8:4, 12, 25, 35, 40; 10:36; 11:20; 13:32; 14:7, 15, 21; 15:35; 16:10; 17:18.
35. See Acts 15:7; 20:24.
36. See Luke 1:1–4.
37. Contra Hengel, *The Four Gospels*, 100–103.

Jesus in the Lukan prologue.[38] Neither the noun nor the verb is present in the Gospel of John.

Researchers have scrutinized the occurrences of the noun "gospel" in ancient corpuses of Christian literature, such as the Apostolic Fathers and the Nag Hammadi Library. The title of the former anthology intimates that the authors had some connection to the apostolic generation, whether it was believed that they had personal relationships with the apostles or carried on their theological legacy. The Nag Hammadi Library was named after the city in Egypt where a jar filled with manuscripts was unearthed in 1945.[39] Whether the gospel denoted an oral proclamation or a literary genre in any of these writings must be tested on a case-by-case basis.

Some cases are clear-cut. A letter ascribed to Clement, the bishop of Rome, that was delivered to the Corinthians reminded them about what Paul had written to them about the "beginning of the gospel."[40] Paul's letter to the Corinthians had scolded them for forming conflicting factions,[41] for they should have been united under the banner of Paul's oral gospel about "Christ crucified." An anonymous homily with Clement's name attached to it in the title prefaces a saying of Jesus in a text with the words "for the Lord says in the gospel."[42] This author had a Gospel book. In the apologetic

---

38. Keith (*The Gospel*, 123–29) describes the criticism of the earlier Gospels for not arranging their material "in order" (cf. Luke 1:3) as an example of "competitive textualization."

39. For critical caution about the exaggerations in the story of the discovery of the Nag Hammadi codices, see Mark Goodacre, "How Reliable is the Story of the Nag Hammadi Discovery?" *JSNT* 35.4 (2013): 303–22.

40. See *1 Clem* 47:2. For the text, see Holmes, *Apostolic Fathers*, 109.

41. See *1 Clem* 47:3 (cf. 1 Cor 1:12).

42. See *2 Clem* 8:5. For the text, see Holmes, *Apostolic Fathers*, 149. According to Koester, this is the singular exception among the Apostolic Fathers in applying the term "gospel" to a written document. See Koester, *Synoptische Überlieferung*, 11; Koester, *Ancient Christian Gospels*, 17. Koester (*Ancient Christian Gospels*, 17–18, 18n.1) seems to sideline the import of this evidence. He notes that only the second part of the saying about those who are faithful with a little will be faithful with much parallels the first part of Luke 16:10. This leads him to conjecture that the author of *2 Clement* had access to a sayings collection that drew on the Gospels of Matthew and Luke but was not previously designated as a "gospel" before *2 Clement* was written. Finally, he dates the writing of *2 Clement* to 150 CE or later on the grounds that it presupposes harmonized quotations of the Gospels of Matthew and Luke. For further debate about the source(s) of *2 Clem* 8:5, see A Committee of the Oxford Society of Historical Theology, *Apostolic Fathers*, 133; Köster, *Synoptische Überlieferung*, 99–102; Gregory, *The Reception*, 137; Petersen, "Die Evangelienüberschriften," 261; Aune, "The Meaning," 11–12; Andrew F.

Epistle to Diognetus, the anonymous "disciple" (*mathētēs*) of an uncertain date who composed it was thrilled by how the Law was reverenced, the grace of the prophets was recognized, and the faith of the *euangelia* ("gospels") was established.[43] The plural is used for plural Gospel writings. In the late second-century *Treatise on the Resurrection*, the author reminded his pupil Rheginos that he had read about the glorious appearances of Moses and Elijah in the Gospel.[44] The allusion could be to any of the three Synoptic accounts of Jesus's transfiguration.[45]

Other cases are debatable. Ignatius, a bishop of Antioch, sent letters to various Christ congregations while being transferred as a prisoner to Rome to be torn apart by the beasts in the coliseum during the reign of Trajan.[46] He juxtaposed the *euangelion* with the Law of Moses and the prophets.[47] Despite the written character of his scriptural "archives" (*archeia*),[48] he seems to have been juxtaposing inanimate textual objects with a living "gospel." The sole archive that he prized above all else was the incarnate Jesus and his saving death and resurrection.[49] He was not

Gregory and Christopher M. Tuckett, "*2 Clement* and the Writings that Later Formed the New Testament" in *The Reception of the New Testament in the Apostolic Fathers*, 269–70; Pokorny, *From the Gospel*, 180; Young, *Jesus Tradition*, 255–56. For criticism of Koester's late dating of *2 Clement* and the counterargument that it might predate Marcion, see Kelhoffer, "ΕΥΑΓΓΕΛΙΟΝ," 13–15.

43. See *Diogn.* 11:6. For the text, see Holmes, *Apostolic Fathers*, 300. The neglect of this example in other surveys of the gospel terminology is noted in Keith, *The Gospel*, 120.

44. See *Treat. Res.* 1.48.7–11. For the text, see Malcolm L. Peel, "The Treatise on the Resurrection (I,4)" in *The Nag Hammadi Library in English* (3rd rev. ed.; ed. James M. Robinson; San Francisco: Harper & Row, 1988), 56. According to Koester, this is the singular exception among the Nag Hammadi Library in applying the term "Gospel" to a written document. See Koester, *Ancient Christian Gospels*, 23.

45. See Mark 9:2–8; Matt 17:1–8; Luke 9:28–36. Tuckett (*Nag Hammadi*, 68–71) finds some limited traces of Matthean redaction in the *Treatise on the Resurrection*, indicating that its author may at least be dependent on Matthew's Gospel.

46. For a few studies on Ignatius of Antioch, see William R. Schoedel, *Ignatius of Antioch: A Commentary on the Letters of Ignatius* (Hermeneia; ed. Helmut Koester; Philadelphia: Fortress, 1985); Allen Brent, *Ignatius of Antioch: A Martyr Bishop and the Origin of the Episcopacy* (London: T&T Clark, 2007). Ignatius expected to meet such a fate in *Rom* 5:1 and this came to pass according to Eusebius (*H.E.* 3.36.3) and Jerome (*Vir. ill.* 16).

47. See Ignatius, *Smyrn.* 5:1; 7:2; *Philad.* 5:2. Hengel (*The Four Gospels*, 63–64) argues that Ignatius was here referring to written Gospels.

48. See Ignatius, *Philad.* 8:2.

49. See Ignatius, *Philad.* 8:2 (cf. 5:1). See Schoedel, *Ignatius*, 208n.6, 234, 234n.22, 242; Koester, *Ancient Christian Gospels*, 8; Petersen, "Die Evangelienüberschriften," 261; Aune, "The Meaning," 11; Pokorny, *From the Gospel*, 178.

unaware of the Gospel of Matthew. He attests that Jesus was baptized to fulfill all righteousness, alluding to Jesus's reply when John the Baptizer tried to dissuade him from getting baptized in Matthew's Gospel.[50] Mark's Gospel presented John's rite as a "baptism of repentance for the forgiveness of sins."[51] Matthew's redactional insertion of a conversation between Jesus and the Baptizer over why Jesus chose to be baptized by John was designed to ward off any problematic theological implications that readers might draw from Mark's baptism account.[52]

There are four references to a *euangelion* in an antique Jewish instructional manual or church order entitled "The Lord's Teaching through the Twelve Apostles to the Nations," better known under the abridged title of the *Didache* ("Teaching").[53] There is an academic consensus that it is a composite document, though the question of how many stages of growth the text underwent before it reached its final form is where the consensus ends.[54] The four references were from the same editorial hand. This is evidenced in the parallel constructions in the commands "to pray" (*proseuchesthe*) or "to act" (*poiēsate*) "in this manner" (*houtō*) "as the Lord commanded in his gospel" (*hōs ekeleusen ho kurios en tō euangeliō autou*), "according to the decree of the gospel" (*kata to dogma tou euangeliou*),

---

50. See Ignatius, *Smyrn.* 1:1 (cf. Matt 3:15).

51. See Mark 1:4.

52. See Matt 3:14–15. Although Koester developed the criterion that an intertextual relationship can be established if a Gospel writer's redactional activity is reproduced in a later text, he doubted that Ignatius was directly dependent on Matthew's text in this instance. See Köster, *Synoptische Überlieferung*, 59; cf. Hagner, "Sayings," 240. Paul Foster ("The Epistles of Ignatius of Antioch and the Writings that Later Formed the New Testament" in *The Reception of the New Testament in the Apostolic Fathers*, 174–76) rightly counters that this passage from Ignatius easily passes Koester's redactional criterion. Other scholars who have concluded that Ignatius was dependent on Matt 3:15 include the Oxford Society in 1905 (*Apostolic Fathers*, 76–77), Massaux (*The Influence*, 1.89), Köhler (*Die Rezeption*, 77–79), and Schoedel (*Ignatius*, 222).

53. See *Did.* 8:2; 11:3; 15:3–4. For a few studies on the *Didache*, see Jonathan A. Draper, ed., *The Didache in Modern Research* (Leiden: Brill, 1996); Kurt Niederwimmer, *The Didache* (Hermeneia; trans. Linda M. Maloney; ed. Harold W. Attridge; Minneapolis: Fortress, 1998); Huub Van De Sandt and David Flusser, *The Didache: Its Jewish Sources and its Place in Early Judaism and Christianity* (Minneapolis: Fortress, 2002); Aaron Milavec, *The Didache: Text, Translation, Analysis, and Commentary* (Collegeville: Liturgical, 2003); Jonathan Draper and Clayton N. Jefford, *The Didache: A Missing Piece of the Puzzle in Early Christianity* (Atlanta: SBL, 2015).

54. For a helpful overview of the debate, see Niederwimmer, *The Didache*, 42–52.

or "as you have in the gospel of our Lord" (*hōs echete en tō euangeliō tou kyriou hēmōn*).[55]

Depending on the verse in the *Didache*, the *euangelion* could be defined as either the "gospel" message that Jesus preached or a "Gospel" text with guidelines for Christ-like conduct.[56] It seems less likely that the verses alternated between these two definitions if the same editor was responsible for all four references. *Euangelion* may have retained its kerygmatic meaning for an oral message that was proclaimed.[57] Conversely, if it denoted a written Gospel, the Gospel of Matthew is the most likely candidate.[58] One intriguing theory for why Matthew's text came to be known as a Gospel before the final editing of the *Didache* is that a scribe had copied the Gospels of Mark and Matthew together and got the wrong impression that the Markan incipit was the title covering both works.[59]

---

55. Niederwimmer, *The Didache*, 49; Alan J. P. Garrow, *The Gospel of Matthew's Dependence on the Didache* (JSNTS 254; London: T&T Clark, 2004), 129–30, 131–33.

56. Even the scholars who argue that *Did.* 8:2 or 11:3, or both, referred to an oral gospel allow that 15:3–4 may be referencing a written text. See Köster, *Synoptische Überlieferung*, 10–11, 203, 209, 240; Draper, "The Jesus Tradition in the *Didache*" in *The Didache in Modern Research*, 76, 79, 85–86; Niederwimmer, *The Didache*, 51, 135, 173, 204; Koester, *Ancient Christian Gospels*, 16–17; Sandt and Flusser, *The Didache*, 50, 294–95; Bruce E. Brooks, "Before and After Matthew" in *The Didache: A Missing Piece of the Puzzle in Early Christianity*, 258n.26, 275n.83; 279. Still, Draper ("The Jesus Tradition," 76) and Koester ("Ancient Christian Gospels," 17) are open to the option that *Did.* 15:3–4 was referring to the oral gospel as well.

57. See Hagner, "Sayings," 241; Gundry, "ΕΤΑΓΓΕΛΙΟΝ," 322–23; Milavec, *The Didache*, 65; Aaron Milavec, "Synoptic Tradition in the *Didache* Revisited" *JECS* 11.4 (2003): 459; Aune, "*Gospel Tradition* 11; Young, *Jesus Tradition*, 218–19. Note that Gundry's and Aune's position is that this was the oral message that Jesus proclaimed within Matthew's narrative.

58. See Massaux, *The Influence*, 3.145, 154–55; Köhler, *Die Rezeption*, 30–36; Christopher M. Tuckett, "Synoptic Tradition in the Didache" in *The New Testament in Early Christianity* (ed. Jean-Marie Sevrin; Leuven: Leuven University Press, 1989), 198–99; Stanton, *Jesus and Gospel*, 55; Hengel, *The Four Gospels*, 63–64, 252n.270; Garrow, *The Gospel of Matthew's Dependence*, 133–37; Kelhoffer, "ΕΥΑΓΓΕΛΙΟΝ," 17–22; Christopher Tuckett, "The *Didache* and the Writings that Later Formed the New Testament" in *The Reception of the New Testament in the Apostolic Fathers*, 106, 107, 109–10; Petersen, "Die Evangelienüberschriften," 262n.40; Pokorny, *From the Gospel*, 179. Richard Glover ("The Didache's Quotations and the Synoptic Gospels" *NTS* 5 [1958]: 19, 28), however, argues that the "Gospel" in the *Didache* was a written sayings collection.

59. Kelhoffer, "ΕΤΑΓΓΕΛΙΟΝ," 31, 33–34.

The allusions to Matthew's directives about showing hospitality to itinerant apostles and prophets, fostering peace in the assembly by gently admonishing erring members and silencing unrepentant ones, and almsgiving in the editorial layer of the *Didache* are fairly loose.[60] The best case for the editor's literary dependence on the Gospel of Matthew is in the prayer that is recited after the imperative to pray "as the Lord commanded in his gospel," which can be translated as follows:[61]

> *"Our Father in heaven, hallowed be your name, your kingdom come, your will be done on earth as it is in heaven. Give us today our daily bread, and forgive us our debt, as we also forgive our debtors; and do not lead us into temptation, but deliver us from the evil one; for yours is the power and the glory forever."*

There is near verbatim agreement between the wording of the Lord's Prayer in the *Didache* and the Gospel of Matthew. The few variations in wording are minor. The Father is located "in the heavens" (*en tois ouranois*) in Matthew's Gospel and "in heaven" (*en tō ouranō*) in the *Didache*. There is a petition for the forgiveness of "the debts" (*ta opheilēmata*) in Matthew's Gospel and "the debt" (*tēn opheilēn*) in the *Didache*. The petitioners hope that our debts will be canceled, just as "we forgave" (*aphēkamen*) or "we forgive" (*aphiemen*) our debtors in Matthew's Gospel and the *Didache* respectively. The prayer in the *Didache* finishes with the doxology that is missing from some manuscript witnesses of the Gospel of Matthew. The shorter version of the Lord's Prayer in Luke's Gospel can be safely eliminated from contention as the source for the *Didache*.[62]

The parallels between the two texts may be due to both authors sharing a common liturgical tradition.[63] The slight variations in wording may

---

60. See *Did.* 11:3–4 (cf. Matt 10:11, 40–42); 15:3 (cf. Matt 5:22; 18:15–17); 15:4 (cf. Matt 6:1–4).

61. See *Did.* 8:2 (cf. Matt 6:9–13). For the text, see Holmes, *Apostolic Fathers*, 357.

62. See Luke 11:2–4.

63. The following arguments are found in Koester, *Synoptische*, 203–9; Glover, "The Didache's Quotations," 18–19; Draper, "Jesus Tradition," 85–86; Niederwimmer, *The Didache*, 134–38; Sandt and Flusser, *The Didache*, 50, 294–95; Milavec, "Synoptic Tradition," 448, 451; Young, *Jesus Tradition*, 218–24. Garrow (*The Gospel of Matthew's Dependence*," 165–77) argues that the Lord's Prayer in *Did.* 8:2 was derived from an oral

count against a direct literary relationship between them. It is hard to explain why a redactor would find it necessary to alter Matthew's plural "heavens" or "debts" to the singular "heaven" or "debt" or the tense of the verb "forgive" from aorist to present on redaction-critical grounds. The doxology in the *Didache* points to a liturgical setting. The audience is advised to recite the Lord's Prayer thrice a day, so they would have memorized it and would not need to look it up in a written Gospel.[64] Those who do not pray the prescribed prayer or fast on the wrong days of the week are castigated as "hypocrites."[65] The "hypocrites" did not have the same motivations in Matthew's Gospel when trumpeting their fasts, charitable gifts, and public prayers for human praise.[66] Jesus's denunciation of the longwinded prayers that his non-Jewish contemporaries addressed to their deities in the Gospel of Matthew is absent from the *Didache* too.[67] If the Didachist's exhortation to pray like Jesus prayed in the Gospel was a secondary redactional insertion, its intent may have been to demand that the wording of the Lord's Prayer in the communal liturgy be aligned exactly to Matthew's wording.[68]

On the other hand, the version of the Lord's Prayer in Matthew's Gospel could have originally influenced the wording of the liturgical tradition that the audience of the *Didache* had learned by heart.[69] The minor variations that surfaced in it may be due to faulty memories or intentional grammatical corrections. The deity's location "in the heavens" could have been reworded to the singular "heaven" to correspond with Matthew's line about obeying the divine will on earth as it is done "in heaven" (*en ouranō*). The present tense of the verb "forgive" stresses the continual obligation to

---

tradition that was more primitive than the version of the prayer in Matt 6:9–13, yet he does not rule out an intertextual relationship between the two sources. He just reverses the direction of influence, so that Matt 6:1–18 conflated *Did.* 8:1–3 with Mark 11:25 and 12:40–44.

64. See *Did.* 8:3.

65. See *Did.* 8:1–2.

66. See Matt 6:2, 5, 16.

67. See Matt 6:7.

68. Garrow, *The Gospel of Matthew's Dependence*, 139.

69. The following arguments are found in Clayton N. Jefford, *The Sayings of Jesus in the Teaching of the Twelve Apostles* (Leiden: Brill, 1989), 137–38; Kelhoffer, "ΕΥΑΓΓΕΛΙΟΝ," 17–22; Tuckett, "The *Didache*," 104–6; Olegs Andrejevs, "A Source-critical Analysis of the Lord's Prayer: Multiple Autonomous Recensions or Q?" *ETL* 96.4 (2020): 664–66.

forgive, not just as a precondition for receiving divine forgiveness. If the Two Source Hypothesis is correct, the Lord's Prayer in the Gospels of Matthew and Luke may derive from Q. Some of the wording in the Matthean version of it may reflect the evangelist's editing of Q, such as the expansion of the petition "your kingdom come" with "your will be done on earth as it is in heaven."[70] The placement of the Lord's prayer within the wider context of exposing religious hypocrisy in Matthew's Gospel may also be redactional. This may show that the communal liturgy that the Didachist drew on had replicated Matthean redactional elements. The same would be true if Matthew had redacted Luke's Gospel directly.[71] If Luke was directly dependent on Matthew's Gospel, this argument would be weakened as it would be impossible to determine if Matthew's wording was traditional or redactional if Matthew's own source for the prayer was unrecoverable.[72] In the end, if the term *euangelion* was used for a written "Gospel" in the final form of the *Didache*, then its editor must have at least perceived the obvious affinities between the Lord's Prayer in the community's liturgy and the Lord's Prayer in Matthew's Gospel.

What is not debatable is that Marcion had a text that he reckoned to be a Gospel. According to his hostile patristic biographers,[73] Marcion was a wealthy shipowner from Pontus. He donated a substantial sum of money to the Christ assemblies in Rome, but his gift was declined and he was expelled

---

70. See Matt 6:9–13//Luke 11:2–4. For the argument that Q's wording of the prayer is more closely preserved in Luke 11:2–4, see Andrejevs, "A Source-critical Analysis," 666–67.
71. MacEwan (*Matthean Posterity*, 80–81), however, still allows that Matthew's "debts" may be more primitive than Luke's sins if Matthew was influenced by a liturgical tradition in addition to copying Luke's Gospel.
72. For scholars arguing that Luke edited and shortened Matthew's prayer, see Farmer, *The Gospel*, 45–51; Goulder, "New Paradigm," 2.496–98; Watson, *Gospel Writing*, 172; Ken Olson, "The Lord's Prayer: Abridged Version" in *Marcan Priority without Q*, 101–18. Goodacre (*The Case*, 64) allows that Luke may have known the Lord's prayer in another form through a liturgical tradition.
73. For critical studies on Marcion's life and thought, see Adolf von Harnack, *Marcion: Das Evangelium vom fremden Gott. Eine Monographie zur Geschichte der Grundlegung der katholischen Kirche* (2nd ed.: TU 45; Leipzig: Hinrichs, 1924); R. Joseph Hoffmann, *Marcion: On the Restitution of Christianity: An Essay on the Development of Radical Paulinist Theology in the Second Century* (AAR 46; Chico: Scholars Press, 1984); Sebastian Moll, *The Arch-Heretic Marcion* (WUNT, 250; Tübingen: Mohr Siebeck, 2010); Judith M. Lieu, *Marcion and the Making of a Heretic: God and Scripture in the Second Century* (Cambridge: Cambridge University Press, 2015).

from fellowshipping with them.[74] His "excommunication" has been dated to around 144 CE.[75] This is based on a quip from Tertullian of Carthage (ca. 155–220 CE), a rhetorically-trained Christian author who wrote a number of influential Latin works, that Marcion exhibited his impiety when the pious Roman Emperor Antoninus ruled (ca. 138–61 CE) and an interval of 115 years and six and a half months separated Christ from Marcion.[76] Justin's shock that "even until now" Marcion was aided by demons in spreading his blasphemies against the creator far and wide may allow for his ministry to be dated earlier.[77] Marcion divided Jesus's loving heavenly father from the just, wrathful creator of the world reverenced in the Jewish Scriptures. His opponents accused him of peddling an expurgated version of Luke's Gospel and ten Pauline epistles in a collection called the *Apostolikon* to promote his theology. His Gospel must have closely approximated Luke's text for the accusation that he purged it of the passages that were not conducive to his theological outlook to stick.[78] He admired the apostle Paul, so he may have misunderstood his hero's endorsements of "my gospel"[79] or "our gospel"[80] as the written Gospel that had come into his possession.[81]

It is unlikely that Marcion was the originator of the titular usage of the noun gospel. Some of the texts already surveyed predate Marcion's ministry and their references to a written Gospel cannot be discounted. Moreover, Justin grants that the "memoirs of the apostles" were popularly dubbed "Gospels" in his time.[82] It would have been controversial if the application

---

74. See Tertullian, *Marc.* 4.4.3; *Praescr.* 30.
75. Harnack, *Marcion*, 26.
76. See Tertullian, *Marc.* 1.19.
77. See Justin, *1 Apol.* 26.5; 58.1–2. See Hoffmann, *Marcion*, 45; Joseph B. Tyson, *Marcion and Luke-Acts: A Defining Struggle* (Columbia: University of South Carolina Press, 2006), 29. Moll (*The Arch-Heretic*, 39) and Lieu (*Marcion*, 15n.2) are more cautious about using this passage from Justin to date Marcion's ministry. Justin may not have been pointing out the longevity of Marcion's ministry. He may have just been registering his amazement that false teachers were still introducing new, demonically-inspired falsehoods in his lifetime, long after the original "heresiarchs" Simon the magician and his disciple Menander had died.
78. See, for example, Irenaeus, *Haer.* 1.27.2; Tertullian, *Marc.* 1.1.4–5; 4.2–6; Epiphanius, *Pan.* 42.9.1.
79. See Rom 2:16.
80. See 2 Cor 4:3; 1 Thess 1:5; 2 Thess 2:14.
81. Campenhausen, *The Formation*, 147–63; Koester, *Ancient Christian Gospel*, 35–36.
82. See *1 Apol.* 66.3; cf. *Dial.* 10.2; 100.2.

of the term "gospel" to a text was recently borrowed from Marcion.[83] The relative clause "which are called Gospels" (*ha kaleitai euangelia*) was not a scribal insertion into Justin's first reference to the apostolic memoirs.[84] Justin crafted his *First Apology* in the form of a legal petition to Antoninus Pius, his sons, and the Roman Senate on behalf of the maligned Christians.[85] In his first reference to the "memoirs of the apostles," he was explaining what the Eucharist or the "thanksgiving meal" celebrates. The bread and the chalice symbolize Jesus's broken body and shed blood and are taken in "remembrance" of his sacrifice.[86] In this context, it would have been natural to clarify the idiomatic literary meaning assigned to the rare noun "gospel" by comparing it to a memoir. The preceding chapter has a clarifying gloss about "the ones who are called by us deacons" (*hoi kaloumenoi par' hemin diakonoi*).[87] Justin's Jewish dialogue partner was also cognizant of the titular usage of "gospel." Trypho was impressed by Jesus's high ethical standards "in the so-called Gospel" (*en tō legomenō euangeliō*).[88]

When all the data is taken into consideration, scholars may need to jettison simplistic models of a linear trajectory in which gospel terminology evolved from an oral proclamation to a literary genre. There may not have been a single catalyst for why Christian writers, at different times and places, extended the meaning of the gospel from the good news that was proclaimed about the kingdom of God or the lordship of Jesus to written texts about Jesus. Even in the late second century, Irenaeus could employ speaking verbs such as "preach" (*kēryssō*) or "announce" (*apangellō*) for the gospel that the apostles or their colleagues orally delivered.[89] The polysemy of the term was crucial to Irenaeus's thinking that authentic apostolic books about Jesus

---

83. See Hengel, *The Four Gospels*, 247–48n.247; Pokorny, *From the Gospel*, 182, 186.
84. Contra Osborn, *Justin Martyr*, 124.
85. Parvis, "Justin Martyr," 6–7.
86. Justin's wording is closer to Luke 22:19 than to the other Synoptic texts, but it is not absolutely certain that the "memoir" where he found his Eucharistic liturgy was Luke's Gospel. See Gregory, *Reception*, 278–80.
87. See *1 Apol.* 65.5. See Abramowski, "Memoirs," 323; Kok, "Justin Martyr," 11. Justin's use of the plural *euangelia* ("gospels") disproves Otto Piper's case that Justin defined the "gospel" solely in terms of the singular message of God's ongoing saving activity that was articulated in an indeterminate number of writings. See Otto Piper, "The Nature of the Gospel according to Justin Martyr" *JR* 41.3 (1961): 162–66.
88. See Justin, *Dial.* 10.2.
89. Reed, "ΕΥΑΓΓΕΛΙΟΝ," 20, 24–26. See Irenaeus, *Haer.* 3.1.1; 3.12.12; 3.14.1.

and genuine apostolic oral traditions handed down by their ecclesiastical successors complement each other in testifying to the unitary truth of the Christian gospel.[90] Given its elasticity, the gospel could encompass both oral and written traditions about Jesus's life, teachings, sacrificial death, and postmortem vindication.[91]

The "Memoirs of the Apostles"

Justin reconceptualized the Gospels as the "memoirs" (*apomnēmoneumata*) from the apostles themselves as a collective group.[92] His aim might have been to repackage these texts for the educated elites by cataloging them in an identifiable literary genre.[93] Justin appreciated the *Memoirs of Socrates* by the Athenian philosopher Xenophon (ca. 430–354 BCE).[94] He praised the Athenian philosopher Socrates (ca. 479–399 BCE) for his partial comprehension of divine "reason" (*logos*), the very *logos* that became incarnate in the person of Jesus.[95] Granted, the genitives are functioning differently in the titles of Xenophon's and Justin's memoirs. That is, Xenophon's memoirs were about Socrates, whereas the apostles were the authors of their memoirs and Jesus was their principal subject.[96] Further, the title *Memoirs of Socrates* may not be original to Xenophon.[97]

---

90. Reed, "ΕΥΑΓΓΕΛΙΟΝ," 46.
91. Aune, "The Meaning," 13.
92. See Justin, *1 Apol.* 66.3; 67.3; *Dial.* 100.4; 101.3; 102.5; 103.6, 8; 104.1; 105.1, 5, 6; 106.1, 3, 4; 107.1.
93. Theodor Zahn, *Geschichte des neutestamentlichen Kanons. Erster Band: Das Neue Testament vor Origenes. Zweite Hälfte* (Erlangen: Deichert, 1889), 1.ii.471–76.
94. See Justin, *2 Apol.* 11.3–5. See Zahn, *Geschichte*, 1.ii.471–76; Niels Hydahl, "Hegesipps Hypomnemata" ST 14 (1960): 77–83; Willis A. Shotwell, *The Biblical Exegesis of Justin Martyr* (London: SPCK, 1965), 25; Barnard, *Justin Martyr*, 56; Kennedy, "Classical," 136–37; Abramowski, "The Memoirs," 327–28; Dungan, *The Synoptic Problem*, 31–33; Gabriella Aragione, "Justin, 'philosophe' chrétien, et les 'Mémoires des Apôtres qui sont appelés Évangiles'" *Apoc.* 15 (2004): 47–52; Fialová, "Scripture," 169; Keith, *The Gospel*, 53.
95. See Justin, *1 Apol.* 5.3; *2 Apol.* 10.5–8.
96. Richard Heard, "The *Apomnēmoneumata* in Papias, Justin and Irenaeus" *NTS* 1 (1954): 125.
97. Koester (*Ancient Christian Gospels*, 39) notes that this title only surfaces in late manuscripts and a pseudonymous letter ascribed to Xenophon. The Roman author Aulus Gellius (ca. 125–80 CE) designated Xenophon's memorabilia with the Latin term *comentarii*, which may have been used as a synonym for the Greek term *apomnēmoneumata*.

Xenophon's work was categorized as *apomnēmoneumata* ("memoirs") by the first century in the rhetorical exercises of the Alexandrian sophist Aelius Theon.[98] The plural form of the noun *apomnēmoneuma* ("memoir") may have been applied to the memoirs of the philosophers before the era of the Second Sophistic from 60 to 230 CE.[99] None of this disqualifies the Gospels from fitting in the general category of the philosophers' memorabilia.[100]

Even so, the terms *hypomnēmata* and *apomnēmoneumata* could be applied to a much broader range of literary genres in antiquity. What united this disparate assortment of writings together is that they were pre-literary textual objects, insofar as they were not ready for publication as finished and polished works, and they had a utilitarian function in serving as memory aids.[101] The noun *apomnēmoneuma* itself is etymologically related to the verb *apomnēmoneuō* ("remember"). Justin may have been influenced by Papias's terminology about how Mark "remembered" (*apemnēmoneusen*) Peter's sermons about Jesus.[102] Both Justin and Papias may have classified their texts about Jesus as commemorative writings.[103] Similarly, Clement of Alexandria expanded on Mark's circumstances in Rome where he drafted up his "notes" (*hypomnēma*).[104]

Bauckham (*Jesus*, 213) adds that Justin does not refer to Xenophon's work as the *Memoirs of Socrates*.

98. See Aelius Theon, *Prog.* 66.15; 126.34. See Aragione, "Justin," 47–48.

99. Contra Koester, *Ancient Christian Gospels*, 39. Heard ("The *Apomnēmoneumata*," 125) and Koester (*Ancient Christian Gospels*, 39) translate *apomnēmoneumata* in Plutarch's biographies as recorded "anecdotes" (e.g., *Pomp.* 2.5; *Cat. Maj.* 9.5). Dungan (*The Synoptic Problem*, 31–32) and Aragione ("Justin," 48–49) counter that a third-century CE biographer of the Greek philosophers, Diogenes Laertius, noted the *apomnēmoneumata* of Diodorus Siculus, a Greek historian in the first century BCE (D. L. 4.2). Cirafesi and Fewster ("Justin's Ἀπομνημονεύματα, 192–95) undercut the entire premise of Koester's argument by insisting that *hypomnēmata*, *apomnēmoneumata*, and *commentarii* could be used as interchangeable terms for memorial writings.

100. Hydahl, "Hegesipps Hypomnemata," 79; Abramowski, "The Memoirs," 329.

101. Cirafesi and Fewster, "Justin's Ἀπομνημονεύματα, 195; Larsen, *Gospels*, 11–36; Larsen and Letteney, "Christians," 394–99.

102. Heard, "The *Apomnēmoneumata*," 125–26; cf. Koester, *Ancient Christian Gospels*, 39–40.

103. Cirafesi and Fewster, "Justin's Ἀπομνημονεύματα," 195.

104. See Eusebius, *H.E.* 2.15.1. Cirafesi and Fewster ("Justin's Ἀπομνημονεύματα," 194) note this parallel but incorrectly attribute it to Papias rather than Clement.

Papias's impact on Justin may be evident in a passage where Justin may have referred to Peter's memoirs. Justin qualified the text in which Jesus christened one of his apostles as Peter, and the two sons of Zebedee as *boanerges* or the "sons of thunder," as the "memoirs of him" (*apomnēmoneumata autou*).[105] The pronoun could be translated as a possessive genitive ("his memoirs"), with Peter being its antecedent. This lines up with how the apostolic authors of the memoirs are always put in the genitive case.[106] Since over half of the references to the "memoirs" do not have the genitive qualifier "of the apostles,"[107] the title "memoir" can stand alone and the pronoun could be translated as an objective genitive ("memoirs about him"). In that case, Jesus is its antecedent.[108] There is an allusion to a singly attested detail in Mark's Gospel. No other Gospel has the nickname "sons of thunder," much less transliterated the Aramaic words underlying it.[109] Although Jesus's act of renaming Simon as "Peter" is narrated more fully in the Gospels of Matthew and John,[110] Mark notes that Jesus gave him this

---

105. See Justin, *Dial.* 106.3.
106. See Justin, *Dial.* 100.4; 101.3; 102.5; 103.6; 104.1; 106.1; 106.4. Shotwell, *The Biblical Exegesis*, 24; Barnard, *Justin Martyr*, 57; Abramowski, "The Memoirs," 334–35; Hengel, *Studies*, 68; Stanton, *Jesus*, 101; Hengel, *The Four Gospels*, 222n.85; Skarsaune, "Justin," 72; Ehrman, *Forgery*, 325; Kok, *The Gospel*, 114. Ehrman (*Forgery*, 325) argues the genitive pronoun *autou* should be translated as a possessive genitive, rather than an objective one, because objective genitives usually occur with nouns of action. A potential weakness of this last argument is that the noun *apomnēmoneuma* is related to the verb *apomnēmoneuō*. In a defunct blog post, Tim Henderson pointed to how the genitive pronoun in the phrase *he akoē autou* ("the news about him") in Mark 1:28 and Matt 4:24 is translated as an objective genitive. This blog post is cited in Kok, *The Gospel*, 114.
107. See Justin, *1 Apol.* 66.3, 67.3; *Dial.* 103.8; 105.1; 105.5; 105.6; 106.3; 107.1.
108. See Paul Foster, "The Relationship between the Writings of Justin Martyr and the So-Called Gospel of Peter" in *Justin Martyr and His Worlds*, 108.
109. See Casey, *Jesus*, 66, 189–90; Kok, *The Gospel*, 114–15. This nickname occurs in Mark 3:17 after James and John are listed among the twelve apostles, but the nickname is omitted in the other lists in Matt 10:2–4, Luke 6:14–16, and Acts 1:13. There is no evidence that the nickname was applied to James and John in the *Gospel of Peter* from the fragmentary evidence in the Akhmim fragment. It is debatable whether Justin counted the *Gospel of Peter* as one of the apostles' memoirs. For further debate about Justin's knowledge of the *Gospel of Peter*, see Peter Pilhofer, "Justin und das Petrusevangelium" *ZNW* 81 (1990): 69–75; Foster, "The Relationship," 108–11; Charles E. Hill, "Was John's Gospel among the Apostolic Memoirs?" in *Justin Martyr and His Worlds*, 91–93; Ehrman, *Forgery*, 118, 325–27; Watson, *Gospel Writing*, 379–80.
110. See Matt 16:18; John 1:42.

sobriquet right before mentioning the moniker of James and John.[111] This tips the scales toward the likelihood that Justin was referring to the Gospel of Mark as Peter's memoirs.

As for how many Gospels Justin numbered among the apostles' memoirs, this is difficult to ascertain. The parallels with the New Testament Gospels are usually imprecise.[112] Justin's quotations may deviate from the Gospels due to his fallible memory or his creative efforts to harmonize them. It cannot be ruled out that he had access to pre-Synoptic or pre-Johannine sources that are no longer extant or to Gospels that were not included in the canon. Quotations from the Gospels could have been intentionally modified and harmonized in didactic contexts, such as in Justin's school where catechumens studied and applied Jesus's teachings.[113] Sometimes Justin may have consulted written collections of Jesus's sayings utilized in catechetical settings and other times Gospel manuscripts.[114] No single pattern emerges from the diverse ways in which he conflated the Gospels, so there may be more than one explanation for why he did not quote them exactly.[115] With these caveats in mind, it remains highly probable that all three Synoptic Gospels were among his memoirs.[116] Most of the references to the memoirs are clustered in a section of Justin's *Dialogue with Trypho the Jew* that reinterpreted a lament in the book of Psalms as a prophecy about Jesus.[117]

---

111. See Mark 3:16.
112. See the history of research in Bellinzoni, *The Sayings*, 1–2; Osborn, *Justin Martyr*, 120–21; Gregory, *The Reception*, 211–22; Joseph Verheyden, "Justin's Text of the Gospels: Another Look at the Citations in *1 Apol.* 15.1–8" in *The Early Text of the New Testament* (ed. Charles E. Hill and Michael J. Kruger; Oxford: Oxford University Press, 2012), 313–20; Kok, "Justin Martyr," 28–30.
113. See Charles E. Hill, "'In These Very Words': Methods and Standards of Literary Borrowing in the Second Century" in *The Early Text of the New Testament*, 280; John S. Kloppenborg, "Conflated Citations of the Synoptic Gospels: The Beginning of Christian Doxological Tradition" in *Gospels and Gospel Traditions in the Second Century: Experiments in Reception* (ed. Jens Schröter and Tobias Nicklas; BZNW, 235; Berlin: de Gruyter, 2018), 76–79.
114. Skarsaune, "Justin," 64–67.
115. Verheyden, "Justin's Text," 318–19; Kloppenborg, "Conflated Citations," 72.
116. On the reception of the Gospels of Matthew and Luke in Justin's writings, see Massaux, *The Influence*, 3.465–570; Köhler, *Die Rezeption*, 161–265; Bellinzoni, *The Sayings*, 8–130; Koester, *Ancient Christian Gospels*, 361–402; Gregory, *The Reception*, 211–92.
117. See Justin, *Dial.* 98–106 (cf. Ps 22). See Bellizoni, *The Sayings*, 118; Abramowski, "The Memoirs," 329–31.

Within this section of the *Dialogue*, there are allusions to each Synoptic Gospel. The sons of Zebedee are nicknamed "sons of thunder" as in Mark's Gospel.[118] The memoirs chronicle how the Magi were led by a star to the birthplace of Jesus. If Justin was reading Matthew's nativity story, he freely revised it from identifying the Magi's homeland as Arabia to locating Mary, Joseph, and Jesus in a cave.[119] He quotes the memoirs as saying that "unless your justice surpasses that of the Scribes and Pharisees, you shall not enter the kingdom of heaven."[120] This is a verbatim quotation of an unparalleled verse in Matthew's Gospel in the Greek.[121] The memoirs have points of contact with Matthew's editing of Mark's scene at Caesarea Philippi.[122] In Mark's Gospel, Peter confesses that Jesus is the Messiah and Jesus commands him to keep this a secret. Justin agrees with Matthew's Gospel that Peter also confessed Jesus's divine sonship, which was revealed to Peter by Jesus's father in heaven. Finally, Justin quotes Jesus's last words from the cross in one memoir, which agrees verbatim with Jesus's dying prayer in Luke's Gospel, "Father, into your hands I commend my spirit."[123]

---

118. See Justin, *Dial.* 106.3 (cf. Mark 3:17).

119. See Justin, *Dial.* 106.4 (cf. 77.4; 78.1–2, 5; 102.2; 103.3; *1 Apol.* 32.12). See Massaux, *The Influence*, 3.75; Köhler, *Die Rezeption*, 235; Koester, *Ancient Christian Gospels*, 383–85.

120. See Justin, *Dial.* 105.6. For this translation, see Thomas B. Falls, *Dialogue with Trypho* (Selections from the Fathers of the Church Volume 3; rev. Thomas P. Halton, ed. Michael Slusser; Washington: The Catholic University of America Press, 2003), 159.

121. See Matt 5:20. See Massaux, *The Influence*, 3.75; Bellinzoni, *The Sayings*, 120; Köhler, *Die Rezeption*, 233.

122. See Justin, *Dial.* 100.4 (cf. Mark 8:29; Matt 16:16). See Massaux, *The Influence*, 3.71; Köhler, *Die Rezeption*, 225.

123. See Justin, *Dial.* 105.5 (cf. Luke 23:46). For this translation, see Falls, *Dialogue*, 159. See Massaux, *The Influence*, 3.92; Bellinzoni, *The Sayings*, 120; Köhler, *Die Rezeption*, 254. The intertextual relationship between Justin and Luke's Gospel is strengthened by the fact that they both modify the future tense of the verb *parathēsomai* ("I will commit") in LXX Ps 30:6 to the present *paratithemai* ("I commit"). Gregory's (*The Reception*, 229) hesitance about including this passage as evidence for Justin's dependence on Luke's Gospel reflects an overabundance of caution. Gregory allows that Justin may have drawn on a pre-Lukan testimony book that had already connected LXX Ps 30:6 to Ps 22 and changed the tense of the verb. This scenario seems overly complicated. Luke 23:46 may have redacted Mark 15:34 (cf. Ps 22:1) by changing Jesus's lament of feeling forsaken to a hopeful thanksgiving psalm. After examining every possible reference to the Gospel of Luke in Justin's literary corpus, Gregory (*The Reception*, 291) accepts that "some, if not a great deal, of Lukan redaction is clearly present in the writings of Justin,

Justin's knowledge of John's Gospel is also demonstrable.[124] In his *First Apology*, he interprets the rite of baptism with reference to Christ's saying that one must be "reborn" (*anagennaō*) to "enter" (*eiserchomai*) the "kingdom of heaven" (*basileia tou ouranōn*).[125] The wording is somewhat different from Jesus's cryptic remark to Nicodemus that one must be "born" (*gennaō*) from "above" or "again" (*anōthen*) to "see" (*horaō*) the "kingdom of god" (*basileia tou theou*) in John's Gospel.[126] Jesus reiterates to Nicodemus that, unless people are born of water and spirit, they will never "enter" (*eiserchomai*) the "kingdom of god" (*basileia tou theou*).[127] Justin might have heard this saying of Jesus in a context where Christian catechumens were getting baptized rather than taking it directly from John's Gospel.[128] This option is less likely due to Justin's follow-up point that it is impossible for those who have been born to re-enter their mothers' wombs. This answers Nicodemus's query about how someone can enter his or her mother's womb a second time.[129]

---

and therefore Justin must be considered to depend on *Luke*, either directly or indirectly, in at least those instances where Lukan redaction is present."

124. The scholars who defend Justin's literary dependence on the Gospel of John include Massaux, *The Influence*, 3.46–47, 94–96; Hengel, *The Johannine Question*, 12–14; Nagel, *Rezeption*, 94–116; Hill, *The Johannine Corpus*, 314–51; Hill, "The Orthodox Gospel," 252–65.

125. See Justin, *1 Apol.* 61.4–5.

126. See John 3:3.

127. See John 3:5. Bellinzoni (*The Sayings*, 136–37) and Koester (*Ancient Christian Gospels*, 257–58) argue that Justin's wording is more primitive in that the phraseology of entering the kingdom of God is more characteristic of the Synoptic Gospels than John's Gospel (cf. Matt 5:20; 7:21; 18:3; 19:23–24; Mark 9:47; 10:15, 23–25; Luke 18:17, 25) and there is no ambiguity as to whether Jesus meant that one should be born again or from above. However, Justin's phrasing of entering the kingdom is paralleled in John 3:5, but he picked up the redactional language of the "kingdom of heaven" from the parallel saying in Matt 18:3. Justin may have also purposely removed the ambiguity from the saying in using the verb "reborn" (*anagennaō*).

128. Bellinzoni, *The Sayings*, 135–38; Koester, *Ancient Christian Gospels*, 257–58, 360–61. On the other hand, Justin may have noticed John's language about the necessity of being born out of water and interpreted the saying in reference to baptism. See J. W. Barker, "Written Gospel or Oral Tradition? Patristic Parallels to John 3:3, 5" *EC* 6 (2015): 547–48.

129. See John 3:4. See Hill, *The Johannine Corpus*, 327–28; Hill, "Was John's Gospel," 88; Kok, *The Gospel*, 180; Barker, "Written Gospel," 549–50; Kok, *The Beloved Apostle*, 86–87.

While this example exhibits Justin's knowledge of the Gospel of John, he may not have counted it as one of the "memoirs of the apostles." It is true that he was confident that he had successfully demonstrated to Trypho that the "unique" (*monogenēs*) son from the "father of the universe," who was the deity's "word" (*logos*) and power, consented to be born from a virgin as detailed in the "memoirs of the apostles."[130] The memoirs, in this instance, definitely covered the virginal conception of Jesus in Matthew's and Luke's infancy narratives.[131] The Immanuel prophecy in the Septuagint translation of the book of Isaiah was Justin's proof that Jesus's miraculous birth fulfilled the Scriptures.[132] The prologue of John's Gospel was likely behind Justin's identification of Jesus as the pre-existent "word" (*logos*).[133] Justin had other scriptural proofs for the existence of this divine hypostasis, which could also be described as the deity's glory, wisdom, or angel.[134] However, he may have interpreted his memoirs, that is the Gospels of Matthew and Luke, through the lens of his Johannine Christology without actually finding the *logos* within the memoirs themselves.[135]

There are a few other allusions to John's Gospel that are worth considering. In his *First Apology*, Justin advised his Roman audience to look up Pontius Pilate's records to verify the trustworthiness of his testimony about Jesus's miracles and the manner of his death.[136] Some of his details, from the placement of Jesus on the "judgment seat" (*bēma*) out of mockery to the nails that pierced Jesus's hands, could have been taken from John's Gospel.[137] Yet the so-called "acts that took place under Pontius Pilate" were

---

130. See Justin, *Dial.* 105.1.
131. See Matt 1:18–25; Luke 1:31–35. See John W. Pryor, "Justin Martyr and the Fourth Gospel" *SC* 9 (1992): 156–57; Kok, *The Beloved Apostle*, 88.
132. See, for example, Justin, *Dial.* 43.4–8; 66.1–4; 68.6–8; 71.1–3; 77.2–78.10.
133. See John 1:1–2; cf. Justin, *1 Apol.* 5.4; 10.6; 21.1; 22.2; 23.2; 32.9–10; 60.7; 63.2, 15; 66.2; *2 Apol.* 6.3; *Dial.* 61.1; 84.2; 100.2.
134. Hill, "Was John's Gospel," 89. See *Dial.* 61.1–62.5.
135. Kok, *The Beloved Apostle*, 88.
136. See Justin, *1 Apol.* 35.9; 48.3.
137. See John 19:13; 20:25. For the debate over whether the Gospel of John or the Gospel of Peter was Justin's source for these two points, see Pilhofer, "Justin," 69–75; Hill, *The Johannine Corpus*, 306–9, 330–32; Foster, "The Writings," 108–11; Ehrman, *Forgery*, 326; Watson, *Gospel Writing*, 379–80; Hill, "The Orthodox Gospel," 261–62; Hill, "Was John's Gospel," 91–93; Kok, *The Beloved Apostle*, 85.

not synonymous with the "memoirs of the apostles."[138] Justin's apologetic was that there were public, secular records confirming the accuracy of the Christian accounts about Jesus.[139] It is doubtful that Pilate's journals were readily accessible or contained material overlapping with the Gospels, but Justin may not have expected anyone to actually check. Pointing to records that were theoretically out there was sufficient to reinforce the faith of his fellow Christians.

One passage in the *Dialogue* about the memoirs written "by his apostles and those who followed them" (*hypo tōn apostolōn autou kai tōn ekeinois parakolouthēsantōn*) might imply that there were four memoirs, two by the apostles and two by their assistants.[140] If so, it lines up nicely with the traditional ascriptions of two of the Gospels to the apostles Matthew and John and two to Mark and Luke, the assistants of the apostles Peter and Paul. Justin added how one of the memoirs narrated that, on the night when Jesus was arrested, he was overcome with extreme anxiety and sweated drops of blood. Luke may have been the apostle's assistant who shared this detail.[141] Justin ran through a typical Christian worship service for his Roman audience in his *First Apology*. When Christians gathered together on Sundays, they listened to the public, liturgical reading of the "memoirs of the apostles" alongside the Hebrew prophets.[142] This may be a sign that the four Gospels had already attained a scriptural status in Justin's day.[143] On the contrary, it

---

138. Contra Hill, *Johannine Corpus*, 332–35; Hill, "Was John's Gospel," 90–91.
139. See Osborne, *Justin Martyr*, 133; Koester, *Ancient Christian Gospels*, 41–42; Abramowski, "Memoirs," 333.
140. See Justin, *Dial.* 103.8. Hengel, *Studies*, 68; Hengel, *The Johannine Question*, 13; Hengel, *The Four Gospels*, 20, 44; Stanton, *Jesus*, 100–101; Hill, *The Johannine Corpus*, 338–40; Skarsaune, "Justin," 72; Kruger, *The Question*, 169–70. I disagree with Falls (*Dialogue*, 157) in translating "those who followed them" as "their successors."
141. Skarsaune, "Justin," 72. However, it is textually uncertain whether Justin would have had a manuscript of Luke's Gospel that had this reading in it in Luke 22:44. See Gregory, *The Reception*, 281–82.
142. See Justin, *1 Apol.* 67.3.
143. Metzger, *The Canon*, 145; Hengel, *The Four Gospels*, 116, 162–63, 279n.472; Stanton, *Jesus*, 99–100, 105; Hill, "Was John's Gospel," 88; Kruger, *The Question*, 172; Fialová, "'Scripture,'" 174. One of the most recent defenders of this position is Jacob A. Rodriguez, "Justin and the Apostolic Memoirs: Public Reading as Covenant Praxis" *EC* 11.4 (2020): 496–515. He argues that the public reading of the apostolic memoirs in Justin's Christian community underpinned their self-understanding as the new covenant people and was akin to the public readings of the *Torah* in the Jewish synagogues.

may be anachronistic to think that Justin put the apostles' memoirs on par with the Hebrew Bible. Their primary importance for him may be that they verified that the prophecies in the Hebrew Bible had come to pass in history and exhibited the literacy of the apostles and their learned successors.[144]

The passage may not mean that there were four memoirs originating with either the apostles *or* their assistants. After all, he viewed Mark's Gospel as Peter's memoirs.[145] He had little interest in the person of Mark himself as the secretary who put Peter's words into writing. He also never explicitly identified Paul as an apostle or Luke as Paul's assistant.[146] He is silent about the "apostle to the Gentiles" and his letters.[147] For Justin, there were twelve apostles.[148] In his understanding, an apostle had to be personally trained by Jesus during his lifetime to recall his teachings and actions and illustrate their significance in the light of the Scriptures.[149] Paul may not have measured up to Justin's criteria for an apostle. There is a parallel in how Paul was the protagonist in the latter half of the book of Acts, but its author refrained from calling him an apostle except for in a single verse that seems to include Paul and Barnabas among the apostles.[150] Accompanying Jesus from his baptism to his ascension to heaven was the singular criterion for electing the twelfth

---

144. Shotwell, *The Biblical Exegesis*, 28; Gamble, *The New Testament Canon*, 29, 29n.18; Koester, *Ancient Christian Gospels*, 41–42; Cirafesi and Fewster, "Justin's Ἀπομνημονεύματα," 20–26.

145. This is conceded by Stanton, *Jesus*, 101–02.

146. For the following arguments that Justin did not regard Paul as an apostle, see Kok, "Justin Martyr," 35–36.

147. Four possible reasons for Justin's silence on Paul are listed in Andreas Lindemann, *Paulus in ältesten Christentum* (BHT 58; Tübingen: Mohr Siebeck, 1979), 353. First, Justin may have been ignorant of the Pauline Epistles. Second, Justin may have sidelined the Pauline Epistles because they were treated as authoritative writings by his adversary Marcion. Third, Justin may not have mentioned Paul when dialoguing with Trypho, because his Jewish interlocutor would not have regarded Paul as an authoritative figure. Fourth, Justin may have reworked Paul's theology into his own arguments about the nature of the new covenant and the inclusion of the nations in it without the requirement to adopt the *Torah* without giving Paul his due credit.

148. See Justin, *1 Apol.* 39.3; 42.4; 45.5; 50.12; 53.3; *Dial.* 42.1.

149. See, for example, *1 Apol.* 50.12; *Dial.* 76.6. Skarsaune, "Justin," 68–70. In contradiction to these criteria, Skarsaune ("Justin," 70) allows that Justin may have regarded Paul as an apostle based on his interpretation of *Dial.* 103.8 as referring to Luke as the assistant of the apostle Paul.

150. See Acts 14:14.

apostle in Acts.[151] Justin may not have classed the Gospel of John among the apostolic memoirs. The only passage that he explicitly ascribed to John, an apostle of Christ, was the one in the book of Revelation about Christ's millennial reign before the final judgment.[152] It is uncertain how many texts Justin may have included, in addition to the Synoptic Gospels, among the apostolic memoirs.

There is no contrast in Justin's statement in the *Dialogue* between the memoirs that are either directly or indirectly apostolic. The conjunction *kai* ("and") indicates that all of the memoirs about Jesus were jointly coproduced by the apostles *and* their assistants.[153] Justin may have taken the Lukan prologue to be saying that the apostolic eyewitnesses handed down their testimony to the assistants of the written word.[154] It is more likely that Papias's prologue was in the background of Justin's statement. The apostles Peter and Matthew were assisted by Mark and unaccredited translators. He may have pictured all the apostles dictating to literate amanuenses who transcribed their memoirs. It is unfair that the contributions of secretaries were commonly underappreciated in antiquity. Thus, Justin overlooks Mark and just names Peter as the source of his memoirs. It is noteworthy that Papias's traditions about Mark and Matthew had at last found a foothold in Justin's writings.

The *Gospel According to Matthew*

In the decades between the writings of Justin and Irenaeus, named authors were attached to all four canonical Gospels. Irenaeus had biographical tidbits about each evangelist.[155] Matthew published his Gospel for the Hebrews in their own language while the apostles Peter and Paul were founding the Christ assemblies in Rome. Mark, Peter's disciple and interpreter, "handed down" Peter's preaching in writing.[156] He did so after Peter's and Paul's

---

151. See Acts 1:21–22.
152. See Justin, *Dial.* 81.4 (cf. Rev 20:1–6). See Kok, *The Beloved Apostle*, 80–81.
153. Watson, *Gospel Writing*, 476n.106; Kok, *The Gospel*, 200; Kok, *The Beloved Apostle*, 82.
154. Heckel, *Vom Evangelium*, 92n.242, 328n.332.
155. See Irenaeus, *Haer.* 3.1.1.
156. Unlike the Gospels of Matthew, Luke, and John, Mark's Gospel is not designated by Irenaeus as a "book" (*biblion*) that was published. See Larsen, *Gospels*, 95–96; Larsen and Letteney, "Christians," 402–3. This may be an echo of the elder John's opinion about

"departure" from this life.[157] Luke recorded his own book about Jesus. There was evidence that Luke was Paul's inseparable companion, Irenaeus deduced, in the book of Acts and in the epistles to the Colossians and to Timothy.[158] The first-person plural pronoun "we" in Acts seemed to imply that the narrator was a firsthand participant on Paul's travels and Luke stayed loyal to Paul when he was imprisoned in Rome. John, the Lord's disciple who leaned on his chest at the Last Supper, published his Gospel during his residence in Ephesus.

Irenaeus modified Papias's traditions about Mark and Matthew. He dated the writing activities of the first two evangelists in relation to the timing of Peter's and Paul's martyrdom in Rome, with Matthew preceding Mark in undertaking the task of writing about Jesus.[159] He may have learned about the line of succession from the apostles Peter and Paul who planted churches in Rome to their ecclesiastical successors when he visited the bishop Eleutherus in the imperial capital. This does not validate the thesis

---

the rough state of Mark's notes in contrast to publishable books. Likewise, according to Clement of Alexandria, Mark's *hypomnēma* or "notes" were intended for private circulation among Peter's Roman auditors (cf. Eusebius, *H.E.* 2.15.1; 6.14.6).

157. This is probably a euphemism for the deaths of Peter and Paul. See Kok, *The Gospel*, 202–3. Conversely, Furlong (*The John*, 15–16) notes that the present tense of the participle *kēryssomena* could suggest that Peter was presently preaching when Mark's Gospel was written down, which agrees with other Patristic traditions that Peter was still alive when it was disseminated (cf. Clement, in Eusebius, *H.E.* 2.15.2; 6.14.7). He conjectures that the original text only referred to Peter's departure from the city of Rome, but a scribe misunderstood the verb as a euphemism for Peter's death. This scribe switched the singular genitive pronoun *toutou* ("of this one") to the plural *toutōn* ("of these ones"), so that the text was now referring to the departure of both Peter and Paul from this life when they were executed along with the rest of the victims of Nero's pogrom against the Christians in the city of Rome. There may be no need to propose a hypothetical textual amendment. Peter and Paul were widely revered as martyrs who gave their lives founding the churches in Rome by this date. During the pontificate of Zephyrinus (ca. 199–217 CE), Gaius of Rome pointed out that there were monuments built for Peter and Paul over at the Vatican Hill and Ostian Way (see Eusebius, *H.E.* 2.25.6–7). Papias's tradition was that Mark set out to record his notes about Peter's preaching after serving as Peter's translator for some time but was silent regarding whether or not Peter was still alive at this point. Irenaeus interpreted the silence to mean that Mark was writing after Peter's demise, while Clement interpreted it to mean that Peter was no longer present in Rome when Mark was writing his Gospel there.

158. See Irenaeus, *Haer.* 3.14.1 (cf. Acts 16:10–17; 20:5–15; 21:1–18; 27:1–37; 28:1–16; Col 4:14; 2 Tim 4:11).

159. See Black, *Mark*, 100; Watson, *Gospel Writing*, 128; Kok, *The Gospel*, 117, 202.

that he received his information about the evangelists from a Roman Christian archive.[160] From the limited extant evidence, it cannot be demonstrated that he had independent information about the origins of the Gospels from his own teacher Polycarp.[161] Instead, he hazily recalled a handful of Polycarp's stories about the elder John and reused them to fill in the apostle John's backstory. He must have had another source, in addition to Papias, on the evangelists behind the third and fourth Gospels. The best option is that he had seen these four names in the scribal titles affixed to the Gospels in a codex. Earlier scribes may have reached the same verdict that Irenaeus did about the referents of the "we" in Acts and the beloved disciple in the fourth Gospel when coming up with the names of the third and fourth evangelists.

The four Gospels may have been placed together in a "fourfold gospel canon" in the second half of the second century CE.[162] Papias should not be enlisted as a witness to this collection.[163] Marcion's combination of a Gospel and a ten-letter *Apostolikon* demanded a response. Justin was familiar with the four Gospels as well as other oral and written sources about Jesus, but the "memoirs of the apostles" included the Synoptic Gospels but not John's Gospel.[164] Tatian, Justin's pupil, harmonized all four Gospels in his *Diatessaron* ("through the four"). A missing portion at the start of the late second-century Muratorian Canon likely rehearsed the traditions about the Gospels of Matthew and Mark. This Roman fragment refers to the "third" and "fourth" Gospels.[165] Irenaeus's numerological arguments about four zones, winds, and cherubim may seem like a stretch, but they were put into

---

160. Contra Hengel, *The Four Gospels*, 36, 38, 66–68.

161. Contra Perumalil, "Are Not Papias," 336–37.

162. See Gamble, *The New Testament Canon*, 24–36; Patzia, *The Making*, 64–67; Hengel, *The Four Gospels*, 53–56; Petersen, "Die Evangelienüberschriften," 271, 274; Aune, "The Meaning," 19–24.

163. Contra Lightfoot, *Supernatural Religion*, 32–58; Baum, "Papias als Kommentator," 265–66; Hill, "What Papias Said," 582–628; Heckel, *Vom Evangelium*, 261–65; Hill, *The Johannine Corpus*, 387–94; Hill, "The 'Orthodox Gospel,'" 287–94; Hill, "Papias," 312; Furlong, "Theodore of Mopsuestia," 209–29; Furlong, *The Identity*, 139–53.

164. See Shotwell, *The Biblical Exegesis*, 24; Barnard, *Justin Martyr*, 63; Osborn, *Justin Martyr*, 121; Koester, *Ancient Christian Gospels*, 257–58, 360–61; Kok, *The Beloved Apostle*, 84–90. Contra Hengel, *The Johannine Question*, 13; Hengel, *The Four Gospels*, 20, 44; Stanton, *Jesus*, 100–101; Hill, *The Johannine Corpus*, 338–40; Skarsaune, "Justin," 72; Kruger, *The Question*, 169–70.

165. See MF 2, 9.

the service of justifying "the fourfold gospel" (*tetramorphon to euangelion*) that had been established.[166] The acceptance of all four Gospels may have been a demonstration of unity between Christians in the East and West after the Quartodeciman crisis.[167] This conflict over the dating of Easter between the Christians in Asia Minor and Rome was due to the former following the Johannine chronology in celebrating Easter on the Jewish day of Passover.

There is a theory that the entire New Testament was canonized by a single group of editors in reaction to the Marcionite and Quartodeciman controversies.[168] These editors were supposedly responsible for the names of the authors attached to every New Testament book, the abbreviations of the *nomina sacra* or "sacred words," and the transmission of New Testament writings in codices.[169] The evidence that the Gospels of Matthew and John were copied far more frequently than Mark's Gospel, the different orderings of the Gospels in the surviving canonical lists, and the presence of the *nomina sacra* in canonical and noncanonical writings undermines this theory.[170] Papias did not need the whole canon to link the elder John's tradition about Mark to Peter's "son" Mark in the first Epistle of Peter. The list of canonical books did not need to be finalized by the time of Irenaeus for him to identify the third evangelist as the Luke in Paul's letters to the Colossians and to Timothy. The preference for the codex format over the roll need not be due to the ease with which Christians could bind multiple canonical writings, such as the four Gospels or the Pauline letters, together in codices.[171] The early adoption of the codex as a vehicle for transmitting Christian texts may show that they were initially not put on the same literary level as classical works of literature that were inscribed on rolls.[172]

---

166. See Irenaeus, *Haer.* 3.11.8.

167. Watson, *Gospel Writing*, 468–72.

168. Trobisch, *The First Edition*, 105–6.

169. Trobisch, *The First Edition*, 8–77.

170. Hengel, *The Four Gospels*, 46, 243n.216; Petersen, "Die Evangelienüberschriften," 253–60.

171. This theory is advanced by T. C. Skeat, "The Origin of the Christian Codex," *ZPE* 102 (1994): 267; Harry Y. Gamble, *Books and Readers in the Early Church: A History of Early Christian Texts* (New Haven: Yale University Press, 1995), 62–63. Their arguments are critiqued in Larsen and Letteney, "Christians," 389–94.

172. Larsen and Letteney, "Christians," 407–10.

Irenaeus attests to the longer form of the titles, such as the *Gospel According to Matthew*, affixed to the Gospels in the oldest surviving papyri.[173] It was later abbreviated to the shorter form *According to Matthew*. The convention for published books was that the author's name preceded the title and was put in the genitive case. The Gospel titles put the noun *euangelion* in the singular and have the preposition *kata* ("according to") followed by the name of an evangelist in the accusative case. Whenever a similar formula appears in other ancient writings,[174] it tends to denote the editor or corrector of a text.[175] The formula may have been adapted to express the theological conviction that there was only one valid gospel or presentation of the "good news" about Jesus's saving work that was, nevertheless, communicated from the distinct vantage points of the four

---

173. See Irenaeus, *Haer.* 1.26.2; 3.11.7, 9; 3.12.12. The evidence that the shorter form of the Gospel headings is an abbreviation of the longer form is reviewed in Hengel, *Studies*, 66; Heckel, *Vom Evangelium des Markus*, 207–8; Trobisch, *The First Edition*, 38, 126n.142; Hengel, *The Four Gospel*, 48, 238n.195; Petersen, "Die Evangelienüberschriften," 254–55, 268; Aune, "The Meaning," 16–17; Simon Gathercole, "The Titles of the Gospels in the Earliest New Testament Manuscripts" *ZNW* 104 (2013): 62–71. Contra Theodor Zahn, *Geschichte des neutestamentlichen Kanons: Erster Band: Das Neue Testament vor Origenes Erste Hälfte* (Erlangen: Deichert, 1888), 1.i.164–67; Adolf von Harnack, *The Origin of the New Testament: And the Most Important Consequence of the New Creation* (trans. J. R. Wilkinson; Eugene: Wipf & Stock, 2004), 68–70.

174. For the parallels to the Gospel headings, see Hengel, *Studies*, 65–66, 163n.8; Hengel, *The Four Gospels*, 48, 65–66; 239n.198, n.200, 240n.201; Matthew D. C. Larsen, "Correcting the Gospel: Putting the Titles of the Gospel in Historical Context" in *Rethinking "Authority" in Late Antiquity: Authorship, Law, and Transmission in Jewish and Christian Tradition* (ed. A. J. Berkovitz and Mark Letteney; New York: Routledge, 2018), 80–86, 95n.3. The philologist Didymus of Alexandria uses the formula to identify the correctors of the Iliad (e.g., *Schol.* B 258a). 2 Macc 2:13 refers to the registers and records "according to Nehemiah." The verse may mean that Nehemiah owned these records, not that he wrote them. The translators responsible for the Greek translations of the Hebrew Bible, not the original authors of the biblical books, were identified with the formula "according to the seventy," "according to Theodotian," "according to Aquila," or "according to Symmachus." The physician Galen uses the formula to note that another physician, Mnemon of Side in Pamphylia, corrected book three of Hippocrates's *Epidemics* (*In Hipp. Epid. III Comment.* 2.4 [17.1b.606K]). Two parallels should be discounted. Neither Diodorus Siculus (*Bib. Hist.* 2.32.2) nor Josephus (*Ap.* 1.18) use the formula for Herodotus's and Thucydides's authorship of their respective histories, but for the stories that the historians were retelling "according to" their individual perspectives.

175. Larsen, "Correcting," 80.

evangelists.[176] Or, in keeping with how the formula is used elsewhere, it may express that there were four acceptable reiterations of the same pluriform gospel.[177] Irenaeus could use the conventional formula for book titles when it came to the Gospels that he despised, such as the *Gospel of Judas* or the *Gospel of Truth*.[178] The difference is that he did not regard these texts as legitimate renditions of the true gospel.[179]

The counterargument for dating the standard Gospel titles before the formation of the fourfold gospel canon is that there seem to have been no competing titles or authorial attributions for the Gospels. There was no centralized authority structure for all Christians in the Roman Empire that could have dictated to everyone what the Gospel titles should be. The unanimity with regards to the named evangelists associated with the Gospels and the unconventional way that the titles were formulated may suggest that the titles were attached to the Gospels shortly after they began circulating.[180] When Christians stored multiple Gospels in book cupboards in major urban locations, the practical benefit of the titles was that it enabled them to tell one Gospel apart from another.[181] However, the standard titles in the extant manuscripts were not absolutely necessary for this purpose. The first verse of each Gospel could have functioned as a title, helping Christian readers to distinguish one Gospel from another.[182] There did not need to be a centralized system of governance for the titles to have been broadly disseminated through the codices in which the four Gospels were bound together. From Irenaeus onwards, the patristic authors who championed the fourfold Gospel canon also defended the names of the evangelists attached to each Gospel in the codices.

The Gospel titles in the manuscripts are unattested in the first half of the second century. Papias named a few evangelists, but did not refer to

---

176. See Zahn, *Geschichte*, 1.i.166–67; Harnack, *The Origin*, 70–71; Gamble, *Books and Readers*, 153–54; Heckel, *Vom Evangelium*, 208–10; Trobisch, *The First Edition*, 38, 43, 47–56; Aune, "The Meaning," 14, 24; Kok, *The Gospel*, 68; Kok, "Justin Martyr," 17.

177. Larson, "Correcting," 93.

178. See Irenaeus, *Haer.* 1.31.1; 3.11.9.

179. Aune, "The Meaning," 19; Larsen, "Correcting," 93.

180. Hengel, *The Four Gospels*, 50–56; cf. Petersen, "Die Evangelienüberschriften," 259–60.

181. Hengel, *The Four Gospels*, 53–55, 121–27, 130, 136–40; Petersen, "Die Evangelienüberschriften," 271–73.

182. Gregory, *The Reception*, 51; Kok, *The Gospel*, 67–68; Kok, "Justin Martyr," 17.

their compilations of the oracles as Gospels. Ignatius of Antioch and the editor of the *Didache* seem to have been uninformed about Papias's identifications of two of the evangelists. For the bishop of Antioch, the Gospel of Matthew continued to circulate as an anonymous text. The editor of the *Didache* did not name the author of this Gospel. Marcion's Gospel was likewise anonymous. Justin was aware that his memoirs were commonly called Gospels and that they originated with the apostles, but he tends to assign them to the apostles collectively except for his solitary reference to Peter's memoirs. Theophilus, a bishop of Antioch (ca. 169–82 CE), was one of the first Christians to attribute a direct quote from John's Gospel to a named evangelist. Theophilus commended a spirit-bearing person named John and his theology about the *logos* ("word") in the apology that he addressed to his non-Christian friend Autolycus.[183]

Marcion's Gospel is a useful test case. Tertullian heaped scorn on Marcion for arbitrarily appropriating one of the four Gospels. Moreover, Tertullian was amused that the Gospel that Marcion picked was written by an inferior "apostolic man" like Luke, not an apostle like Matthew or John, though he went on to admit that Marcion did not actually attach a name to his Gospel.[184] Tertullian had the benefit of hindsight when mocking Marcion, for the four-Gospel canon and the traditional authors associated with each text had become well established by his time. Neither was common knowledge in Marcion's day. In a textualized dialogue between a Catholic and a Marcionite Christian dating to the fourth century, the Marcionite Megethus believed Christ and Paul to be the cocreators of Marcion's Gospel.[185]

This is not the place to dive into the debate that has been reopened over whether Marcion tampered with the canonical text of the Gospel of Luke or whether both it and Marcion's Gospel were independently derived from the same *Vorlage*.[186] More relevant here is the question about why Marcion's

---

183. See *Autol.* 2.22. This is noted in Koester, *Ancient Christian Gospels*, 27n.1.
184. See *Marc.* 4.2.3; 4.3.4–5.
185. See Adamantius, *Dial.* 1.8.
186. See Harnack, *Marcion*, 52–73, 177–240; Hoffmann, *Marcion*, 113–45; Gregory, *Reception*, 173–209; Tyson, *Marcion and Luke-Acts*, 38–47; 79–117; Matthias Klinghardt, "Markion vs. Lukas: Plädoyer für die Wiederaufnahme eines alten Falles" *NTS* 52.4 (2006): 484–513; Klinghardt, "The Marcionite Gospel and the Synoptic Problem: A New Suggestion" *NovT* 50.1 (2008): 1–27; Moll, *The Arch-Heretic Marcion*, 89–102;

Gospel lacked a title. He may have purposely deleted Luke's name from his Gospel because he reviled Luke as a forger.[187] His objective may have been to purify Paul's Gospel because he held that it had been corrupted by Luke's interpolations into it. He may have also not spelled out who this Gospel was "according to" because he had no other Gospel in his canon that he needed to differentiate it from.[188] It may be more likely that the Gospel that Marcion got a hold of in Pontus circulated anonymously.[189] He need not have naively believed that it had a heavenly author and was bequeathed to Paul.[190] He just did not try to peer behind its deliberate anonymity. Since the book of Acts

---

Vinzent, *Christ's Resurrection*, 88–90; Jason D. BeDuhn, "The Myth of Marcion as Redactor: The Evidence of 'Marcion's' Gospel against an Assumed Marcionite Redaction" *ASE* 29.1 (2012): 21–48; Vinzent, *Marcion*; Vinzent, "Marcion's Gospel and the Beginnings of Early Christianity" *ASE* 32.1 (2015): 55–87; Lieu, *Marcion*, 188–233; Dieter T. Roth, *The Text of Marcion's Gospel* (NTTSD 40; Leiden: Brill, 2015), 437–38; Matthias Klinghardt, *Das älteste Evangelium und die Entstehung der kanonischen Evangelien* (2 vols; TANZ 60; Tübingen: Francke, 2015), 1.125–378; Daniel A. Smith, "Marcion's Gospel and the Resurrected Jesus of Canonical Luke 24" *ZAC* 21.1 (2017): 41–62; Smith, "Marcion's Gospel and the Synoptics: Proposals and Problems" in *Gospels and Gospel Traditions in the Second Century: Experiments in Reception* (ed. Jens Schröter et al.; BZNW, 235; Berlin: de Gruyter, 2018), 129–73; Shelly Matthews, "Does Dating Luke-Acts into the Second Century Affect the Q Hypothesis?" in *Gospel Interpretation and the Q-Hypothesis* (ed. Mogens Müller and Heike Omerzu; LNTS, 573; London: T&T Clark, 2018), 253–64; Dieter T. Roth, "Marcion's Gospel and the Synoptic Problem in Recent Scholarship" in *Gospel Interpretation and the Q-Hypothesis*, 267–82; Kok, "Justin Martyr," 14–15. The most problematic thesis, in my view, is the one advanced by Vinzent. His hypothesis is that Marcion was the author of his Gospel and that his *Urevangelium* or "proto-Gospel" was the source of the Synoptic tradition. This radical thesis demands that the Synoptic Gospels be redated after Marcion's ministry, but Papias sets the *terminus ad quem* ("limit to which") for dating the Gospels of Mark and Matthew. The internal evidence within the Gospels of Mark and Matthew may point to a date either shortly before or after the destruction of the Jerusalem temple (e.g., Mark 13:2//Matt 24:2; Mark 13:14//Matt 24:15–16; Matt 22:7), when not everyone from the apostolic generation had yet died off (e.g., Mark 9:1//Matt 16:28; Matt 10:23). Before Marcion's Gospel can be factored into the Synoptic Problem, there needs to be a critical reconstruction of the text that commands widespread assent among the scholarly community. For a sober reconstruction of Marcion's Gospel, see Roth, *The Text*, 410–36.

187. Harnack, *Marcion*, 41; Hengel, *The Four Gospels*, 32.
188. Moll, *The Arch-Heretic*, 90.
189. Gregory, *Reception*, 205. Harnack, *Marcion*, 39; Hoffmann, *Marcion*, 140–41; Gregory, *Reception*, 190–91; Vinzent, *Christ's Resurrection*, 82, 82n.50; BeDuhn, "The Myth," 28; Lieu, *Marcion*, 212–13; Klinghardt, *Das älteste Evangelium*, 31–32.
190. Moll, *Arch-Heretic*, 90.

and the Pastoral Epistles were not part of his canon, the key proof texts from each that were used to identify the third evangelist as Luke were not available to Marcion.[191] It was the scribes behind the fourfold gospel canon, and later Irenaeus, who connected these dots in identifying the third evangelist as Luke, the inseparable companion of Paul.

As for the titles of the Nag Hammadi Gospels, they were affixed to them by scribes in imitation of the canonical Gospel titles.[192] For example, the title of the *Gospel According to Thomas* is secondary. Its incipit, which begins with "these are the secret sayings which the living Jesus spoke" (*houtoi hoi logoi hoi apokryphoi hous elalēsen Iēsous ho zōn*) and credits Thomas with recording them, once functioned as its title.[193] Its thirteenth logion might have been in polemical dialogue with Papias's authorial traditions. In this passage, Jesus requested that his disciples tell him who he is like. Peter answered that Jesus resembles a righteous angel and Matthew that he is like a wise philosopher. Thomas's answer was that Jesus is incomparable. Thomas's confession about Jesus's uniqueness was more worthy of him than the declarations by the apostolic authorities behind the Gospels of Mark and Matthew.[194] Peter's role in this passage is to be expected, because it is parodying the scene when Jesus asked his disciples about what the crowds were saying about him and Peter came to the realization that he was the Messiah.[195] It is harder to explain Matthew's inclusion in this scene unless the author of this passage was cognizant about Papias's tradition about the evangelist Matthew and was panning Matthew's Gospel.[196] This may still be an overreading. So long as one accepts

---

191. Hoffmann, *Marcion*, 140–41; Tyson, *Defining Struggle*, 40.

192. Koester, *Ancient Christian Gospels*, 20–23. Petersen ("Die Evangelienüberschriften," 267, 271–74) protests that this conclusion reflects a canonical bias, but he does not advance a case for why these scribal titles should be dated earlier or independent of the canonical Gospels. Indeed, he accepts that the title of another Gospel text, the *Gospel of Judas*, was formulated in opposition to the titles of the canonical Gospels (cf. p. 474).

193. Koester, *Ancient Christian Gospels*, 21. The Greek text is partially preserved in Papyrus Oxyrhynchus 654.

194. Bauckham, *Jesus*, 236–37.

195. See Mark 8:13–20; Matt 16:13–20; Luke 9:18–21; cf. John 6:66–71.

196. Simon Gathercole, *The Composition of the Gospel of Thomas* (Cambridge: Cambridge University Press, 2012), 169–74. See the list of scholars who support this interpretation in Gathercole, "The Alleged Anonymity," 469n.82. Although they differ drastically from Gathercole in dating an earlier form of the *Gospel of Thomas* before the end of the first century and arguing for the independence of some of its sayings from the Synoptic

the premise that there are traces of Matthean redactional material in some sayings in the *Gospel of Thomas*,[197] the author of this saying may have known that Matthew is prominently highlighted in the call narrative in the Gospel of Matthew. Two prominent members of the Twelve in the Synoptic Gospels were selected to be foils for Thomas and his superior wisdom. Papias's traditions about Peter and Matthew may not have been in the background at all.

In the first half of the second century, Papias seems to have been a lone voice in the wilderness in naming two of the evangelists. The texts could be called Gospels in this period of time, but they were kept strictly anonymous. Justin's advocacy of the memoirs of the apostles and their assistants marked a turning point. He evinced his familiarity with Papias's traditions when positively referencing the memoirs of Peter. Once Matthew's name was attached to the first of the four Gospels bound together in the codices in the time between Justin and Irenaeus, the rest was history. Matthew's authorship was upheld by all the defenders of the fourfold gospel canon. It had become the consensus position.

---

tradition, Stephen J. Patterson, James M. Robinson, and Hans-Gebhard Bethge allow that *log*. 13 had the Gospel of Matthew in view and was polemicizing against the Christians who championed its theology. See Stephen J. Patterson, James M. Robinson, and Hans-Gebhard Bethg, *The Fifth Gospel: The Gospel of Thomas Comes of Age* (new ed.; London: Bloomsbury T&T Clark, 2012), 35.

197. See Gathercole, *The Composition*, 168–84; Goodacre, *Thomas*, 66–81.

5

THE ASCRIPTION OF THE *GOSPEL ACCORDING TO THE HEBREWS* TO MATTHEW

THE GOSPEL OF Matthew was part of an intramural Jewish conversation over Jesus's qualifications as a messianic figure and a teacher of *Torah*.[1] Its Jesus is a new Moses.[2] His parents temporarily resettled in Egypt to save him from a tyrannical despot who ordered the slaughter of the baby boys in Jesus's birthplace.[3] When Jesus was an adult, he imparted new decrees on a mountain.[4] After hiking up a mountain with three disciples, he was transfigured before them and a heavenly voice boomed "listen to him" in the three Synoptic Gospels.[5] In addition to his glimmering garments, Jesus's face shone in the Gospel of Matthew just like Moses's did when he descended from Mount Sinai.[6] In this Gospel's unique passages,[7] Jesus cleared up his intention to fulfill, not to abolish, "the Law or the Prophets" in his Sermon on the Mount. Heaven and earth will pass away before the smallest stroke of the pen is subtracted from the Law of Moses. Anyone who relaxes any

---

1. See the review of scholarship of the "Matthew within Judaism" paradigm in Anders Runesson and Daniel M. Gurtner, "Introduction: The Location of Mattthew-within-Judaism Perspective in Past and Present Research" in *Matthew within Judaism: Israel and the Nations in the First Gospel* (Atlanta: SBL, 2020), 1–14. This is a fine collection of essays from some of the leading scholarly proponents of this paradigm.
2. For an in-depth treatment of the Mosaic typology in the Gospel of Matthew, see Dale C. Allison, *The New Moses: A Matthean Typology* (new ed.; Eugene: Wipf & Stock, 2013), 137–270. Bacon (*Studies*, 165–249; Idem, "The 'Five Books,'" 65–66) was the first scholar to put forward the thesis that the outline of Matthew's Gospel was modeled on the Pentateuch.
3. See Matt 2:13–16.
4. See Matt 5:1–7:29.
5. See Matt 17:1–8; Mark 9:2–8; Luke 9:28–36. The imperative "listen to him" in all three Synoptic Gospels is an allusion to Deut 18:15 and establishes Jesus's identity as the prophet like Moses.
6. See Exod 34:29–35.
7. For the following passages, see Matt 5:17–20; 23:2–12.

commandments will be demoted to the least position in the kingdom of heaven. Potential disciples had to exceed the righteousness of the scribes and Pharisees in their obedience to the commandments. Jesus granted that the Pharisees had legitimate authority to guide people on how to obey the commandments by virtue of sitting in Moses's seat. He rebuked certain Pharisees for their alleged hypocrisy in not living up to the standards that they set for others or flaunting their titles or social status by wearing enlarged phylacteries and long tassels.

The Gospel of Matthew has been rightly included in academic surveys of the Jewish Gospels.[8] The earliest patristic writers distinguished it from another Jewish Gospel that was not titled "according to Matthew," but "according to the Hebrews." The oldest quotations from the *Gospel According to the Hebrews* that we have come from Clement, Origen, and Didymus of Alexandria in Egypt. These three Alexandrian scholars dating from the late second to the fourth century did not ascribe this text to a named evangelist.[9] When categorizing the undisputed, disputed, and spurious Christian writings in the fourth century, Eusebius decided that the *Gospel According to the Hebrews* belonged in the third category, though its classification was debated.[10] It was two fourth-century Christian writers, Epiphanius and Jerome, who thought that they were quoting the *Gospel According to the Hebrews* and mistook it as either an older edition or a mutilated copy of Matthew's Gospel.[11]

---

8. See, for instance, Craig Evans, "The Jewish Christian Gospel Tradition" in *Jewish Believers in Jesus: The Early Centuries* (ed. Oskar Skarsaune and Reidar Hvalvik; Peabody: Hendrickson, 2007), 242–44.

9. See Clement, *Str.* 2.9.45.5; Origen, *Comm. Jo.* 2.12.87; Didymus the Blind, *Comm. Ps.* 184.9–10.

10. See Eusebius, *H.E.* 3.25.5.

11. See Epiphanius, Pan. 29.9.4; 30.3.7; 30.13.2; 30.14.3; Jerome, *Epist.* 20.5; *Vir. ill.* 3; *Tract. Ps.* 135; *Matt.* 12.13; *Is.* 11.1–3; *Pelag.* 3.2. Coogan ("The Ways," 1–18) differs from my approach in judging the patristic writers to have been referencing varying recensions of the Gospel of Matthew in Jewish and proto-orthodox Christian circles. It was in the fourth century that figures such as Eusebius, Epiphanius, and Jerome tried to carve out a sharp distinction between the textual recensions that were circulating among the "Hebrews," "Ebionites," or "Nazoreans" from their canonical version of Matthew's text. My counterproposal is that the Gospel of Matthew and the *Gospel According to the Hebrews* were separate works entirely, but Epiphanius and Jerome mistakenly related the references to the latter text to the older traditions about an original edition of the Gospel of Matthew in a Semitic language that may have never existed in the first place.

The complications with reconstructing the *Gospel According to the Hebrews* is that it has been lost apart from the fragments cited by patristic and medieval writers and scribes. What is more, they were under the impression that they all had the same *Gospel According to the Hebrews*, but modern scholars are less certain over whether they were actually citing one,[12] two,[13] or three[14] distinct Gospels. Epiphanius and Jerome muddied the waters further in associating the *Gospel According to the Hebrews* with Matthew. They misapprehended the traditions that Matthew's Gospel was translated from a Semitic language and privileged by a *Torah*-observant Jewish-Christian faction known as the Ebionites or "Poor Ones."

---

12. The Patristic consensus that there was a single, primitive *Gospel According to the Hebrews* has some modern defenders. See R. A. Pritz, *Nazarene Jewish Christianity: From the End of the New Testament Period Until Its Disappearance in the Fourth Century* (Jerusalem: Magnes Press, 1988), 83–94; P. L. Schmidt, "'Und es war geschrieben auf Hebräisch, Griechisch und Lateinisch': Hieronymus, das Hebräer-Evangelium und seine mittelalterliche Rezeption" *Filologia Mediolatina* 5 (1998): 49–93; Beatrice, "Apostolic Fathers" 158–60, 169–76; Wolfram Kinzig, "The Nazoraeans" in *Jewish Believers in Jesus: The Early Centuries* (ed. Oscar Skarsaune and Reider Hvalvik;Peabody: Hendrickson, 2007), 473; Edwards, *The Hebrew Gospel*, 1–124.

13. In this hypothesis, the *Gospel According to the Hebrews* should be differentiated from the Greek Gospel that is cited by Epiphanius. Modern scholars have entitled Epiphanius's text as the *Gospel of the Ebionites* because he claimed that this was the Gospel in the Ebionites' possession. See Mimouni, *Early Judaeo-Christianity*, 175–91, 221–33; Luomanen, *Recovering*, 83–89, 101–39; Kok, "Did Papias of Hierapolis Use," 38–47; Gregory, *The Gospel*, 8–17, 31–261.

14. There are two competing hypotheses. Alfred Schmidtke rejects the distinction between the *Gospel According to the Hebrews* and the *Gospel of the Ebionites*. He distinguishes the *Gospel According to the Hebrews* from the *Gospel of the Twelve* known to Origen and the *Gospel of the Nazoreans* known to Jerome. See Alfred Schmidtke, *Neue Fragmente und Untersuchungen zu den judenchristlichen Evangelien: Ein Beitrag zur Literatur und Geschichte der Judenchristen* (TU 37.1; Leipzig: Hinrichs, 1911), 1–302; Schmidtke, "Zum Hebräerevangelium" *ZNW* 35 (1936): 24–44. Hans Waitz distinguishes between the *Gospel According to the Hebrews* that circulated in Alexandria, the *Gospel of the Ebionites* known to Epiphanius and to Origen under the title of the *Gospel of the Twelve*, and the *Gospel of the Nazoreans* known to Jerome. See Hans Waitz, "Das Evangelium der zwölf Apostel: (Ebioniteevangelium)" *ZNW* 13.4 (1912): 338–48, *ZNW* 14.1 (1913): 38–64, and *ZNW* 14.2 (1913): 117–32; cf. Waitz, "Neue Untersuchung über die sogen. Judenchristlichen Evangelien" *ZNW* 36 (1937): 60–81. Waitz's hypothesis won over most scholars, though it has been modified at points. See Vielhauer and Strecker, "Jewish Christian Gospels," 134–78; Klijn, *Jewish Christian Gospel Tradition*, 3–146; Klauck, *Apocryphal Gospels*, 36–54; Frey, "Die Fragmente judenchristlicher Evangelien," 560–92.

Irenaeus and the Ebionites' Misuse
of Matthew's Gospel

Because of Papias, Irenaeus presumed that the Gospel of Matthew had been translated from the apostle Matthew's native language into Greek.[15] By his time, this Gospel was grouped together with three other Gospels in a collection that was heralded as authoritative and mutually interpretive. Although Irenaeus gave the impression that the fourfold gospel commanded universal Christian assent, he bitterly complained that there were sectarians who misappropriated one of the four Gospels and discarded the other three. They were basing their idiosyncratic viewpoints, in his view, on selective readings of one Gospel in isolation from the other three.[16] The Ebionites and Marcion had polar opposite perspectives on the continuity or discontinuity between Jesus and his Jewish heritage, so Irenaeus represented the Ebionites as championing Matthew's Gospel and Marcion as propagating a bowdlerized copy of Luke's Gospel. His insinuation was that schismatics who severed their ties with the catholic or universal community of Christian believers could be unmasked due to their exclusive preference and misinterpretation of one of the four canonical Gospels. His fundamental point would be ruined if it turned out that the Gospel of Matthew was not the Ebionites' prized possession.[17]

Irenaeus's project was to construct a genealogy of "heresy." Since the truth precedes falsehood in his worldview, the deviations from the apostles'

---

15. See Irenaeus, *Haer.* 3.1.1.
16. See Irenaeus, *Haer.* 3.11.7.
17. See Klijn and Reinink, *Patristic Evidence*, 20, 23–24; Klijn, *Jewish Christian Gospel Tradition*, 4; Sakari Häkkinen, "Ebionites" in *A Companion to Second-Century Christian "Heretics"* (SVC 76; ed. Antti Marjanen and Petri Luomanen; Leiden: Brill, 2005), 260; Oskar Skarsaune, "The Ebionites" in Oskar Skarsaune and Reidar Hvalvik, eds., *Jewish Believers in Jesus: The Early Centuries*, 435–36, 460; James Carleton Paget, *Jews, Christians and Jewish Christians in Antiquity* (WUNT 251; Tubingen: Mohr Siebeck, 2010), 327, 328, 329n.28, 352; Frey, "Die Fragmente judenchristlicher Evangelien,", 573–74; Frey, "Die Fragmente des Ebionäervangeliums" in *Antike christliche Apokryphen in deutscher Übersetzung*, 608; Gregory, *The Gospel*, 181. Contra Vielhauer and Strecker, "Jewish Christian Gospels," 136; Richard Bauckham, "The Origin of the Ebionites" in *The Image of the Judaeo-Christians in Ancient Jewish and Christian Literature* (ed. Peter J. Tomson and Doris Lambers-Petry; WUNT 158; Tübingen: Mohr Siebeck, 2003), 163–64; Beatrice, "The Gospel," 173; Edwards, *The Hebrew Gospel*, 10–12, 18–19, 26; Broadhead, *Jewish Ways*, 386–88; Mimouni, *Early Judaeo-Christianity*, 222.

authentic message can be discerned and weeded out. In his portrayal of his competitors, they were the founders of philosophical schools, each with their own unique ethos.[18] They were placed in their own line of succession that went back to the arch-heretic Simon, the magician who was first confronted by Peter in Samaria.[19] In reality, the Ebionites may not have been a unified Jewish "sect" at all. "Ebionites" may have been one of the popular self-designations among Jewish Christ-followers in general in this period.[20] Irenaeus may not have realized that it transliterated the Aramaic equivalent of the Hebrew plural noun for "poor ones." Hence, he passed on the opportunity to provide a scathing etymology for the title as based on the Ebionites' "poor" intellectual faculties, moral characters, or literalistic hermeneutics.[21] Nor did he follow his typical procedure of naming the Ebionites' founder. Other heresiologists compensated for this oversight by fabricating a group founder named Ebion.[22]

The Ebionites' self-designation cannot be traced back to the first decades of the Jesus movement. The "pillars" of the Jerusalem Christ association, namely Jesus's brother James and the apostles Peter and John, extended to Paul the right hand of fellowship after his vision of Jesus. Paul was authorized to evangelize the nations. Their one requirement was that Paul should not neglect the poor, which may have motivated him to raise a collection of money for the poor saints in Jerusalem.[23] This was Paul's description of their material poverty; it was not a self-chosen designation.[24] There may have been

---

18. Skarsaune, "The Ebionites," 420–21.
19. See Irenaeus, *Haer.* 1.23.1–4 (cf. Acts 8:9–13, 18–24).
20. Skarsaune, "The Ebionites," 421–24.
21. For such insults directed against the Ebionites, see Origen, *Cels.* 2.1; *Princ.* 4.3.8; *Comm. Matt* 16.12; *Hom. Gen.* 3.5; Eusebius, *H.E.* 3.27.1, 6; Epiphanius, *Pan.* 30.17.2–3.
22. See, for example, Tertullian, *Praescr.* 10.8; 33.3–5, 11; *Virg.* 6.1; *Carn. Chr.* 14; 18; 24. Häkkinen ("Ebionites," 251) argues that Hippolytus of Rome may have invented Ebion in his lost *Syntagma*, since Ebion appears in the *Refutation of All Heresies* (7.35). This latter text, though, has likely been misattributed to Hippolytus.
23. See Gal 2:10; Rom 15:26.
24. Contra Hans-Joachim Schoeps, *Jewish Christianity: Factional Disputes in the Early Church* (trans. Douglas A. Hare; Philadelphia: Fortress, 1969), 11, 102; Michael Goulder, "A Poor Man's Christology" *NTS* 45 (1999): 333–34; Luomanen, *Recovering*, 23. This position was refuted in Leander E. Keck, "The Poor Amongst the Saints in the New Testament" *ZNW* 56 (1965): 100–129; Keck, "The Poor Amongst the Saints in Jewish Christianity and Qumran" *ZNW* 57 (1966): 54–78; cf. Bauckham, "The

Ebionites in the fourth century who insisted that the roots of their title went back to the earliest Christ community in Jerusalem, who sold all of their personal property and held their possessions in common.[25] They may have come up with this explanation for their group's name after reflecting on the idealization of the Christ congregation in Jerusalem in Acts.[26] The popularity of their title may be due to the recurring denunciations of the unjust oppression of those at the bottom of the socioeconomic scale in the Hebrew Bible and the hope for a great eschatological reversal when the poor and humble would be blessed.[27]

In his longest excerpt on the Ebionites,[28] Irenaeus sketched out their customs. He specified their diligent study of the prophetic writings, their rite of circumcision, and their adoration of the city of Jerusalem as the house of God. The posture of their prayers may have been facing in the direction where the Jewish capital once stood.[29] They loathed Paul as a turncoat who apostasized from the Mosaic Law. Just as Irenaeus was uninformed about the meaning of the term Ebionite, this seems like a superficial account of the Ebionites' practices. He may have not had any firsthand acquaintance with the Ebionites. His sparse information about them may have been culled from an older catalog of heresies.[30] What disturbed him the most was that the Ebionites reckoned that Joseph was Jesus's biological father.[31] Their translation

Origin," 178; Skarsaune, "The Ebionites," 425; Broadhead, *Jewish Ways*, 188–89; Paget, *Jews*, 345–46; Gregory, *The Gospel*, 289.

25. See Epiphanius, *Pan.* 30.17.2–3 (cf. Acts 2:43–47; 4:32–37). See Goulder, "A Poor Man's Christology," 332–33; Skarsaune, "The Ebionites," 452.

26. Keck, "The Poor Amongst the Saints in Jewish Christianity," 59; Bauckham, "The Origin," 178; Luomanen, *Recovering*, 35; Paget, *Jews*, 346.

27. See, for example, 1 Sam 2:8 (cf. Ps 113:7–8); Job 24:4; Ps 9:18; 12:5; 35:10; 37:11; 69:33; 72:12–13; Prov 30:14; Isa 25:4; 32:7; Jer 20:13; Ezek 22:29; Amos 5:12; Matt 5:3, 5; Luke 6:20, 24. For further discussion on the Ebionites' self-designation, see Schoeps, *Jewish Christianity*, 11, 101–2; Bauckham, "The Origin," 177–80; Häkkinen, "Ebionites," 247; Skarsaune, "The Ebionites," 421, 425–27; Broadhead, *Jewish Ways*, 188–89; Paget, *Jews*, 344–47; Gregory, *The Gospel*, 289.

28. See Irenaeus, *Haer.* 1.26.2.

29. Schoeps, *Jewish Christianity*, 113; Klijn and Reinink, *Patristic Evidence*, 20; Häkkinen, "Ebionites," 271; Paget, *Jews*, 357.

30. The best guess is that Irenaeus had an updated version of Justin's *Syntagma against All the Heresies*. Justin tolerated *Torah*-observant Christ-followers so long as they did not try to proselytize non-Jewish Christians, so the Ebionites were likely absent from Justin's heresiological catalog before it was revised. See Häkkinen, "Ebionites," 251; Paget, *Jews*, 318.

31. See Irenaeus, *Haer.* 3.21.1.

of the book of Isaiah had a "young woman" give birth to Immanuel.[32] For Irenaeus, the virginal conception of Jesus was integral to his doctrine of recapitulation. Consequently, the Ebionites did not grasp that the divinity had to fully enter into our fallen humanity in order to redeem the human condition.[33] By disallowing that Jesus's divine and human natures were united in one person, they refused the mixture of wine and water in the heavenly chalice and stuck to their old leaven in their insistence on Jesus's natural birth.[34]

The Ebionites reduced Jesus to a mere mortal, as did Cerinthus of Ephesus and Carpocrates of Alexandria.[35] In the cosmologies of these two latter thinkers,[36] the supreme deity was not involved in creating the physical universe that imprisons human souls. They blamed an inferior divine power or malevolent angels respectively for making matter. On this point, the Ebionites' theology that the creator of the universe elected Israel could not be farther apart from the theologies of Cerinthus and Carpocrates. All the same, Cerinthus and Carprocrates judged that Jesus was conceived like everybody else through the ordinary processes of procreation. The only thing that set him apart from every other human being was his virtue as a wise, righteous person. A celestial power that Cerinthus identified as the "Christ" possessed Jesus at his baptism and empowered him to reveal the means of salvation from this material prison or perform miraculous feats. Cerinthus supposed that the Christ aeon vacated Jesus's body before it expired on the cross and was raised to life again.

There is a text-critical issue about whether Irenaeus really surmised that the Ebionites' opinions about Jesus were the same as the opinions of Cerinthus and Carpocrates. The Latin translation of *Against Heresies* states that they were "not similar" (*non similiter*), but the early third-century Roman author of the *Refutation of All Heresies* was copying Irenaeus's Greek text and states that they were "similar" (*homoiōs*).[37] At most, the similarities seem more apparent than real. The Ebionites may have held that Jesus was

---

32. See Irenaeus, *Haer.* 3.21.1.
33. See Irenaeus, *Haer.* 4.33.4.
34. See Irenaeus, *Haer.* 5.1.3.
35. See Irenaeus, *Haer.* 1.25.2.
36. The following summary is based on Irenaeus, *Haer.* 1.25.1; 1.26.1. For further discussion, see Michael J. Kok, "Classifying Cerinthus's Christology" *JECH* 9.1 (2019): 35–39.
37. See *Ref.* 7.34.1; 10.22.1. The reasons for doubting the attribution of this text to Hippolytus are rehearsed in M. David Litwa, *Refutation of All Heresies* (Atlanta: SBL, 2016), xxxii–xlii.

appointed to be the Christ, which means "anointed one," at his baptism in the same way that Israelite prophets, priests, and rulers were anointed by the spirit of Yahweh. They did not hold that Jesus was temporarily inhabited by a spirit that was itself called Christ.[38] The reason for the Christ aeon's descent in the thinking of Cerinthus and Carpocrates was to reveal a previously unknown spiritual realm inhabited by a totally transcendent deity far beyond the physical universe. Since they theorized that divine beings were impassible, or incapable of suffering, the Christ aeon had to abandon the human Jesus to his fate on the cross. The Ebionites were not beholden to their cosmological dualism between spirit and matter. According to Irenaeus, the theologians who divided the human Jesus from the impassible Christ preferred Mark's Gospel over Matthew's.[39] Mark's narrative started at Jesus's baptism, where the spirit descended like a dove "into" (*eis*) him, and Jesus's last words from the cross was a lament that God had forsaken him.[40] All of these arguments may support the Latin reading *non similiter*.[41] However, Irenaeus would not have brought up the Ebionites in the midst of his exposés of Carpocrates and Cerinthus unless he detected some kinship between their beliefs that Jesus was an ordinary human who was possessed by a spirit at his baptism. At a minimum, they all disbelieved in the virgin birth. A scribal copyist misread Irenaeus's comparison and inserted "not" before the word "similar."[42]

---

38. See Paget, *Jews*, 352; Kok, "Classifying," 36, 39. Contra Goulder, "A Poor Man's Christology," 335–37; Häkkinen, "Ebionites," 268–69; Luomanen, *Recovering Jewish Sects*, 20–21, 46; Michael F. Bird, *Jesus the Eternal Son: Answering Adoptionist Christology* (Grand Rapids: Eerdmans, 2017), 119. For corroborating evidence that the Ebionites held the same Christology as Cerinthus and Carpocrates, Tertullian (*Carn. Chr.* 14) scoffs at Ebion's misuse of a proof-text in Zech 1:14 LXX, in which an angel was indwelling in the prophet Zechariah, in support of a possessionist Christology. It is not clear, however, that Tertullian actually had an Ebionite source for this Christological view that Jesus was indwelled by an angel. Epiphanius (*Pan.* 30.3.6; 13.7; 14.4; 16.3) describes how the Ebionites believed that the divine Christ possessed Jesus at his baptism, but he was misreading Irenaeus's comparison.
39. See Irenaeus, *Haer.* 3.11.7.
40. See Mark 1:10; 15:34. For the reception of these verses, see Kok, *The Gospel*, 243–45.
41. See Klijn and Reinink, *Patristic Evidence*, 20.
42. See Häkkinen, "Ebionites," 265n.49; Skarsaune, "The Ebionites," 428; Luomanen, *Recovering Jewish-Christian Sects*, 20–21; Paget, *Jews*, 352; Bird, *Jesus the Eternal Son*, 114n.18; Kok, "Classifying Cerinthus's Christology," 38.

Irenaeus sidestepped the tension between the Ebionites' exclusive preference for the Gospel of Matthew and their rejection of Matthew's infancy narrative. He did not charge them with cutting out Matthew's opening chapters, but he scoffed at how oblivious they were to what Matthew reported about Jesus's supernatural birth.[43] His polemic that there were four marginal Christian sects who misappropriated one Gospel each, so the Ebionites usurped the Gospel of Matthew and those who maintained the distinction between the human Jesus and the divine Christ picked the Gospel of Mark, is artificial. The Ebionites were not a single sect, but were diverse Jewish Christ believers. Some of them may have grown rather fond of Mark's Gospel. It lacked an infancy narrative altogether. It just started with Jesus's anointing for his messianic office by the spirit at his baptism.[44] The lament that Jesus shouted out from the cross could be voiced by any innocent human sufferer.[45]

Some scholars may overlook how amenable Mark's Gospel may have been to the Ebionites because they pigeonhole it as a "Pauline" Gospel.[46] This minimizes the differences between the theologies of Mark and Paul.[47] Unlike Mark, Paul reapplies the language about preexistent divine wisdom to Jesus as the agent through whom the world was created and represents Jesus as the second Adam who liberates Adamic humanity from the curse.[48] Unlike Paul, one of Mark's favorite Christological titles is "the son of the human" (*ho huios tou anthrōpou*), an allusion to Daniel's vision of a human-like figure who rides the clouds.[49] Mark's attention on Jesus's sacrificial death is not incompatible with *Torah*-observance.[50] When the covenant people were oppressed by the Seleucids, the willingness of a mother and her seven sons to be tortured and killed for their allegiance to the Law of Moses assuaged

---

43. See Irenaeus, *Haer.* 3.11.7.
44. See Mark 1:9–11.
45. See Mark 15:34.
46. For a recent monograph contending that Mark's Gospel is a Pauline work, see Mar Pérez I Díaz, *Mark, a Pauline Theologian* (WUNT 2.521; Tübingen: Mohr Siebeck, 2020).
47. For the following Christological differences, see Kok, *The Gospel*, 95–101.
48. See, for example, Rom 5:12–21; 1 Cor 8:6.
49. See, for example, Mark 8:38; 13:26; 14:62. Paul shifts to the title Lord when engaging the same underlying tradition in 1 Thess 4:15–17.
50. See, for example, Mark 8:31; 9:30–31; 10:33–34, 45.

the deity's wrath against the nation.[51] The anticipation that the gospel would be spread to all the nations and the elect would be gathered from the ends of the earth is in line with the eschatological ingathering of the nations to worship Yahweh alongside the people of Israel.[52] When the Pharisees asked why Jesus does not observe the tradition of the elders about washing their hands, he reprimanded them for extolling their nonbiblical oral traditions at the expense of Moses's commandments.[53] His aphorism that nothing that enters a person from the outside can render him or her unclear, and the parenthetical aside that he was thereby "cleansing all foods," may not be an echo of Paul's principle that no foods are unclean in themselves.[54] Paul intervened in a situation where Jews and non-Jews were eating together in Rome. In Mark's Gospel, Jesus, the disciples, and the Pharisees were chatting about whether ritual impurity could be transmitted from unwashed hands via a liquid to the eater in an intra-Jewish social context, where everyone had grown up with the dietary restrictions about clean and unclean food. Jesus's answer was that unwashed hands cannot contaminate kosher food, thus cleansing it.[55] His retort was that it is what comes out of a person, as in bodily discharges and immoral actions, that is ritually defiling.[56]

Some Ebionites may have had a predilection for the Gospel of Mark and others for the Gospel of Matthew. Some of them proof-texted a verse in Matthew's Gospel for why anyone who self-identifies as a disciple of Jesus must imitate their teacher's *Torah*-observant way of life.[57] Since Irenaeus does

---

51. See 2 Macc 7:1–42; 4 Macc 17:7–22. See Casey, *Aramaic Sources*, 209; Crossley, *The Date*, 49.
52. See Mark 13:10, 27; 14:9; cf. Isa 2:2–4; 60:3–16; 66:18–24; Mic 4:1–4; Zeph 3:9; Zech 8:20–23; 14:16–21; *Tob.* 13:11.
53. See Mark 7:1–23.
54. See Mark 7:15, 18–23; Rom 14:14. For the numerous exegetes who interpret Jesus's aphorism, and Mark's parenthetical explanation of it, as rendering all foods clean, see John van Maaren, "Does Mark's Jesus Abrogate Torah? Jesus' Purity Logion and its Illustration in Mark 7:15–23" *JJMJS* 4 (2017): 23–24n.5.
55. Crossley, *The Date*, 191–204; Daniel Boyarin, *The Jewish Gospels: The Story of the Jewish Christ* (New York: The New Press, 2012), 102–28; Maaren, "Does Mark's Jesus," 26–40.
56. Maaren, "Does Mark's Jesus," 31–35.
57. See Matt 10:24–25 (cf. Pseudo-Tertullian, *Adv. Omn. Haer.* 3; Origen, *in Matt. comm. ser.* 79; Pseudo-Hieronymus, *Indic. de haer.* 10; Epiphanius, *Pan.* 28.5.1; 30.26.2; 30.33.4). Broadhead (*Jewish Ways*, 211) underscores that this point is independently multiply attested.

not charge the Ebionites with tampering with Matthew's text, some of them must have been comfortable with Matthew's nativity story. Again, they were diverse Jewish Christ-followers who did not all have the same beliefs and practices. Origen and Eusebius, in fact, report that there was a split between the Ebionites who denied or affirmed the virginal conception of Jesus.[58]

A more skeptical theory is that Origen invented the idea that there were two branches of the Ebionites because he was influenced by the textual variant in Irenaeus's extract on the Ebionites. He deduced that some Ebionites were similar and others dissimilar to Cerinthus and Carpocrates.[59] At one point, he seems to be following Irenaeus when noting that both schools of the Ebionites hated Paul.[60] At other points, his wording seems closer to the text of the *Refutation*. They both observed that the Ebionites's Jesus was "similar" (*homoiōs*) to the rest of humanity and not born of a virgin.[61] In the *Refutation*, the Ebionites' insistence that Jesus had to obey the Mosaic Law "to have been made righteous" (*dedikaiōsthai*) is not far from Cerinthus's reasoning for why Jesus was divinely chosen because he was "more righteous" (*dikaioteros*) than everyone else.[62] However, even if Origen was aware of the textual variant over whether the Ebionites' opinions were similar or not to

---

58. See Origen, *Cels.* 5.61; Eusebius, *H.E.* 3.37.3. Eusebius was not an independent witness to the two schools of the Ebionites, but he goes farther than Origen in his argument that neither group affirmed Jesus's preexistence or divinity. On this point, he may have been dependent on another commentary by Origen in which he noted that the Ebionites and the Valentinians denied the orthodox Christology of the Johannine prologue. See Pritz, *Nazarene Jewish Christianity*, 27; Klijn and Reinink, *Patristic Evidence*, 25; Petri Luomanen, "The Nazarenes: Orthodox Heretics with an Apocryphal Canonical Gospel?" in *The Other Side: Apocryphal Perspectives on Ancient Christian 'Orthodoxies'* (NTOA 117; ed. Candida R. Moss, Tobias Nicklas, Christopher Tuckett, and Joseph Verheyden; Göttingen: Vandenhoeck & Ruprecht, 2017), 70–72.

59. Klijn and Reinink, *Patristic Evidence*, 26; Luomanen, *Recovering Jewish Christian Sects*, 19–20, 28–29.

60. See Origen, *Cels.* 5.61; cf. *Hom. Jer.* 19.12. Petri Luomanen, "The Nazarenes: Orthodox Heretics with an Apocryphal Canonical Gospel?" in *The Other Side: Apocryphal Perspectives on Ancient Christian 'Orthodoxies'* (NTOA 117; ed. Candida R. Moss, Tobias Nicklas, Christopher Tuckett, and Joseph Verheyden; Göttingen: Vandenhoeck & Ruprecht, 2017), 68.

61. Compare Origen, *Cels.* 5.65 and *Ref.* 7.33.1. See Luomanen, "The Nazarenes," 68–69.

62. See *Ref.* 7.33.1; 7.34.1–2. See Luomanen, "The Nazarenes," 68–69. The major difference, though, is that Cerinthus may not have measured Jesus's righteousness against the standards of the Mosaic Law and the Ebionites did not distinguish the human Jesus from the divine Christ.

the opinions of Cerinthus and Carpocrates, there is not a single passage in *Against Heresies* or the *Refutation* where any Ebionites upheld that Jesus was born of a virgin. Origen did not glean his second group of Ebionites from the prior heresiological sources. He must have learned that some Ebionites accepted the virgin birth independently from Irenaeus through his personal correspondence with them.[63]

Irenaeus manufactured a Christian sect on the fringes out of the Ebionites and the rest of the heresiologists followed suit. Eusebius could not accept that this heretical sect was basing their beliefs and practices on the orthodox Gospel of Matthew. He corrected Irenaeus by alleging that their Gospel was actually the spurious *Gospel According to the Hebrews*.[64] Anyone who wished to harmonize Irenaeus's and Eusebius's statements about the Ebionites could now submit that Matthew's Greek text and the *Gospel According to the Hebrew* were varying versions of the same underlying exemplar.

Epiphanius and the Nazorean and Ebionite Versions of Matthew's Gospel

Epiphanius was born in the early fourth century near Eleutheropolis in Palestine. After studying rhetoric and monasticism in Egypt, he returned home to govern a monastery for thirty years. He was appointed bishop of Constantia in Cyprus around 367 CE. He became embroiled in theological and ecclesiastical controversies. For instance, he detested Origen's theology. He was invited to participate in a council in Constantinople that planned to censure the bishop there for welcoming four Egyptian monks who espoused Origen's theological views. He died sailing back from there to Cyprus around 402 or 403 CE. His *magnum opus* is the *Panarion*, a "medicine chest" of orthodox anecdotes for eighty heresies stretching from the time of Adam to the present.[65] Even by the standards of heresiological discourse, his tendentiousness

---

63. Häkkinen, "Ebionites," 254–55; Skarsaune, "The Ebionites," 445; Broadhead, *Jewish Ways*, 195; Paget, *Jews*, 328, 35.

64. See Eusebius, *H.E.* 3.27.4.

65. For a study on Epiphanius's life and thought, see Andrew S. Jacobs, *Epiphanius of Cyprus: A Cultural Biography of Late Antiquity* (Oakland: University of California Press, 2016), 8–25; cf. Pritz, *Nazarene Jewish Christianity*, 29; Joseph Verheyden, "Epiphanius on the Ebionites" in The Image of the Judaeo-Christians in Ancient Jewish and Christian Literature, 182–84; Broadhead, *Jewish Ways*, 174; Luomanen, *Recovering*, 30–31.

and carelessness when muddling up what his opponents believed and prac-
ticed seems extreme.[66] In the twenty-ninth and the thirtieth chapters of his
Panarion, he set his sights on two supposed Jewish factions known as the
Nazoreans and the Ebionites. The former group had the ability to read the
Gospel of Matthew in Hebrew, though Epiphanius was unsure if they cut
out its opening genealogy.[67] The latter group had a corrupted version of the
Gospel of Matthew without its genealogy and nativity story and brazenly put
it forward as the original version of the text "according to the Hebrews."[68]

His convoluted account of the origins of the Nazoreans is perplexing.[69] The gist of it is that Jesus's disciples were originally known as
Nazoreans. This included Paul.[70] Some of them moved to Egypt after Jesus's
ascension under the leadership of the evangelist Mark. There is a lengthy
digression about how they changed their title to the Jesseans because Jesse
was the father of King David.[71] The Nazoreans were renamed Christians
at Antioch.[72] Epiphanius contradicts himself when he relates that the
Nazoreans originated in Pella after the Jewish War. Some Jewish Christ followers had fled there to escape the Roman siege of Jerusalem that ended
with the destruction of the temple in 70 CE.[73] This is why Epiphanius
could not work out whether the Nazoreans existed before or after Cerinthus
became an adversary of the apostles.[74] He assured his readers that Ebion, the

---

66. See the negative assessments of Epiphanius's legacy in Jacobs, *Epiphanius of Cyprus*, 1–4.
    Yet Jacobs observes that Epiphanius's vituperative rhetoric fits imperial Roman attitudes
    toward otherness (pp. 7–8).
67. See Epiphanius, *Pan.* 29.9.4.
68. See Epiphanius, *Pan.* 30.3.7; 13.2; 14.3.
69. For attempts to recap Epiphanius's historical account of the Nazoraeans, see Klijn and
    Reinink, *Patristic Evidence*, 44–45; Pritz, *Nazarene Jewish Christianity*, 35–43; Martinus
    C. de Boer, "The Nazoreans: Living at the Boundary of Judaism and Christianity" in
    Tolerance and Intolerance in Early Judaism and Christianity (ed. Graham N. Stanton and
    Guy G. Stroumsa; Cambridge: Cambridge University Press, 1998), 245–46; Kinzig, "The
    Nazoraeans," 479–80; Broadhead, *Jewish Ways*, 174–75; Luomanen, *Recovering*, 53–57.
70. See Epiphanius, *Pan* 29.1.2–3; 6.2–8.
71. See Epiphanius, *Pan.* 29.1.3–4.9; 5.1–4
72. See Epiphanius, *Pan.* 29.4.10.
73. See Epiphanius, *Pan.* 29.7.7–8.
74. See Epiphanius, *Pan.* 29.1.1. Epiphanius (*Pan.* 28.2.3–5; 4.1–2; 6.1–6) reimagined
    Cerinthus as the leader of the opposition against the apostles and Paul when they
    approved of a "law-free" mission to the nations. The older tradition from Irenaeus is
    that Cerinthus was the opponent of the aged John, the Lord's disciple (cf. *Haer.* 3.3.4),

imaginary founder of the Ebionites, began his career among the Nazoreans in Pella.[75] After his lengthy excurses about the group's name and history, he narrowed in on their core theological tenets. They had the same canonical division between the Old and New Testaments and were able to read the Law, the Prophets, and the Writings in Hebrew.[76] They professed that a solitary divine being created everything that exists and that Jesus is the creator's "son" or "servant" (*pais*). They expected that the dead would be raised.[77] What set them apart from non-Jewish Christians was their social praxis. They circumcised their sons, rested on the Sabbath, and abided by all of the Jewish legal statutes.[78]

Epiphanius's account of the Nazoreans' beliefs is more straightforward than his account of their history and may be historically reliable.[79] Yet this confidence in the historicity of Epiphanius's account may be misplaced insofar as his concise synopsis of their Jewish practices are fairly stereotypical. Identity markers such as circumcision, the Sabbath, or dietary restrictions were often attacked by anti-Jewish Christian polemicists. Many Jews and Christians awaited the future, corporate resurrection of the dead. His lack of personal acquaintance with the Nazoreans is apparent when he was unable to find out their stance on the doctrine of the virgin birth.[80] He had heard that they were cursed at dawn, at midday, and in the evening in the prayers of those who attend the synagogue.[81] He was no more tolerant of their presence among Christians. His regrettable verdict was that they could not be numbered among the believers in Christ if they maintained their Jewish ethnic and cultural identities.[82] The hybridity of

---

but Epiphanius switched Cerinthus with Ebion as the one in the bathhouse (cf. *Pan.* 30.24.1–7).

75. See Epiphanius, *Pan.* 30.1.1; 2.1.
76. See Epiphanius, *Pan.* 29.7.2, 4.
77. See Epiphanius, *Pan.* 29.7.3.
78. See Epiphanius, *Pan.* 29.5.4; 7.2; 8.1–7.
79. Broadhead (*Jewish Ways*, 177–78) judges the core of Epiphanius's report on the Nazoraeans in *Pan.* 29.7.2–8 to be generally accurate and externally corroborated by Jerome.
80. See Epiphanius, *Pan.* 29.7.6. See Pritz, *Nazarene Jewish Christianity*, 35; Klijn and Reinink, *Patristic Evidence*, 46; Kinzig, "The Nazoraeans," 473; Luomanen, *Recovering*, 62–63; Gregory, *The Gospel*, 295; Luomanen, "The Nazarenes," 295.
81. See Epiphanius, *Pan.* 29.9.2.
82. See Epiphanius, *Pan.* 29.7.1; 9.1.

the Nazoreans was perceived to be dangerous for those who were invested in the construction of sharp social boundaries between the Jewish and Christian communities.[83]

The Nazoreans could be regarded as the successors of the Jerusalem apostles.[84] The earlier heresiological sources were silent about them because none of the heresiologists targeted them for abuse before Epiphanius.[85] If the Ebionites split from the Nazoreans in Pella over a Christological dispute, there may be a historical core to the legend that Ebion was once a Nazorean.[86] This split may be behind Justin's notice that there was a division between Jewish Christ-followers over whether they should compel non-Jewish Christians to Judaize by adopting the *Torah* or behind Origen's and Eusebius's notices about the two schools of the Ebionites who differed over the doctrine of the virgin birth.[87] The problem is that Justin's two groups were not divided over Christology, Origen's two groups reviled Paul, and Eusebius's two groups did not accept Jesus's divinity.[88] It may be problematic to read back Epiphanius's Nazoreans into these earlier conflicts or grant his assumption that they originated in Pella.

---

83. Daniel Boyarin, *Border Lines: The Partition of Judaeo-Christianity* (Philadelphia: University of Pennsylvania Press, 2004), 207–9.

84. See Pritz, *Nazarene Jewish Christianity*, 14–17, 39, 75; Boer, "The Nazoreans,", 243–45, 252; Bauckham, "The Origin," 162–63; Kinzig, "The Nazoraeans," 481; Broadhead, *Jewish Ways*, 163, 178–79, 186; Mimouni, *Early Judaeo-Christianity*, 63–66.

85. Pritz, *Nazarene Jewish Christianity*, 75; Boer, "The Nazoreans," 252; Bauckham, "The Origin," 163; Broadhead, *Jewish Ways*, 178–79.

86. Pritz, *Nazarene Jewish Christianity*, 337–38.

87. See Justin, *Dial.* 47.1–4; Origen, *Cels.* 5.61; 5.65; Eusebius, *H.E.* 3.27.3. See Pritz, *Nazarene Jewish Christianity*, 20–21, 23–24, 25–28; Bauckham, "The Origin," 163; Broadhead, *Jewish Ways*, 181; Mimouni, *Early Judaeo-Christianity*, 96, 98, 107, 111.

88. Paget, *Jews*, 356; Luomanen, "The Nazarenes," 67. Pritz (*Nazarene Jewish Christianity*, 20) and Skarsaune ("The Ebionites," 429–30, 432–33) note that Justin disapproved of Jewish Christians who confessed that Jesus was the exalted Messiah but not a preexistent divine being. Nevertheless, Justin only excludes the Jewish Christ-followers who demand that the non-Jewish Christians Judaize from those who will inherit salvation. Eusebius's assertion that the second group of Ebionites did not identify Jesus as God's word and wisdom may have depended on Origen's comment that the Christology of the Ebionites and the Valentinians fell short of the depiction of Jesus in the Johannine prologue (cf. *Comm. Tit.* 3.11). See Pritz, *Nazarene Jewish Christianity*, 27; Klijn and Reinink, *Patristic Evidence*, 25; Luomanen, "The Nazarenes," 25. Still, neither Origen's nor Eusebius's second group of Ebionites is a perfect match for the Nazoraeans if they accepted an orthodox Christology and the canonicity of Paul's letters.

The Nazoraeans may have been Epiphanius's living contemporaries, but he carved out a lengthy history for them on the basis of his reading of the book of Acts and Eusebius's *Ecclesiastical History*.[89] In Acts, the Christ followers are first called Christians at Antioch and Paul is put on trial as a ringleader of the Nazoreans.[90] The followers of Jesus praise the maker of heaven and earth, who raised and glorified Jesus as a "servant" or "son" (*pais*), and were not guilty of anything except for putting their hope in the resurrection of the dead.[91] Mark's ministry among the Therapeutae in Egypt and the flight of the Jewish Christ-followers to Pella is related by Eusebius.[92] Eusebius located the Ebionites in the village of Kochaba, which is where Ebion moved to according to Epiphanius.[93]

Unlike his profile of the Nazoreans, Epiphanius's profile of the Ebionites bears little resemblance to his predecessors. Epiphanius's Ebionites could not make up their minds over whether Jesus was a human who was possessed by a heavenly being, a prophet like Moses who pronounced the abolition of the sacrificial system, a reincarnation of the original human Adam, or a gigantic archangel.[94] They did not just live in accordance with the Jewish legislations in circumcising their sons and resting on the Sabbath.[95] They ritually immersed in water daily, especially if they had physical contact with non-Jews or engaged in sexual activity.[96] They were adverse to eating meat.[97] They consumed water, not wine, during the Eucharist.[98] They suspected that an interpolator inserted false passages pertaining to the sacrificial cult into the Pentateuch and rejected all the Hebrew prophets between Moses's successor

---

89. Verheyden, "Epiphanius," 184–85n.13; Luomanen, *Recovering*, 53–57, 63–65; cf. Klijn and Reinink, *Patristic Evidence*, 46n.1; Gregory, *The Gospel*, 296–297; Luomanen, "The Nazarenes," 61.
90. See Acts 11:26; 24:5.
91. See Acts 3:13, 26; 4:24, 27, 30; 23:6; 24:15, 21.
92. See Eusebius, *H.E.* 2.16.1–17.24; 3.5.3.
93. See Eusebius, *Onom.* 301.32–34; Epiphanius, *Pan.* 30.2.8.
94. See Epiphanius, *Pan.* 30.2.2; 3.1–6; 14.4–5; 16.2–4; 17.6–7; 18.5–6.
95. See Epiphanius, *Pan.* 30.2.2; 17.5; 26.1–2.
96. See Epiphanius, *Pan.* 30.2.4–5; 15.3; 16.1.
97. See Epiphanius, *Pan* 30.15.3–4; 18.7–9.
98. See Epiphanius, *Pan.* 30.16.1. This has nothing to do with Irenaeus's image of the commixture of the wine and water in the chalice as a metaphor for Jesus's dual nature. Contra Schoeps, *Jewish Christianity*, 113; Klijn and Reinink, *Patristic Evidence*, 20; Luomanen, *Recovering*, 21–22. See Häkkinen, "Ebionites," 266n.50; Skarsaune, "The Ebionites," 430, 434, 434n.40.

Joshua and Jesus as false prophets.[99] This is nothing like Irenaeus's Ebionites who diligently or overscrupulously studied the prophetic writings.[100]

Too much intellectual energy has been expended puzzling out how Irenaeus's Ebionites evolved into Epiphanius's Ebionites.[101] Epiphanius drew on a bewildering variety of sources, including the *Circuits of Peter*,[102] the *Ascent of James*,[103] the *Book of Elchasai*,[104] a Gospel,[105] and an apocryphal

---

99. See Epiphanius, *Pan.* 30.15.2; 16.5, 7; 18.4–5, 7–9. For the theory of false pericopes in the Pentateuch, see Schoeps, *Jewish Christianity*, 82–84, 88–92.

100. See Irenaeus, *Haer.* 1.26.2. See Klijn and Reinink, *Patristic Evidence*, 20; Skarsaune, "The Ebionites," 437; Luomanen, *Recovering*, 46–47; Paget, *Jews*, 358. The adjective *curiosius* should not be translated as "curious." Contra Schoeps, *Jewish Christianity*, 88; Häkkinen, "Ebionites," 259–60.

101. See, for instance, Bauckham, "The Origen," 163–80; Luomanen, *Recovering*, 41–49, 161–65; Mimouni, *Early Judaeo-Christianity*, 220–33, 238–47.

102. See Epiphanius, *Pan.* 30.15.1–3. The *Circuits of Peter* might have been the title of the *Grundschrift* or "Basic Writing" redacted in the Pseudo-Clementine *Homilies* and *Recognitions*. See F. Stanley Jones, "Jewish Christianity of the *Pseudo-Clementines*" in *A Companion to Second-Century Christian "Heretics"*, 315–34.

103. See Epiphanius, *Pan.* 30.16.7. There is disagreement about whether the *Ascent of James* was the source behind *Recognitions* 1.27.1–71.6 or 1.33.3–71.6. See R. E. Van Voorst, *The Ascents of James: History and Theology of a Jewish Christian Community* (SBLDS 112; Atlanta: Scholars Press, 1989), 45–46 (cf. Klijn and Reinink, *Patristic Evidence*, 31; Häkkinen, "Ebionites," 265; Bauckham, "The Origin," 165) and F. S. Jones, *An Ancient Jewish Christian Source on the History of Christianity: Pseudo-Clementine Recognitions 1:27–71* (SBLTT 37; Christian Apocrypha Series 2; Atlanta: Scholars Press, 1995), 35, 147–48. The title may be based on James's ascent up the stairs of the temple to deliver a speech about his brother's Christological identity and anti-cultic message. Note that both Van Voorst (*The Ascent*, 179–80) and Jones (*An Ancient Jewish Christian Source*, 166–67) contest Epiphanius's identification of the source as an Ebionite text, but see the rebuttal of Bauckham ("The Origin," 165–71). At the very least, it is an anti-Pauline, Jewish source. Paul is the unnamed "hostile person" who threw James down from the top of the temple stairs, preventing him from persuading the crowd, and hunted down Jesus's followers in Damascus (1.70.1–71.4).

104. See Epiphanius, *Pan.* 30.17.4. To explain how this apocalyptic book came into the Ebionites' possession, Epiphanius makes up a story about how Elxai joined Ebion's followers (cf. *Pan.* 30.3.2; 17.5). Luomanen (*Recovering*, 43) makes the case that the Ebionites could have crossed paths with Elchasaite missionaries, but it is more likely that Epiphanius was the one to construct the "Elchasaite bridge" to link the Ebionites and the Elchasaites together. This metaphor is used in Broadhead, *Jewish Ways*, 203. See Klijn and Reinink, *Patristic Evidence*, 28–38, 43; Verheyden, "Epiphanius," 187n.23; Häkkinen, "Ebionites," 257, 259; Skarsaune, "Ebionites," 453; Broadhead, *Jewish Ways*, 203–6; Paget, *Jews*, 335.

105. See Epiphanius, *Pan.* 30.13.2–3, 4, 6, 7–8; 14.3, 5; 16.5; 22.4. However, Skarsaune ("Ebionites," 457–58) argues that Epiphanius discovered this Gospel at a late stage and

Acts of the Apostles.[106] The resulting portrait of the Ebionites was a mess. His blunder was assuming that the sources at his disposal were all Ebionite in character, compounding Irenaeus's inaccurate representation of the Ebionites as a single sect.[107] Epiphanius misrepresented his sources. It served his polemical agenda to compare Ebion to a "monstrosity with many shapes" and a "many-headed hydra" and to denigrate Ebion's self-contradictory philosophy as irresponsibly syncretistic.[108] From his point of view, the Ebionites were neither orthodox Christians nor orthodox Jews, for they discredited the sections within the Hebrew Bible that did not accord with their vegetarian and anti-cultic standpoints.[109] He fabricated conversations with the Ebionites out of whole cloth.[110] Since his reconstruction of the Ebionites departed so much from his heresiological predecessors, he constructed the Nazoreans as the representatives of a Jewish form of the Christian faith in its simplest, stereotypical form.[111]

Given his penchant for misattributing sources to the Ebionites, his assertion that he had gotten a hold of a defective copy of Matthew's Gospel that they titled the *Gospel According to the Hebrews* ought to be handled with caution.[112] His citations from it do not overlap with the rest of the patristic citations of the *Gospel According to the Hebrews* and harmonize the Synoptic Gospels to a much greater extent. Some modern scholars, therefore, have

---

inserted it into an earlier draft of his chapter on the Ebionites at 30.13–14. He attributes the rest of the fragments to the *Circuits of Peter*. However, he does not deal with the reference to the "gospel" (*euangelion*) outside the section in 30.16.5.

106. See *Pan.* 30.16.6. This may have been Epiphanius's source for a slanderous rumor about Paul. See Verheyden, "Epiphanius," 200; Häkkinen, "Ebionites," 264, 270. According to the rumor, Paul was a Greek individual from Tarsus who desired to marry the high priest's daughter and was willing to become a Jewish proselyte. When his feelings were not reciprocated, he became enraged and wrote against the Jewish customs that he once planned to embrace wholeheartedly.

107. See Klijn and Reinink, *Patristic Evidence*, 28–38, 43; Verheyden, "Epiphanius," 185–208; Häkkinen, "Ebionites," 256–57, 259–65; Skarsaune, "Ebionites," 423–24, 450–561; Broadhead, *Jewish Ways*, 198–206; Paget, *Jews*, 329–41.

108. Verheyden, "Epiphanius," 182.

109. Verheyden, "Epiphanius," 183.

110. See Epiphanius, *Pan.* 30.15.4; 18.7, 9. See Skarsaune, "The Ebionites," 453.

111. Luomanen, *Recovering*, 65–66.

112. Contra Schmidtke, *Neue Fragment*, 242–246; Pritz, *Nazarene Jewish Christianity*, 83, 84–85, 86–87; Kinzig, "The Nazoraeans," 473; Beatrice, "Apostolic Fathers," 158–59, 169–76, 188–89; Edwards, *Hebrew Gospel*, 26–27, 65–75, 102–7.

relabeled it the *Gospel of the Ebionites*.[113] The title may be a misnomer if he came across this Gospel at Cyprus and was wrong in thinking that its author was an Ebionite.[114] The fragmentary evidence of the *Gospel of the Ebionites* does not show any signs of harmonizing the Synoptic Gospels with John's Gospel, but this may be a precarious reason for dating it before the harmony of all four Gospels in the *Diatessaron* in the latter half of the second century.[115]

In the first fragment that Epiphanius cited from it, the apostles as a group, or one of them in particular, muse in the first person about how Jesus chose "us" when he was around thirty years old.[116] The twelve apostles were chosen to be a testimony to Israel.[117] This is why some, but not all, scholars equate the *Gospel of the Ebionites* with the text that Origen entitled the *Gospel of the Twelve*.[118] Matthew is named last and Jesus

---

113. Daniel A. Bertrand, "L'Évangile des Ebionites: une harmonie évangelique antérieur au Diatessaron," *NTS* 26 (1980): 550–63; Vielhauer and Strecker, "Jewish Christian Gospels," 166–71; Klijn and Reinink, *Patristic Evidence*, 30–31; Klijn, *Gospel Tradition*, 27–28, 30, 38–39, 41, 65–77; Klauck, *Apocryphal Gospels*, 51–54; Bauckham, "The Origin of the Ebionites," 164, 172; Verheyden, "Epiphanius," 188–200; Häkkinen, "Ebionites," 262–63; Skarsaune, "The Ebionites," 457–61; Luomanen, *Jewish-Christian Sects*, 83, 145–61, 251–52; Paget, *Jews*, 339–41; Mimouni, *Early Judaeo-Christianity*, 177–78, 181–82, 221–33; Kok, "Did Papias of Hierapolis Use," 43–44; Gregory, *The Gospel*, 8, 10, 171–261. For example, one can compare the harmonization of the Synoptic baptism accounts in the *Gospel of the Ebionites* below (cf. 30.13.7–8) with the dissimilar account of Jesus's baptism in the Hebrew Gospel that the Nazoreans used according to Jerome (*Comm. Isa.* 11.1–3).
114. Skarsaune, "The Ebionites," 461.
115. For critiques of dating the *Gospel of the Ebionites* earlier than the Diatessaron on these grounds, see H. J. W. Drijvers and G. J. Reinink, "Taufe und Licht: Tatian, Ebionäerevangelium und Thomasakten" in *Text and Testimony: Essays on New Testament and Apocryphal Literature in Honour of A. F. J. Klijn* (ed. T. Baarda, A. Hilhorst, G. P. Lutikhuizen, and S. J. van der Woude; Kampen: J. H. Kok, 1988), 104; Gregory, *The Gospel*, 182; contra Bertrand, "L'Évangile des Ebionites," 551; Klijn, *Jewish Christian Gospel Tradition*, 29; Mimouni, *Early Judaeo-Christianity*, 223.
116. See Epiphanius, *Pan.* 30.13.2–3. Jesus's age is specified in Luke 3:23. Interestingly, the elders in Asia Minor who saw John, the Lord's disciple, took John 8:57 to imply that Jesus lived into his forties (cf. Irenaeus, *Haer.* 2.22.5).
117. The closest parallel is the double tradition saying about Jesus's disciples sitting on twelve thrones, judging the twelve tribes of Israel in the eschaton (cf. Matt 19:28//Luke 22:30).
118. See Origen, *Hom. Luc.* 1.2. See Waitz, "Das Evangelium der zwölf Apostel," 347; Waitz, "Neue Untersuchung," 71; Bertrand, "L'Évangile des Ebionites," 553–54; Evans, "The Jewish Christian Gospel Tradition," 250; Mimouni, *Early Judaeo-Christianity*, 222. Other scholars are skeptical about this identification. See Schmidtke, *Neue Fragment,*

addresses him in the second person, reminding him that he was sitting at his customs house when he was called. Epiphanius may have adduced this as evidence that this was the Ebionites' corrupted version of Matthew's Gospel.[119] The text has replicated a Matthean redactional trait by locating Matthew, not Levi, at the tollbooth.[120] Yet it does not explicitly state that the tax collector Matthew was the author. This Gospel could have been pseudonymously ascribed to any one of the twelve apostles or to the whole group collectively.

Epiphanius was shocked that this Gospel excluded Jesus's geneology,[121] since the Ebionites were so adamant about Jesus's mere humanity.[122] In Epiphanius's excerpts from the *Gospel of the Ebionites* on John's baptizing ministry, there are parallels to unique details in all three Synoptic Gospels. It sets up the scene as follows:

> *"It happened in the days of Herod king of Judea that there came*
> *John baptizing a baptism of repentance in the Jordan river, who is*
> *said to be of the family of Aaron the priest, son of Zachariah and*
> *Elisabeth, and all went out to him."*[123]

When Epiphanius repeats this summary about John baptizing in the days of Herod, the king of Judea, he adds that this also took place

---

170–75; Schmidtke, "Zum Hebräerevangelium," 31–32; Vielhauer and Strecker, "Jewish Christian Gospels," 166; Klijn, *Jewish Christian Gospel Tradition*, 28; Klauck, *Apocryphal Gospels*, 53–54; Gregory, *The Gospel*, 180, 204. Vielhauer and Strecker ("Jewish Christian Gospels," 166) are not even sure that this fragment belongs to the *Gospel of the Ebionites* because the other fragments do not employ the first-person pronoun, but its style may differ from the rest of the fragments because it was the incipit that identified the pseudonymous apostolic author(s) of the text. See Frey, "Die Fragmente des Ebionäervangeliums," 611; Gregory, *The Gospel*, 195.

119. Klijn, *Jewish-Christian Gospel Tradition*, 66; Verheyden, "Epiphanius," 195–96; Gregory, *The Gospel*, 204.

120. See Matt 9:9 (contra Mark 2:14; Luke 5:27).

121. See Epiphanius, *Pan.* 30.14.3.

122. Verheyden, "Epiphanius," 193. This is one of the reasons why Skarsaune ("The Ebionites," 458) argues that Epiphanius discovered this Gospel after writing an earlier draft of his chapter on the Ebionites. He may have initially expected that the Ebionites were trying to prove from Matthew's genealogy that Jesus was the descendant of David because he was the biological son of Joseph.

123. See Epiphanius, *Pan.* 30.13.6. For this translation, see Gregory, *The Gospel*, 207.

when Caiaphas was the high priest.[124] Luke introduces John's parents as Zechariah, a priest in the order of Abijah, and Elizabeth, the descendant of Aaron.[125] Luke also dated John's baptizing ministry to the time of the tetrarchy of Herod Antipas and the high priesthood of Annas and Caiaphas.[126] Technically Caiaphas was appointed as the high priest in 18 CE, but his father-in-law Annas who was the ex-high-priest may have still wielded some political clout. Herod the Great, the king of Judea from 37 to 4 BCE, was mixed up with Herod Antipas, the tetrarch of Galilee from 4 BCE to 39 CE, in the *Gospel of the Ebionites*. The mistake was due to jumping from Luke's first reference to a Herod when Zechariah was serving as a priest to Luke's second reference to a Herod when the Baptizer was in the wilderness.[127] By doing so, the author rejected not only Luke's genealogy but the entire infancy narrative as well. John the Baptizer is characterized in the *Gospel of the Ebionites* in the following manner:

> *"It happened that John was baptizing, and there went out to him Pharisees, and they were baptized, and all Jerusalem. And John had a garment of camel's hair and a leather belt about his waist. And his food . . . was wild honey, the taste of which was manna, like a cake in oil."*[128]

---

124. See Epiphanius, *Pan.* 30.14.3. For the translated text, see Gregory, *The Gospel*, 207–8.

125. See Luke 1:5–24, 57–80.

126. See Luke 3:1–2.

127. See Luke 1:5; 3:1. See Bertrand, "L'Évangile des Ebionites," 555; Klijn, *Jewish Christian Gospel Tradition*, 69; Verheyden, "Epiphanius," 192n.48, 194n.57; Mimouni, *Early Judaeo-Christianity*, 227; Gregory, *The Gospel*, 213–14. David B. Sloan challenges the thesis that the *Gospel of the Ebionites* was dependent on Luke's Gospel, arguing that the reverse is the case. See David B. Sloan, "What if the Gospel of the Hebrews was Q?" Paper presented to the Q Section at the Annual Meeting of the Society of Biblical Literature (Boston, November 2017), 7. This paper can be found online at www.reconstructingq.com/gospel-of-the-hebrews.pdf. He posits that Luke may have reproduced the incipit of his source in 3:1–3 but made corrections and improvements along the way. In this case, Luke corrected Herod Antipas's political title and added Annas alongside Caiaphas. However, it seems easier to explain how a much later author, ignorant of the political situation in Galilee during the adult years of John the Baptizer, made an inadvertent error in skipping from Luke 1:5 to 3:1.

128. See Epiphanius, *Pan.* 30.13.4. For this translation, see Gregory, *The Gospel*, 218.

This excerpt draws on the Gospels of Mark and Matthew.[129] It follows Mark's sequence in first introducing John, then summarizing how the people of Jerusalem went out to be baptized by him, and lastly describing John's clothing and diet.[130] But it is only in Matthew's Gospel that the Pharisees approach John to be baptized.[131] One notable difference from these Gospels, however, is the description of the honey that the Baptizer ate. It tasted like a cake dipped in oil, which was an allusion to the manna that the ancient Israelites ate during their sojourn in the wilderness.[132] There is a pun between the words for "cake" (*egkris*) and "locust" (*akris*) that really only works in Greek.[133] This Greek pun makes it unlikely that this Gospel was translated from a Semitic language.[134] Finally, the aftermath of Jesus's baptism is narrated as follows:

> "When the people had been baptized, there came also Jesus, and he was baptized by John. And, as he came up from the water, there opened the heavens and he saw the Holy Spirit in a form of a dove, coming down and entering into him. And a voice from heaven, saying, 'you are my son, the beloved one, in you I am well pleased.' And again, 'today I have begotten you.' And immediately there shone around the place a great light. When he saw it… John said to him, 'who are you, lord?' And again, a voice from heaven came to him, 'this is my son, the beloved in whom I am well pleased.' And then… John fell down before him and said, 'I entreat you lord, you baptize me.' But he prevented him, saying, 'Let things be, for in this way it is fitting that all things be fulfilled.'"[135]

---

129. See Bertrand, "L'Évangile des Ebionites," 555; Klijn, *Jewish Christian Gospel Tradition*, 67–68; Mimouni, *Early Judaeo-Christianity*, 226; Gregory, *The Gospel*, 218–22.
130. See Mark 1:4–6. John's widespread fame is narrated after the description of his clothing and diet in Matt 3:1, 4–6. Luke omits the description of John's appearance and his diet of locusts and honey altogether.
131. See Matt 3:7.
132. See LXX Exod 16:31; Num 11:8.
133. Bertrand, "L'Évangile des Ebionites," 555; Vielhauer and Strecker, "Jewish Christian Gospels," 167; Klijn, *Jewish Christian Gospel Tradition*, 68; Klauck, *Apocryphal Gospels*, 51; Evans, "The Jewish Christian Gospel Tradition," 250; Gregory, *The Gospel*, 224.
134. Contra Edwards, *The Hebrew Gospel*, 26–27; Mimouni, *Early Judaeo-Christianity*, 223.
135. See Epiphanius, *Pan.* 30.13.7–8. For this translation, see Gregory, *The Gospel*, 225–26.

This excerpt draws on all three Synoptic Gospels.[136] "The holy spirit" literally, not figuratively, takes the "form" (*eidos*) of a dove and descends "into" (*eis*) Jesus, setting him apart from the rest of the people who were baptized that day. There are echoes of the distinctive vocabulary used in Mark's and Luke's baptism accounts.[137] The voice from heaven addresses Jesus three times.[138] The conversation between Jesus and John again reproduces Matthew's redaction of Mark's Gospel.[139] In Matthew's Gospel, John pleads with Jesus to be baptized by him when they had just met. It may have seemed more appropriate to the author of the *Gospel of the Ebionites* to have John react in this way after seeing the great light that shone around the area and hearing the heavenly voice. The detail about the light, however, is first attested in Tatian's *Diatessaron*. His own teacher, Justin, had already taken some creative license with the Synoptic Gospels in imagining that a fire was kindled in the Jordan river, which Tatian changed to a light shining from heaven.[140]

Although the *Gospel of the Ebionites* has harmonizing features,[141] it was not strictly a harmony of the Synoptic Gospels. It has a distinct theology in

---

136. See Bertrand, "L'Évangile des Ebionites," 557; Vielhauer and Strecker, "Jewish Christian Gospels," 167; Klijn, *Jewish Christian Gospel Tradition*, 71–73; Klauck, *Apocryphal Gospels*, 52–53; Mimouni, *Early Judaeo-Christianity*, 227–28; Evans, "The Jewish Christian Gospel Tradition," 251–52; Gregory, *The Gospel*, 227–40.

137. See Mark 1:10; Luke 3:22.

138. See Mark 1:11; Luke 3:22 (D); Matt 3:17.

139. See Matt 3:14–15.

140. See Justin, *Dial.* 88.3; Ephrem, *Comm.* 4.5. For Tatian's influence on the *Gospel of the Ebionites*, see Drijvers and Reinink, "Taufe und Licht," 92–93, 95, 98–102. The light tradition is also interpolated between Matt 3:15–16 in Codex Vercellensis and Codex Sangermanensis, two Old Latin manuscripts.

141. See Bertrand, "L'Évangile des Ebionites," 553–57; Vielhauer and Strecker, "Jewish Christian Gospels," 167–68; Klijn, *Jewish Christian Gospel Tradition*, 65–73; Klauck, *Apocryphal Gospels*, 52–53; Verheyden, "Epiphanius," 190–99; Evans, "The Jewish Christian Gospel Tradition," 250–52; Mimouni, *Early Judaeo-Christianity*, 224–28; Gregory, *The Gospel*, 196–200, 209–11, 218–20, 227–30. Edwards (*Hebrew Gospel*, 66–72) counters that the Gospel that Epiphanius cited was the source of the Lukan special material, but this contradicts his own conclusion that there are thirteen clear and fourteen possible parallels to Luke's Gospel, six clear and five possible parallels to Matthew's Gospel, and three clear and three possible parallels to Mark's Gospel. He underestimates some of the other parallels to the Gospels of Matthew and Mark. Sloan ("What If," 6–8) equates Epiphanius's Gospel with Q. However, the conversation between John the Baptizer and Jesus and the placement of Matthew at the tollbooth may reflect Matthean redaction. If these details were in Q, it seems strange that Luke missed them. Instead, Luke 3:20 dodges the potentially troublesome implications that

its own right.[142] It pictures Jesus as an ordinary human before he received the spirit at his baptism, which was accompanied by the heavenly light and the proclamations about his divine sonship. In addition to its omission of locusts from John's diet, it tweaks a verse in Luke's Gospel to make Jesus say that he desired to "not" eat the Passover meal with his disciples.[143] Both passages may promote vegetarianism.[144] In another verse from the "Gospel" (*euangelion*), the purpose of Jesus's coming was to abolish sacrifice and his hearers were warned that they would suffer divine wrath if they did not cease sacrificing.[145] In the end, Epiphanius was trying to make sense out of the traditions from Papias that Matthew's Gospel was translated from a Semitic language, from Irenaeus that the Ebionites loved Matthew's Gospel, and from Eusebius that the Ebionites possessed the *Gospel According to the Hebrews*. He was mistaken in thinking that the Gospel that he discovered had anything to do with Matthew, the *Gospel According to the Hebrews*, or the Ebionites. He had stumbled upon a Greek text that was dependent on the Synoptic Gospels and used it along with other sources to construct his peculiar profile of the Ebionites.

Jerome and the Nazoreans' Edition of Matthew's Gospel

One of Epiphanius's friends was his younger contemporary Jerome.[146] Jerome was born in Stridon in Italy around 347 CE. His Christian parents

---

Jesus was baptized by John by locking John up in prison before Jesus's baptism. Likewise, Luke 5:27 agrees with Mark 2:14 in placing Levi at the tollbooth.

142. Verheyden, "Epiphanius," 188; contra Bertrand, "L'Évangile des Ebionites," 550–51, 561–63.

143. See Epiphanius, *Pan.* 30.22.4 (contra Luke 22:15).

144. See Klijn and Reinink, *Patristic Evidence*, 31; Vielhauer and Strecker, "Jewish Christian Gospels," 168; Klijn, *Gospel Tradition*, 41, 68, 77; Klauck, *Apocryphal Gospels*, 51–52; Häkkinen, "Ebionites," 262; Edwards, *The Hebrew Gospel*, 76; Luomanen, *Recovering*, 37; Gregory, *The Gospel*, 223–26, 253–54, 258–59. Skarsaune ("The Ebionites," 459–60) is less certain that the author of the *Gospel of the Ebionites* was a vegetarian. When Epiphanius was refuting the Ebionites' vegetarianism, he noted that Jesus ate meat and drank wine in contrast to the Baptizer (30.19.1–3; cf. Matt 11:18–19). Locusts may not have qualified as meat for him. Skarsaune attributes the latter passage in *Pan.* 30.22.4 about the Passover to the *Circuits of Peter*.

145. See Epiphanius, *Pan.* 30.16.5.

146. For a study on Jerome's life and thought, see Stefan Rebenich, *Jerome* (The Early Church Fathers; London: Routledge, 2002), 1–69; Pritz, *Nazarene Jewish Christianity*, 48–51;

ensured that he had a good rhetorical education and he moved to Trier in Gaul, where he planned to embark on a career. It was here that he decided to pursue a Christian vocation. He returned to Aquileia and became connected with a monastic community. Afterwards, he traveled to Syrian Antioch and then retreated to the wilderness of Chalcis ad Belum about twenty-seven kilometers southwest of the Syrian town of Beroea around 375 CE. While enjoying the monastic life, he was trained in Hebrew by a Jewish Christian. He returned to Antioch around 377 CE where he was ordained as a priest and had the privilege of listening to the lectures of Apollinaris, the bishop of Laodicea. He did not anticipate that Apollinaris would be officially condemned at the First Council of Constantinople in 381 CE. Next, he moved to Constantinople, where he became connected with the bishop Gregory of Nazianzus, and then on to Rome where he was hired by the bishop Damasus I to work in the ecclesiastical archive in 382 CE. He traveled further after the death of Damasus and his failed ambition to be ordained as the next bishop of Rome, but he settled in Bethlehem as his final place of residence in 386 CE. He was a gifted linguist and prolific author whose lasting contribution was his translation of biblical books into Latin.

Jerome may have had some personal interactions with the Nazoreans when he lived near Beroea. Although no one before Epiphanius and Jerome gave detailed accounts about the Nazoreans, there is no doubt about the antiquity of their title.[147] This does not mean that a straight line of continuity can be drawn from the Jewish Christ-followers in the first century to the Nazoreans in the fourth century.[148] The Jewish Nazoreans could have also been a tiny faction that was making their peace with the larger body of Catholic Christians in the fourth century.[149] The last option is that the Nazoreans may not have been a sect at all. The title may have been in popular

---

Broadhead, *Jewish Ways of Following Jesus*, 164; Luomanen, *Recovering Jewish Christian Sects*, 67–68.

147. See, for instance, Acts 24:5; Tertullian, *Marc.* 4.8.1. See the extensive analysis of the nomenclature in Simon Claude Mimouni, "Les Nazoréens Recherche Étymologique Et Historique" *Revue Biblique* 105.2 (1998): 216–60.

148. Many scholars make this mistake. See Pritz, *Nazarene Jewish Christianity*, 14–17, 39, 75; de Boer, "The Nazoreans," 243–45, 252; Bauckham, "The Origin," 162–63; Kinzig, "The Nazoraeans," 481; Broadhead, *Jewish Ways*, 163, 178–79, 186; Mimouni, *Early Judaeo-Christianity*, 63–66.

149. Schmidtke, *Neue Fragmente*, 41–42, 105, 124–25, 301–2.

use among non-Greek or non-Latin Christ-followers who did not adopt the title "Christians" for themselves.[150] This is not to say that some of the people known as Nazoreans were not ethnically Jewish.[151]

Jerome seems to corroborate Epiphanius's information about the Nazoreans in his epistolary correspondence with Augustine, the bishop of Hippo, around 394–95 CE.[152] They began trading letters when Augustine objected to Jerome's commentary on Paul's epistle to the Galatians. Jerome had interpreted Paul's public rebuke of Peter as a hypocrite when he discontinued eating with non-Jews when pressured from emissaries from James as a staged conflict.[153] The two apostles pretended to fight over the appropriateness of table fellowship between Jews and non-Jews in the Christ assemblies in order to help their audience come to a resolution on this issue. In Jerome's view, the goal of the apostles was for their audience to realize that they were no longer under the dispensation of the Mosaic law but were formed as a community together by grace. Although Jerome was defending Peter's reputation after he was slammed by a non-Christian critic, Augustine was offended by his allegation that the apostles acted deceitfully. Instead, Augustine admitted that the earliest, ethnically Jewish Christ followers were permitted to keep their customs.

Jerome raised the counterexample of the Nazoreans as part of his counterargument against Augustine.[154] Their affirmations of Jesus's messiahship, divine sonship, virginal conception, suffering under Pilate, and resurrection were orthodox by the standards of the Nicene Creed. Yet they did not stop observing the *Torah*. Like Epiphanius before him, Jerome put the Nazoreans forward as a case study for why it was impossible for people to maintain their Jewish and Christian identities at the same time.

---

150. Kinzig, "The Nazoraeans," 470–71; Luomanen, *Recovering*, 51–53; Gregory, *The Gospel*, 291, 293, 300.
151. Although he argues that the author of the Nazorean commentary on Isaiah was basically aligned with the beliefs and practices of other Catholic Christians, Luomanen concedes that some of the Nazoraeans may have been ethnically Jewish. See Luomanen, "The Nazarenes," 60.
152. For a helpful contextualization of Jerome's comments about the Nazoraeans in his objections to Augustine's exegesis of the Antioch incident in Gal 2:11–14, see Mimouni, *Early Judaeo-Christianity*, 114–25.
153. See Jerome, *Comm. Gal.* 1.prol. II (cf. Gal 2:11–14).
154. See Jerome, *Ep.* 112.13.

They were not welcome in Christian or in Jewish communities, for a benediction had been formulated against them in the synagogue. Elsewhere, Jerome seems to have taken the insertion of Nazarenes in the "blessing against the heretics" (*birkat ha-minim*) in the twelfth benediction of the synagogue prayers as targeting all Christians.[155] Jerome's letter may offer scholars a window into the Nazoreans' creedally-orthodox Christology.[156] Epiphanius admitted that he did not know what the Nazoreans believed about the virgin birth, so Jerome may have had independent information.[157] Nevertheless, since Jerome was trying to score points in an extended debate with Augustine, he may not be an objective source on the Nazoreans' beliefs.[158]

Generally, Jerome was positive, or at least neutral, toward the Nazoreans. One of his gripes about the stupidity of the first-century residents of Nazareth for not discerning that Jesus was more than the son of a carpenter has been misread in reference to the fourth-century Christian Nazoreans.[159] Jerome benefited from the Nazoreans' insights, for he repeatedly consulted a commentary on the book of Isaiah by someone

---

155. There is no evidence that *notzrim* was inserted into the benediction until the fourth century. Some scholars agree with Epiphanius that this revision of the *birkat ha-minim* targeted the Nazoreans. See Reuven Kimelman, "Birkat Ha-Minim and the Lack of Evidence for an Anti-Christian Jewish Prayer in Late Antiquity" in *Jewish and Christian Self-Definition* (2 vols.; ed. E. P. Sanders; Philadelphia: Fortress, 1981), 237–38; Pritz, *Nazarene Jewish Christianity*, 102–7; Joel Marcus, "*Birkat Ha-Minim* Revisited" *NTS* 55.4 (2009): 537–40; Mimouni, *Early Judaeo-Christianity*, 144–47, 154–55. Others argue that it cursed Christians in general. See Lawrence Schiffman, *Who Was a Jew? Rabbinic and Halakhic Perspectives on the Jewish-Christian Schism* (Hoboken: Ktav, 1985), 57–60; Pieter W. Van den Horst, "The Birkat ha-minim in Recent Research" *ExpTim* 105 (1994–1995): 267–68; William Horbury, *Jews and Christians in Contact and Controversy* (Edinburgh: T&T Clark, 1998), 73–77, 109; Boyarin, *Border Lines*, 71–72, 262n.90; Ruth Langer, *Cursing the Christians: A History of the Birkat HaMinim* (Oxford: Oxford University Press, 2012), 31–32, 269–70n.85.
156. Pritz, *Nazarene Jewish Christianity*, 53–55; De Boer, "The Nazoreans," 240; Mimouni, *Early Judaeo-Christianity*, 122–23.
157. Kinzig, "The Nazoraeans," 474.
158. Luomanen, *Recovering*, 27, 68–71; Luomanen, "The Nazarenes," 64–66; Gregory, *The Gospel*, 298.
159. See Jerome, *Comm. Matt.* 13.53–54. This misreading is found in Klijn and Reinink, *Patristic Evidence*, 47. This mistake is corrected in Pritz, *Nazarene Jewish Christianity*, 54–55; Kinzig, "The Nazoraeans," 474n.56; Broadhead, *Jewish Ways of Following Jesus*, 173.

self-identifying as a Nazorean.[160] Its exegesis is marked by the commentator's polemical engagement with the representatives of Rabbinic Judaism. The commentator hoped that the children of Israel might join the tributaries of the church.[161] In the exposition of another Isaianic passage,[162] the light that shone out from the land of Zebulon and the land of Naphthali was the preaching of Christ, which freed the people from the errors of the scribes and Pharisees and shook off the heavy yoke of the Jewish traditions. Then, Paul multiplied the preaching of the gospel to the most distant tribes around the world, freeing them from their enslavement to idols and to the power of death.

The ecclesiology in the commentary seems aligned with a Catholic worldview and the commentator may have demeaned the *Torah* itself as a yoke that was cast aside.[163] However, it is unlikely that the Law of Moses was criticized. It may be the oral traditions of the Pharisees, and their rabbinic successors, that were characterized as burdensome. There may be a parallel in how Jesus could denounce the oral traditions of the Pharisees and exhort his hearers to take on his light yoke, while upholding the Law of Moses as unalterable in Matthew's Gospel.[164] This Nazorean commentator may have tolerated Paul's "law-free" mission to the nations, while remaining *Torah*-observant as a Jewish follower of Jesus.

Jerome is adamant that he received the *Gospel According to the Hebrews*, which was an older Semitic version of Matthew's Gospel, from the Nazoreans to translate. His readers could check out the Gospel for themselves by searching for it in Pamphilus's library in Caesarea.[165] Some of Jerome's citations from the text helped him solve translation issues and show that he was

---

160. See Jerome, *Comm. Isa.* 8.11–15, 19–22; 9.1; 11.1; 29.17–21; 31.6–9. For analysis of the commentary, see Pritz, *Nazarene Jewish Christianity*, 57–70; Klijn and Reinink, *Patristic Evidence*, 49–50; Kinzig, "The Nazoraeans," 475–77; Broadhead, *Jewish Ways*, 166–71; Luomanen, *Recovering*, 71–75.

161. See Jerome, *Comm. Isa.* 31.6–9.

162. See Jerome, *Comm. Isa.* 9.1.

163. Luomanen, "The Nazarenes," 62.

164. See Matt 5:18; 11:29–30; 15:3–9.

165. See Jerome, *Vir. ill.* 3; *Pelag.* 3.2. Some scholars accept that Jerome was telling the truth that he had access to the *Gospel According to the Hebrews*, which he copied and translated. See Pritz, *Nazarene Jewish Christianity*, 83, 86–87; Kinzig, "The Nazoraeans," 473; Beatrice, "Apostolic Fathers," 154–58, 169–76; Edwards, *The Hebrew Gospel*, 28–37, 76–96, 102–7.

working with a source or sources in a Semitic language.[166] At other times, Jerome seems to have been untruthful when he plagiarized past Greek Christian writers who quoted the *Gospel According to the Hebrews* and passed off their citations as his own translations. His alleged translations of the line about the Holy Spirit, described as Jesus's mother, lifting Jesus up by his hairs looks suspiciously like it was borrowed from Origen's commentaries. Origen quotes the *Gospel According to the Hebrews* as saying that the Holy Spirit carried Jesus by one of his hairs to Mount Tabor.[167]

The most blatant example of plagiarism is from a quotation from the risen Jesus that Jerome claimed that he found in the *Gospel According to the Hebrews*. Ignatius of Antioch had professed that "I know" (*oida*) and "I believe" (*pisteuō*) that Jesus was raised in the flesh, for the risen Jesus invited those who were with Peter to "take hold of me, handle me and see that I am not a bodiless daimon."[168] A daimon is a spirit. The reassurance that Jesus did not rise as a "bodiless daimon" (*daimonion asōmatos*) may be Ignatius's free paraphrase of the risen Jesus's assurance to his disciples that he was not a "spirit" (*pneuma*) and had "flesh" (*sarx*) and bones in Luke's Gospel.[169] The variations in wording, however, may make an intertextual relationship hard to demonstrate.[170] Origen found the saying "I am not a bodiless daimon" in a text entitled the *Doctrina Petri* or the *Teaching of Peter*.[171] Eusebius was at a loss about what may have been Ignatius's source for the saying and quotes the larger context in which Ignatius cited the saying in his epistle to the Smyrneans as follows:

> *"For I know and believe that after the resurrection he was in the flesh. And when he came to those who were with Peter, he said to them, 'Take hold of me, handle me and see that I am not a bodiless daimon.'"*[172]

---

166. See, for instance, Jerome, *Ep.* 20.5; *Tract. Ps.* 135; *Comm. Matt.* 2.5; 6.11; 23.35.
167. See, for instance, Jerome, *Comm. Mich.* 7.6; *Comm. Isa* 40.9–11; *Comm. Ezech.* 16.13; cf. Origen, *Comm. Jo.* 2.12.87; *Hom. Jer.* 15.4.
168. See Ignatius, *Smyrn.* 3.1–2. For this translation, see Gregory, *The Gospel*, 275.
169. See Luke 24:39. See Vielhauer and Strecker, "Jewish Christian Gospels," 144–45; Frey, "Die Fragmente judenchristlicher Evangelien," 585.
170. See Gregory, *The Reception of Luke*, 70–75; Beatrice, "Apostolic Fathers," 148.
171. See Origen, *Princ.* I *pref.* 8. For this translation, see Gregory, *The Gospel*, 274–75.
172. See Eusebius, *H.E.* 3.36.11. For this translation, see Gregory, *The Gospel*, 276.

Jerome was happy to be the one to break the news that he had found the saying in the *Gospel According to the Hebrews*. He must have forgotten that Origen ascribed the saying to another source, but the evidence that he dishonestly lifted it from Eusebius is that he also has the words "I saw" (*vidi*) and "I believe" (*credo*) as part of the quote about Jesus not being bodiless after his resurrection.[173] Like Papias, it is unlikely that the early second-century bishop Ignatius was a witness to the *Gospel According to the Hebrews*.[174] Jerome does not admit the extent to which he relied on earlier Greek commentators for his knowledge of the *Gospel According to the Hebrews*. Even so, it may be going too far to deny that Jerome had not obtained some text from the Nazoreans.

The following historical scenario has a ring of plausibility.[175] Jerome had received some samples from the Gospel that the Nazoreans were reading in their own language and translated them. He supposed that the extracts that the Nazoreans supplied him with came from the same work that previous Christian commentators had identified as the *Gospel According to the Hebrews*. Since Eusebius had referred to a Gospel that had "come to us" in the Hebrew language,[176] Jerome took it as a given that the *Gospel According*

---

173. See Jerome, *Vir. ill.* 16; cf. *Comm. Isa.* 65.prol. See Vielhauer and Strecker, "Jewish Christian Gospels," 144–45; Klijn, *Jewish-Christian Gospel Tradition*, 123; Luomanen, *Recovering*, 96, 108; Frey, "Die Fragmente judenchristlicher Evangelien," 585; Kok, "Did Papias of Hierapolis," 45–46; Gregory, *The Gospel*, 275–79.

174. Beatrice ("The Gospel," 154–63) defends the attribution of Ignatius's saying to the *Gospel According to the Hebrews*. He notes that there is a textual variant in a Latin translation of Ignatius's epistle to the Smyrneans that has *vidi* ("I saw"). He adds that the "I" who saw Jesus in the flesh after his resurrection was not Ignatius but the apostle Matthew as the author of the *Gospel According to the Hebrews*. There are a number of problems with this thesis. First, he notes that Matthew may be the speaker who uses the first-person plural pronoun in Epiphanius's citation of his Gospel (cf. *Pan.* 30.13.2–3), but this is not explicit and, in any case, the arguments for distinguishing Epiphanius's *Gospel of the Ebionites* from the *Gospel According to the Hebrews* are convincing. In chapter three, it was shown that Papias was not referring to the content of the *Gospel According to the Hebrews* as Matthew's oracles. Second, Jerome has also included the verb *credo* ("I believe") in the quote because he copied it from Eusebius. Third, this is not a solitary instance of Jerome relying on earlier Greek quotations of the *Gospel According to the Hebrews*.

175. Luomanen, *Recovering*, 100–101; 127–28.

176. See Eusebius, *Theoph. fr.* 4.12, 22. For doubts that Eusebius was referring to the same text as the *Gospel According to the Hebrews*, see Gregory, *The Gospel*, 35–36, 141–42, 143–44.

to the Hebrews was housed in the library at Caesarea and planned to track it down. He greatly exaggerated the extent to which he translated the Nazoreans' entire Gospel. However, this was not out of character for Jerome, for he bragged that he had completed his translations of the Old and New Testament when he had just begun translating them.[177]

What Gospel did the Nazoreans have in their possession if it was not the *Gospel According to the Hebrews*? It may have been another lost Gospel that modern scholars have entitled the *Gospel of the Nazoreans*.[178] No one coined a title like this until the ninth century.[179] This hypothetical Gospel has often been characterized as resembling the Gospel of Matthew, but some of the fragments assigned to it are not paralleled in the Gospel of Matthew.[180] Other fragments that have nothing in common with Matthew's Gospel tend to get assigned to the *Gospel According to the Hebrews* that Jerome only knew secondhand through the commentaries on it that he had read. For instance, Jerome asserted that the *Gospel According to the Hebrews* that he purportedly translated into Greek and Latin narrates that the risen Jesus appeared to his brother James, because "James had sworn that he would not eat bread from that hour in which he had drunk the cup of the Lord, until he would see him rising from those who sleep."[181] The Gospel of Matthew pays almost no attention to James. Jesus's brothers and sisters are briefly named by the residents of Nazareth, who were incredulous that Jesus was claiming to be a prophet when they had known his family from his childhood, and Mary is identified as the mother of James and Joseph.[182]

---

177. See Jerome, *Vir. ill.* 135.
178. Vielhauer and Strecker, "Jewish Christian Gospels," 154–65; Klijn and Reinink, *Patristic Evidence*, 47–49; Klijn, Jewish Christian Gospel Tradition, 29–30, 31–32; Klauck, *The Apocryphal Gospels*, 43–51; Broadhead, *Jewish Ways of Following Jesus*, 164–66, 172–73; Frey, "Die Fragmente des Nazoräerevangeliums," 623–54.
179. Pritz, *Nazarene Jewish Christianity*, 85–86; Edwards, *Hebrew Gospel*, 121–22; Klauck, *Apocryphal Gospels*, 49–50.
180. See, for instance, Jerome, *Comm. Eph.* 5.4; *Comm. Ezech.* 18.5–9; *Pelag.* 3.2.
181. See Jerome, *Vir. Ill.* 2. For this translation, see Gregory, *The Gospel*, 98. This passage is frequently assigned to the *Gospel According to the Hebrews* by defenders of the three Gospel hypothesis. See Vielhauer and Strecker, "Jewish Christian Gospels," 178; Klijn, *Jewish Christian Gospel Tradition*, 79–86; Klauck, *The Apocryphal Gospels*, 42–43; Frey, "Die Fragmente des Hebräerevangeliums," 604–5.
182. See Matt 13:55 (cf. Mark 6:3); 27:56 (cf. Mark 15:40).

The criteria for distinguishing a hypothetical *Gospel of the Nazoreans*, which looked like Matthew's Gospel and was written in a Semitic language, from the "apocryphal" *Gospel According to the Hebrews* may be insufficient.[183] The *Gospel According to the Hebrews* may have contained material that has parallels with both Synoptic and noncanonical traditions, much like the *Gospel of Thomas* does. It could have also been translated into different languages in the process of its transmission. For the most part, Jerome may have quoted earlier commentators on the *Gospel According to the Hebrews*. For instance, Jerome curiously mentions Origen as an avid reader of the *Gospel According to the Hebrews* in the same context that he mentions the tradition about the resurrection appearance to James. He may have taken this passage from one of Origen's commentaries.[184] What the Nazoreans may have passed on to Jerome was a handful of passages from their translation of Matthew's Gospel in their own language that he mistakenly thought were from the *Gospel According to the Hebrews* as well. He relied on their excerpts to sort out textual issues in the Gospel of Matthew in his own commentary on the text, including the location of the village of Bethlehem, the wording of one of the petitions in the Lord's Prayer, the identification of the martyred prophet Zechariah, the meaning of the name Barabbas, or the cause of the tearing of the temple curtain.[185]

Jerome was overconfident that the *Gospel According to the Hebrews* that was cited by earlier patristic authorities, and that he confused with the Nazoreans' copy of Matthew's Gospel, was a primitive edition of the Gospel of Matthew.[186] His confidence eventually waned. He became more circumspect in noting that many Christians maintained that the *Gospel According to the Hebrews* was authored by Matthew.[187] Unlike Epiphanius, Jerome may have realized too late that the *Gospel According to the Hebrews* was a separate

---

183. For the following arguments countering the three Gospel hypothesis, see Luomanen, *Recovering*, 84–85; Kok, "Did Papias of Hierapolis," 41–43; Mimouni, *Early Judaeo-Christianity*, 182–89; Gregory, *The Gospel*, 14–16; Luomanen, "The Nazarenes," 56–59.

184. Luomanen, *Recovering*, 168, 249–50; Gregory, *The Gospel*, 99.

185. See, for example, Jerome, *Comm. Matt.* 2.5; 6.11; 23.35; 27.16; 27.51. See Luomanen, *Recovering*, 109–14.

186. See Jerome, *Vir. ill.* 3; *Tract. Ps.* 135; *Comm. Matt.* 12.13.

187. See Jerome, *Pelag.* 3.2. See Frey, "Die Fragmente des Nazoräerevangeliums," 626; Gregory, *Gospel*, 50.

text from the Gospel of Matthew all along. Whether he finally got a hold of the *Gospel According to the Hebrews*, or the other Hebrew Gospel that Eusebius mentioned in his work *On Divine Manifestation*, remains a mystery.

In conclusion, the apostle Matthew came to be identified as the author of another Gospel, or rather Gospels, outside of the New Testament canon by the fourth century. This was due to confusing the older patristic references to the *Gospel According to the Hebrews* with Papias's tradition that the Gospel of Matthew was originally written "in the Hebrew language." Alas, it turns out that the supposedly lost Aramaic original of the Greek Gospel of Matthew was not preserved for centuries. It probably never existed in the first place. Instead, the *Gospel According to the Hebrews* and the so-called *Gospel of the Ebionites* should be distinguished from the Gospel of Matthew and studied on their own terms.

CONCLUSION

The Theological Implications of an Anonymous Gospel

MATTHEW WAS ONCE an outcast. Toll collectors were notorious for collecting more than their fair share. At best, there was a negative stigma attached to Matthew's occupation. At worst, Matthew was shunned by his neighbors as a traitor who cooperated with their political oppressors and extorted money from them. His tarnished reputation may have been irreparable if Jesus had not recruited him to be one of his twelve apostles. The rehabilitation of Matthew may be inspirational, regardless of whether he had anything to do with the Gospel bearing his name or not. Nonetheless, millions of Christians throughout the last two millennia have esteemed Matthew as one of the four evangelists. The popularity of the Gospel that was attributed to him soared during the patristic period. Some Christians today may resist any efforts to deconstruct the ancient church traditions about the origins of this Gospel.

There are points where the patristic traditions about the Gospel of Matthew remain quite insightful. They rightly highlighted the importance of the tax collector's call narrative in the Gospel. They were wrong that the Greek text had been translated from Aramaic, but they were right that the implied audience of this Gospel was probably Jewish. The Gospel cannot be fully comprehended without some fluency in biblical and Second Temple Jewish texts and traditions. Crediting the Gospel to an apostolic eyewitness of Jesus performed an apologetic function for the Christians who treasured it over competing renditions of the life of Jesus. Apostolicity was one of the criterions that secured its spot in the New Testament canon.

Additionally, a case could be made that the identification of the evangelists is hermeneutically significant to the interpretation of the four Gospels.[1] It aids exegetes in narrowing down who wrote them, when they

---

1. Gregory Goswell, "Authorship and Anonymity in the New Testament Writings" *JETS* 60.4 (2017): 733, 734.

were written, and to whom they were written to rule out anachronistic interpretations.[2] It enables them to link separate texts together such as the Gospel of Luke and Acts or the Johannine corpus.[3] It may strengthen their trust in the historicity of the events that the evangelists recorded.[4] The traditional names of the New Testament writers display the unity and complementarity of their witnesses to the Christ event. For example, Mark is linked to Peter and Paul, while Luke's Gospel acts as a bridge between the Synoptic tradition and the Pauline letters.[5] The function of an authorial tradition is thus to bestow a particular status on a certain discourse in a specific sociocultural context.[6] The fear is that the "death of the author" will result in the endless multiplication of meanings that readers may impute to a text.[7]

Anonymity, though, was the norm in the historiographical books of the Hebrew Bible and in the historiographical writings in the Ancient Near East.[8] It was commonplace in ancient Jewish literature, whether one looks at the Dead Sea Scrolls or at the anonymous sayings in rabbinic literature.[9] If the reader's gaze is shifted too much to the world behind the text, it may detract from the priority of the subject matter within the text.[10] It is the person of Jesus and the salvation that he ushered into the world that takes center

---

2. Goswell, "Authorship," 735.

3. Goswell, "Authorship," 735. Michel Foucault, one of Goswell's dialogue partners, explains that collecting texts in an authorial corpus implies "a relationship of homogeneity, filiation, authentication of some texts by the use of others, reciprocal explication, or concomitant utilization." See Michel Foucault, "What is an Author?" in *Aesthetics, Method and Epistemology: Volume 2* (ed. James Faubion; trans. Robert Hurley; London: Penguin, 2000), 211.

4. Goswell, "Authorship," 735.

5. Goswell, "Authorship," 738–40, 748–49.

6. Foucault, "What is an Author," 211.

7. Goswell, "Authorship," 734. For instance, Roland Barthes ("The Death of the Author" in *Image-Music-Text* [trans. Stephen Heath; New York: Hill & Wang, 1977], 147) exclaims, "Once the Author is removed, the claim to decipher a text becomes quite futile. To give a text an Author is to impose a limit on that text, to furnish it with a final signified, to close the writing." Likewise, Foucault ("What is an Author," 222) characterizes the author as "the ideological figure by which one marks the manner in which we fear the proliferation of meaning."

8. Armin D. Baum, "Anonymity in the New Testament History Books. A Stylistic Device in the Context of Greco-Roman and Ancient Near Eastern Literature" *NovT* 50 (2008): 127–31, 134–39; cf. Goswell, "Authorship," 747–48.

9. Sanders and Davies, *Studying*, 22–23; Crossley, *The Date*, 15–16.

10. Baum, "Anonymity," 142.

stage in the Gospel of Matthew. Through the literary device of an omniscient narrator, this Gospel minimizes the evangelist's individual vantage point in retelling *the* story of Jesus's life, death, and resurrection.[11] It was a foundational narrative from the outset.

The real author is unknown, but the notion of an "implied author" could function as a control on interpretations. The implied author seems to be a *Torah*-observant, Jewish follower of Jesus who was invested in the question of the continuity of the good news about Jesus with the epic history of Israel. There may be a self-reference in the commendation of the "discipled scribe" who labors for the kingdom of heaven and discovers old and new treasures.[12] There was a lively expectation that Jesus might return in glory before the whole first generation of witnesses to his life had passed away.[13] These eyewitnesses could have been involved in the transmission of the oral Jesus traditions before they were written down. There is internal evidence for the date and provenance of the text. There may be an allusion to the fire that engulfed the Jerusalem temple in 70 CE.[14] Papias, Ignatius, and the editor of the *Didache* knew the Gospel of Matthew. This sets a *terminus a quo* ("limit from which") and the *terminus ad quem* ("limit to which") for dating the text. There is a reason why the evangelist noted that Jesus's fame spread throughout Syria and why one of the earliest readers of the Gospel was a bishop from Antioch.[15] Such clues about the date and provenance may help with grammatical-historical exegesis. Even so, a doctrine of biblical inspiration might demand that meaning transcend the intentions of the historically-located author if Scripture is the "living word of God" that speaks to people in ever-changing sociocultural contexts. For Christians who cherish the Gospel of Matthew as part of their Scripture, it may be a worthwhile exercise to test the received traditions about it through a close reading of the text.

---

11. Sanders and Davies, *Studying*, 22–23.
12. See Matt 13:52. See Schreiner, *Matthew*, 9.
13. See Matt 10:23; 16:28 (cf. Mark 9:1; Luke 9:27).
14. See Matt 22:7; cf. Matt 24:2//Mark 13:2.
15. See Matt 4:24; contra Mark 1:28.

BIBLIOGRAPHY

Abramowski, Luise. "The 'Memoirs of the Apostles' in Justin." In *The Gospel and the Gospels*. Edited by Peter Stuhlmacher, 323–35. Grand Rapids: Eerdmans, 1991.

Achtemeier, Paul J. *1 Peter*. Hermeneia. Minneapolis: Fortress, 1996.

Albright, W. F. and Mann, C. S. *Matthew*. AB. Doubleday: New York, 1971.

Allison, Dale C. *The New Moses: A Matthean Typology*. New Edition. Eugene: Wipf & Stock, 2013.

Andrejevs, Olegs. "A Source-critical Analysis of the Lord's Prayer: Multiple Autonomous Recensions or Q?" *Ephemerides theologicae Lovanienses* 96.4 (2020): 661–79.

Annand, Rupert. "Papias and the Four Gospels." *Scottish Journal of Theology* 9 (1956): 46–62.

Aragione, Gabriella. "Justin, 'philosophe' chrétien, et les 'Mémoires des Apôtres qui sont appelés Évangiles,'" *Apocrypha* 15 (2004): 41–56.

Aune, David E. *Jesus, Gospel Tradition and Paul in the Context of Jewish and Greco-Roman Antiquity*. WUNT 303. Tübingen: Mohr Siebeck, 2013.

Bacon, B. W. "The Elder John, Papias, Irenaeus, Eusebius, and the Syriac Translator." *Journal of Biblical Literature* 27 (1908): 1–23.

———. "The 'Five Books' of Matthew against the Jews." *Expositor* 15 (1918): 56–66.

Bacon, Benjamin. *Studies in Matthew*. New York: Henry Holt 1930.

Barker, J. W. "Written Gospel or Oral Tradition? Patristic Parallels to John 3:3, 5." *Early Christianity* 6 (2015): 543–58.

Barnard, L. W. *Justin Martyr: His Life and Thought*. Cambridge: Cambridge University Press, 1967.

Barthes, Roland. *Image-Music-Text*. Translated by Stephen Heath. New York: Hill & Wang, 1977.

Bartlet, Vernon. "Papias's 'Exposition': Its Date and Contents." In *Amicitiae Corolla: A Volume of Essays Presented to James Rendel Harris, D. Litt. on the Occasion of his Eightieth Birthday*. Edited by H. G. Wood, 15–44. London: University of London Press, 1933.

Bauckham, Richard. "The Origin of the Ebionites." In *The Image of the Judaeo-Christians in Ancient Jewish and Christian Literature*. Edited by Peter J. Tomson and Doris Lambers-Petry, 162–81. WUNT 158. Tübingen: Mohr Siebeck, 2003.

————. "Paul and Other Jews with Latin Names in the New Testament." In *The Jewish World Around the New Testament*. Edited by Richard Bauckham, 371–92. WUNT 233. Tübingen: Mohr Siebeck, 2008.

————. "The Gospel of Mark: Origins and Eyewitnesses." In *Earliest Christian History: History, Literature, and Theology. Essays from the Tyndale Fellowship in Honor of Martin Hengel*. Edited by Michael F. Bird and Jason Maston, 145–69. WUNT 2.320. Tübingen: Mohr Siebeck, 2012.

————. *Jesus and the Eyewitnesses: The Gospels as Eyewitness Testimony*. Second Edition. Grand Rapids: Eerdmans, 2017.

Baum, Armin D. "Papias als Kommentator Evangelischer Aussprüche Jesu." *Novum Testamentum* 38 (1996): 257–76.

————. "Der Presbyter des Papias über einen 'Hermeneuten' des Petrus: Zu Eusebius, Hist. eccl. 3,39,15." *Theologische Zeitschrift* 56 (2000): 21–35.

————. "Ein aramäischer Urmatthäus im kleinasiatischen Gottesdienst. Das Papiaszeugnis zur Entstehung des Matthäusevangeliums." *Zeitschrift für die Neutestamentliche Wissenschaft* 92 (2001): 257–72.

————. "Autobiografische Wir- und Er-Stellen in den neutestamentlichen Geschichtsbüchern im Kontext der antiken Literaturgeschichte." *Biblica* 88 (2007): 473–95.

————. "Anonymity in the New Testament History Books. A Stylistic Device in the Context of Greco-Roman and Ancient Near Eastern Literature." *Novum Testamentum* 50 (2008): 120–42.

————. "The Original Epilogue (John 20:30–31), the Secondary Appendix (21:1–23), and the Editorial Epilogues (21:24–25) of John's Gospel. Observations against the Background of Ancient Literary Conventions." In *Earliest Christian History: History, Literature, and Theology. Essays from the Tyndale Fellowship in Honor of Martin Hengel*. Edited by Michael F. Bird and Jason Maston, 227–70. WUNT 2.320. Tübingen: Mohr Siebeck, 2012.

Beatrice, Pier Franco. "The 'Gospel according to the Hebrews' in the Apostolic Fathers." *Novum Testamentum* 48.2 (2006): 147–95.

BeDuhn, Jason D. "The Myth of Marcion as Redactor: The Evidence of 'Marcion's' Gospel against an Assumed Marcionite Redaction." *Annali Di Storia Dell'Esegesi* 29.1 (2012): 21–48.

Bellinzoni, Arthur J. *The Sayings of Jesus in the Writings of Justin Martyr*. NovTSup 17. Leiden: Brill, 1967.

Bernier, Jonathan. *The Quest for the Historical Jesus after the Demise of Authenticity: Toward a Critical Realist Philosophy of History in Jesus Studies.* LNTS 540. London: T&T Clark, 2016.

Bertrand, Daniel A. "L'Évangile des Ebionites: une harmonie évangelique antérieur au Diatessaron." *New Testament Studies* 26 (1980): 548–63.

Biblia Patristica: Index des citations et allusions bibliques dans la literature patristique. 6 vols. Paris: CNRS Editions, 1975–95.

Bird, Michael F. *Jesus the Eternal Son: Answering Adoptionist Christology.* Grand Rapids: Eerdmans, 2017.

Black, C. Clifton. *Mark: Images of an Apostolic Interpreter.* Second Edition. Minneapolis: Fortress, 2001.

Black, Matthew. "The Use of Rhetorical Terminology in Papias on Mark and Matthew." *Journal for the Study of the New Testament* 37 (1989): 31–41.

Boer, Martinus C. de. "The Nazoraeans: Living at the Boundary of Judaism and Christianity." In *Tolerance and Intolerance in Early Judaism and Christianity.* Edited by Graham N. Stanton and Guy G. Stroumsa, 239–62. Cambridge: Cambridge University Press, 1998.

Boxall, Ian. *Matthew through the Centuries.* Wiley Blackwell Bible Commentaries. Hoboken: Wiley, 2019.

Boyarin, Daniel. *Border Lines: The Partition of Judaeo-Christianity.* Philadelphia: University of Pennsylvania Press, 2004.

———. *The Jewish Gospels: The Story of the Jewish Christ.* New York: The New Press, 2012.

Brent, Allen. *Ignatius of Antioch: A Martyr Bishop and the Origin of the Episcopacy.* London: T&T Clark, 2007.

Broadhead, Edwin K. *Jewish Ways of Following Jesus: Redrawing the Religious Map of Antiquity.* WUNT 266. Tübingen: Mohr Siebeck, 2010.

———. *The Gospel of Matthew on the Landscape of Antiquity.* WUNT 378. Tübingen: Mohr Siebeck, 2017.

Brooks, Bruce E. "Before and After Matthew." In *The Didache: A Missing Piece of the Puzzle in Early Christianity.* Edited by Jonathan Draper and Clayton N. Jefford, 247–86. Atlanta: SBL, 2015.

Bruce, F. F. *The Canon of Scripture.* Downers Grove: IVP, 1988.

Burkitt, F. Crawford. *The Gospel History and Its Transmission.* Edinburgh: T&T Clark, 1911.

Butler, B. C. *The Originality of St. Matthew: A Critique of the Two Document Hypothesis.* Cambridge: Cambridge University Press, 1951.

Cadbury, Henry J. "A Possible Case of Lukan Authorship (John 7:53–8:11)." *Harvard Theological Review* 2010 (1911): 237–44.

Campenhausen, Hans von. *The Formation of the Christian Bible*. Philadelphia: Fortress, 1972.

Carlson, Stephen C. "Clement of Alexandria on the 'Order' of the Gospels." *New Testament Studies* 47 (2001): 118–25.

Carlson, Stephen. *Papias of Hierapolis Exposition of Dominical Oracles: The Fragments, Testimonia, and Reception of a Second Century Commentator*. Oxford: Oxford University Press, 2021.

Carson, D. A. *Matthew: Chapters 1 through 12*. EBC. Grand Rapids: Zondervan, 1995.

Carter, Warren. *Matthew: Storyteller, Interpreter, Evangelist*. Peabody: Hendrickson, 2004.

Casey, Maurice. *An Aramaic Approach to Q: Sources for the Gospels of Matthew and Luke*. Cambridge: Cambridge University Press, 2002.

———. *Jesus of Nazareth: An Independent Historian's Account of His Life and Teaching*. London: T&T Clark International, 2010.

Chapman, John. *John the Presbyter and the Fourth Gospel*. Oxford: Clarendon Press, 1911.

Cirafesi, Wally V. and Fewster, Gregory P. "Justin's Ἀπομνημονεύματα and Ancient Greco-Roman Memoirs." *Early Christianity* 7.2 (2016): 186–212.

Collins, Adela. *Mark: A Commentary*. Hermeneia. Minneapolis: Fortress, 2007.

Collins, J. N. "Rethinking 'Eyewitnesses' in the Light of 'Servants of the Word' (Luke 1:2)." *Expository Times* 121 (2010): 447–52.

Colson, F. H. "Τάξει in Papias (The Gospels and the Rhetorical Schools)." *Journal of Theological Studies* 14 (1912): 62–69.

Coogan, Jeremiah. "The Ways that Parted in the Library: The Gospels according to Matthew and according to the Hebrews in Late Ancient Heresiology." *The Journal of Ecclesiastical History* 73 (2022): 1–18.

Cosgrove, Charles H. "A Woman's Unbound Hair in the Greco-Roman World, with Special Reference to the Story of the 'Sinful Woman' in Luke 7:36–50." *Journal of Biblical Literature* 124.4 (2005): 675–92.

Counet, Chatelion. "Pseudepigraphy and the Petrine School: Spirit and Tradition in 1 and 2 Peter and Jude." *HTS Teologiese Studies* 62.2 (2006): 403–24.

Crossley, James G. *The Date of Mark's Gospel: Insight from the Law in Earliest Christianity*. London: T&T Clark, 2004.

Culpepper, R. Alan. *John, the Son of Zebedee: The Life of a Legend*. Minneapolis: Fortress, 2000.

Davies, W. D. and Allison, Dale C. *A Critical and Exegetical Commentary on The Gospel According to Saint Matthew. Volume II: Introduction and Commentary on Matthew VIII—XVII.* ICC. Edinburgh: T&T Clark, 1991.

De Boor, C. *Neue Fragmente des Papias, Hegesippus und Pierius: In bisher unbekannten Excerpten aus der Kirchengeschichte des Philippus Sidetes. Texte und Untersuchungen* 5.2. Leipzig: Hinrichs, 1888.

Deeks, David G. "Papias Revisited." *Expository Times* 88 (1977): 296–301, 324–29.

Díaz, Mar Pérez I. *Mark, A Pauline Theologian.* WUNT 2.521. Tübingen: Mohr Siebeck, 2020.

Doering, Lutz. "Apostle, Co-Elder, and Witness of Suffering: Author Construction and Peter Image in First Peter." In *Pseudepigraphie und Verfasserfiktion in frühchristlichen Briefen: Pseudepigraphy and Author Fiction in Early Christian Letters.* Edited by Jörg Frey, Jens Herzer, Martina Janßen, and Clare K. Rothschild, 645–81. Tübingen: Mohr Siebeck, 2012.

Donahue, John R. "Tax Collectors and Sinners: An Attempt at Identification." *Catholic Biblical Quarterly* 33 (1971): 39–61.

Donovan, J. "Note on the Eusebian Use of 'Logia.'" *Biblica* 3 (1926): 301–10.

Draper, Jonathan A. Editor. *The Didache in Modern Research.* Leiden: Brill, 1996.

———. "The Jesus Tradition in the *Didache*." In *The Didache in Modern Research.* Edited by Jonathan A. Draper, 72–92. Leiden: Brill, 1996.

Drijvers, H. J. W. and Reinink, G. J. "Taufe und Licht: Tatian, Ebionäerevangelium und Thomasakten." In *Text and Testimony: Essays on New Testament and Apocryphal Literature in Honour of A. F. J. Klijn.* Edited by T. Baarda, A. Hilhorst, G. P. Luttikhuizen, and S. J. van der Woude, 91–110. Kampen: J. H. Kok, 1988.

Draper, Jonathan and Jefford, Clayton N. Editors. *The Didache: A Missing Piece of the Puzzle in Early Christianity.* Atlanta: SBL, 2015.

Dungan, David Laird. *A History of the Synoptic Problem: The Canon, the Text, the Composition, and the Interpretation of the Gospels.* New York: Doubleday, 1999.

Edwards, James R. *The Hebrew Gospel and the Development of the Synoptic Tradition.* Grand Rapids: Eerdmans, 2009.

Ehrman, Bart D. "Jesus and the Adulteress." *New Testament Studies* 34 (1988): 24–44.

———. *Apostolic Fathers: Epistle of Barnabas, Papias and Quadratus, Letter to Diognetus, The Shepherd of Hermas.* 2 vols. Loeb Classical Library. Cambridge: Harvard University Press, 2003.

———. *Forgery and Counterforgery: The Use of Literary Deceit in Early Christian Polemics.* Oxford: Oxford University Press, 2013.

Eichorn, Johann Gottfried. "Über die drey ersten Evangelien. Einige Bermerkungen zu ihrer künftigen Behandlung." In *Allgemeine Bibliothek der biblischen Literatur* 5. Leipzig: Weidmann, 1794, 761–996.

Elliott, John. H. *1 Peter.* AB 37B. New Haven: Yale University Press, 2000.

Evans, Craig. "The Jewish Christian Gospel Tradition." In *Jewish Believers in Jesus: The Early Centuries.* Edited by Oskar Skarsaune and Reider Hvalvik, 241–77. Peabody: Hendrickson, 2007.

Falls, Thomas B. *Dialogue with Trypho.* Selections from the Fathers of the Church Volume 3. Revised by Thomas P. Halton. Edited by Michael Slusser. Washington: The Catholic University of America Press, 2003.

Farmer, William R. *The Synoptic Problem: A Critical Analysis.* Dillsboro: Western North Carolina Press, 1976.

———. *The Gospel of Jesus: The Pastoral Relevance of the Synoptic Problem.* Louisville: Westminster John Knox, 1994.

Ferguson, Matthew Wade. "Ancient Historical Writings Compared to the Gospels of the New Testament." *The Secular Modern Web Library.* 2016. https://infidels.org/library/modern/matthew_ferguson/gospel-genre.html.

Fiovlá, Radka. "'Scripture' and the 'Memoirs of the Apostles': Justin Martyr and His Bible." In *The Process of Authority: The Dynamics in Transmission and Reception of Canonical Texts.* Edited by Jan Dušek and Jan Roskovec, 165–78. Berlin: De Gruyter, 2016.

Fleddermann, Harry T. *Q: A Reconstruction and Commentary.* Leuven: Peeters, 2005.

Foster, Paul. "The Epistles of Ignatius of Antioch and the Writings that Later Formed the New Testament." In *The Reception of the New Testament in the Apostolic Fathers.* Edited by Andrew Gregory and Christopher Tuckett, 159–86. Oxford: Oxford University Press, 2005.

———. "The Relationship between the Writings of Justin Martyr and the So-Called Gospel of Peter." In *Justin Martyr and His Worlds.* Edited by Sarah Parvis and Paul Foster, 104–12. Minneapolis: Fortress, 2007.

Foucault, Michel. "What is an Author?" In *Ascetics, Method and Epistemology. Volume 2.* Edited by James Faubion, 205–22. Translated by Robert Hurley. London: Penguin Books, 2000.

France, R. T. *Matthew: Evangelist and Teacher*. Grand Rapids: Zondervan, 1989.

Frey, Jörg. "Die Fragmente judenchristlicher Evangelien." In *Antike christliche Apokryphen in deutscher Übersetzung. I. Band: Evangelien und Verwandtes. Teilband 1*. Edited by Christoph Markschies and Jens Schröter, 560–92. Tübingen: Mohr Siebeck 2012.

———. "Die Fragmente des Hebräerevangeliums." In *Antike christliche Apokryphen in deutscher Übersetzung. I. Band: Evangelien und Verwandtes. Teilband 1*. Edited by Christoph Markschies and Jens Schröter, 593–606. Tübingen: Mohr Siebeck 2012.

———. "Die Fragmente des Ebionäerevangeliums." In *Antike christliche Apokryphen in deutscher Übersetzung. I. Band: Evangelien und Verwandtes. Teilband 1*. Edited by Christoph Markschies and Jens Schröter, 607–22. Tübingen: Mohr Siebeck 2012.

———. "Die Fragmente des Nazoräerevangeliums." In *Antike christliche Apokryphen in deutscher Übersetzung. I. Band: Evangelien und Verwandtes. Teilband 1*. Edited by Christoph Markschies and Jens Schröter, 623–54. Tübingen: Mohr Siebeck 2012.

Furlong, Dean. "Theodore of Mopsuestia: New Evidence for the Proposed Papian Fragment in *Hist. eccl.* 3.24.5–13." *Journal for the Study of the New Testament* 39.2 (2016): 209–29.

———. *The John also called Mark: Reception and Transformation in Christian Tradition*. Tübingen: Mohr Siebeck, 2020.

———. *The Identity of John the Evangelist: Revision and Reinterpretation in Early Christian Sources*. Minneapolis: Lexington Books, 2020.

Gamble, Harry Y. *The New Testament Canon: Its Making and Meaning*. Minneapolis: Fortress, 1985.

———. *Books and Readers in the Early Church: A History of Early Christian Texts*. New Haven: Yale University Press, 1995.

Garrow, Alan J. P. *The Gospel of Matthew's Dependence on the Didache*. JSNTS 254. London: T&T Clark, 2004.

Gathercole, Simon J. *The Composition of the Gospel of Thomas*. Cambridge: Cambridge University Press, 2012.

———. "The Alleged Anonymity of the Canonical Gospels." *Journal of Theological Studies* 69.2 (2018): 447–76.

Glover, Richard. "The Didache's Quotations and the Synoptic Gospels." *New Testament Studies* 5 (1958): 12–29.

Goodacre, Mark. *The Synoptic Problem: A Way through the Maze*. London: T&T Clark, 2001.

———. *The Case against Q*. Harrisburg: Trinity, 2002.

————. *Thomas and the Gospels: The Case for Thomas's Familiarity with the Synoptics*. Grand Rapids: Eerdmans, 2012.

————. "How Reliable is the Story of the Nag Hammadi Discovery?" *Journal for the Study of the New Testament* 35.4 (2013): 303–22.

Goodspeed, E. J. *Matthew, Apostle and Evangelist*. First Edition. Philadelphia: John C. Winston, 1959.

Goswell, Gregory. "Authorship and Anonymity in the New Testament Writings." *Journal of the Evangelical Theological Society* 60.4 (2017): 733–49.

Goulder, Michael. *Midrash and Lection in Matthew*. London: SPCK, 1974.

————. *Luke: A New Paradigm*. Sheffield: JSOT, 1989.

————. "A Poor Man's Christology." *New Testament Studies* 45 (1999): 332–48.

Grant, F. C. *The Gospels: Their Origins and Growth*. New York: Harper, 1957.

Grant, Robert M. "Papias and the Gospels." *Anglican Theological Review* 25 (1943): 171–72.

Gregory, Andrew. *The Reception of Luke and Acts in the Period before Irenaeus*. WUNT 2.169. Tübingen: Mohr Siebeck, 2003.

————. *The Gospel according to the Hebrews and the Gospel of the Ebionites*. Oxford: Oxford University Press, 2017.

Gregory, Andrew and Tuckett, Christopher. Editors. *The Reception of the New Testament in the Apostolic Fathers*. Oxford: Oxford University Press, 2005.

————. "*2 Clement* and the Writings that Later Formed the New Testament." In *The Reception of the New Testament in the Apostolic Fathers*. Edited by Andrew Gregory and Christopher Tuckett, 251–92. Oxford: Oxford University Press, 2005.

Gundry, Robert. *The Use of the Old Testament in St. Matthew's Gospel: With Special Reference to the Messianic Hope*. Leiden: Brill, 1975.

Gundry, Robert H. *Matthew: A Commentary on his Handbook for a Mixed Church Under Persecution*. Second Edition. Grand Rapids: Eerdmans, 1994.

————. "ΕΤΑΓΓΕΛΙΟΝ: How Soon a Book?" *Journal of Biblical Literature* 115 (1996): 321–25.

————. "The Apostolically Johannine Pre-Papian Tradition Concerning the Gospels of Mark and Matthew." In *The Old is Better: New Testament Essays in Support of Traditional Interpretations*. Edited by Robert H. Gundry, 49–73. WUNT 178. Tübingen: Mohr Siebeck, 2005.

————. *Peter: False Disciple and Apostate according to Saint Matthew: Second Edition with Responses to Reviews*. Eugene: Wipf & Stock, 2018.

Hagner, Donald A. "The Sayings of Jesus in the Apostolic Fathers and Justin Martyr." In *Gospel Perspectives, Volume 5: The Jesus Tradition Outside the Gospels*. Edited by David Wenham, 233–68. Sheffield: JSOT, 1984.

————. *Matthew 1–13*. Dallas: Word, 1993.

Häkkinen, Sakari. "Ebionites." In *A Companion to Second Century Christian "Heretics."* SVC 76. Edited by Antti Marjanen and Petri Luomanen, 247–78. Leiden: Brill, 2005.

Harnack, Adolf Von. *Marcion: Das Evangelium vom fremden Gott. Eine Monographie zur Geschichte der Grundlegung der katholischen Kirche*. Second Edition. TU 45. Leipzig: Hinrichs, 1924.

————. *The Origin of the New Testament: And the Most Important Consequence of the New Creation*. Translated by J. R. Wilkinson. Eugene: Wipf & Stock, 2004.

Harris, J. Rendel. *Testimonies: Part I*. Cambridge: Cambridge University Press, 1906.

————. *Testimonies: Part II*. Cambridge: Cambridge University Press, 1920.

Head, Peter M. and Williams, P. J. "Q Review." *Tyndale Bulletin* 54.1 (2003): 119–44.

Heard, Richard. "The *Apomnēmoneumata* in Papias, Justin, and Irenaeus." *New Testament Studies* 1 (1954): 122–29.

Heckel, Theo K. *Vom Evangelium des Markus zum viergestaltigen Evangelium*. WUNT 120. Tübingen: Mohr Siebeck, 1999.

Hengel, Martin. *Studies in the Gospel of Mark*. Philadelphia: Fortress, 1985.

————. *The Johannine Question*. Translated by John Bowden. London: SCM, 1989.

————. *The Four Gospels and the One Gospel of Jesus Christ*. Translated by John Bowden. London: SCM, 2000.

Hill, Charles E. "What Papias Said about John (and Luke): A New 'Papian' Fragment." *Journal of Theological Studies* 49 (1998): 582–629.

————. *The Johannine Corpus in the Early Church*. Oxford: Oxford University Press, 2004.

————. "Papias of Hierapolis." *Expository Times* 117 (2006): 309–15.

————. "Was John's Gospel among Justin's Apostolic Memoirs?" In *Justin Martyr and His Worlds*. Edited by Sarah Parvis and Paul Foster, 88–94. Minneapolis: Fortress, 2007.

————. "The 'Orthodox Gospel': The Reception of John in the Great Church Prior to Irenaeus." In *The Legacy of John: Second-Century Reception of the Fourth Gospel*. Edited by Tuomas Rasimus, 233–300. Leiden: Brill, 2009.

————. "'In These Very Words': Methods and Standard of Literary Borrowing in the Second Century." In *The Early Text of the New Testament.* Edited by Charles E. Hill and Michael J. Kruger, 313–35. Oxford: Oxford University Press, 2012.

Hill, David. *The Gospel of Matthew.* Grand Rapids: Eerdmans, 1972.

Hoek, Annawies Van den. "The 'Catechetical' School of Early Christian Alexandria and Its Philonic Heritage." *Harvard Theological Review* 90.1 (1997): 59–87.

Hoffmann, R. Joseph. *Marcion: On the Restitution of Christianity: An Essay on the Development of Radical Paulinist Theology in the Second Century.* AAR 46. Chicago: Scholars Press, 1984.

Holmes, B. T. "Luke's Description of John Mark." *Journal of Biblical Literature* 54 (1935): 65–68.

Holmes, Michael W. *The Apostolic Fathers: Greek Texts and English Translations.* Third Edition. Grand Rapids: Baker Academic, 2007.

Holtzmann, Heinrich Julius. *Die synoptischen Evangelien. Ihr Ursprung und geschichtlicher Charakter.* Leipzig: Wilhelm Engelmann, 1863.

Horbury, William. *Jews and Christians in Contact and Controversy.* Edinburgh: T&T Clark, 1998.

Horrell, David G. "The Product of a Petrine Circle? A Reassessment of the Origin and Character of 1 Peter." *Journal for the Study of the New Testament* 86 2002): 29–60.

Horst, Pieter W. Van den. "The Birkat ha-minim in Recent Research." *Expository Times* 105 (1994–95): 363–68.

Hughes, Kyle R. "The Lukan Special Material and the Tradition History of the *Pericope Adulterae.*" *Novum Testamentum* 55 (2013): 232–51.

Hydahl, Niels. "Hegesipps Hypomnemata." *Studia Theologica* 14 (1960): 70–113.

Ilan, Tal. *Lexicon of Jewish Names in Late Antiquity: Part I: Palestine 300 BCE – 200 CE.* TSAJ 91. Tübingen: Mohr Siebeck, 2002.

Jacobs, Andrew S. *Epiphanius of Cyprus: A Cultural Biography of Late Antiquity.* Oakland: University of California Press, 2016.

Jefford, Clayton N. *The Sayings of Jesus in the Teaching of the Twelve Apostles.* Leiden: Brill, 1989.

Jones, F. S. *An Ancient Jewish Christian Source on the History of Christianity: Pseudo-Clementine Recognitions 1:27–71.* SBLTT 37. Christian Apocrypha Series 2. Atlanta: Scholars Press, 1995.

————. "Jewish Christianity of the *Pseudo-Clementines.*" In *A Companion to Second Century Christian "Heretics."* SVC 76. Edited by Antti Marjanen and Petri Luomanen, 315–34. Leiden: Brill, 2005.

Keck, Leander E. "The Poor Amongst the Saints in the New Testament." *Zeitschrift für die neutestamentliche Wissenschaft* 56 (1965): 100–129.

―――. "The Poor Amongst the Saints in Jewish Christianity and Qumran." *Zeitschrift für die neutestamentliche Wissenschaft* 57 (1966): 54–78.

Keener, Craig S. *The Gospel of Matthew: A Socio-Rhetorical Commentary.* Grand Rapids: Eerdmans, 2009.

Keith, Chris. "Recent and Previous Research on the Pericope Adulterae (John 7.53–8.11)." *Currents in Biblical Research* 6.3 (2008): 377–404.

―――. "The Initial Location of the Pericope Adulterae in Fourfold Tradition." *Novum Testamentum* 51 (2009): 209–31.

―――. *The Gospel as Manuscript: An Early History of the Jesus Tradition as Material Artifact.* Oxford: Oxford University Press, 2020.

Kelhoffer, James A. "'How Soon a Book' Revisited: ΕΤΑΓΓΕΛΙΟΝ as a Reference to "Gospel" Materials in the First Half of the Second Century." *Zeitschrift für die neutestamentliche Wissenschaft* 95 (2004): 1–34.

Kennedy, George. "Classical and Christian Source Criticism." In *The Relationship among the Gospels: An Interdisciplinary Dialogue.* Edited by William O. Walker, 125–55. San Antonio: Trinity University Press, 1978.

Kiley, Mark. "Why 'Matthew' in Matt 9:9–13." *Biblica* 65.3 (1984): 347–51.

Kilpatrick, George D. *The Origins of the Gospel according to St. Matthew.* Oxford: Clarendon, 1946.

Kimelman, Reuven. "Birkat Ha-Minim and the Lack of Evidence for an Anti-Christian Jewish Prayer in Late Antiquity." In *Jewish and Christian Self Definition.* 2 vols. Edited by E. P. Sanders, 226–44. Philadelphia: Fortress, 1981.

Kinzig, Wolfram. "The Nazoraeans." In *Jewish Believers in Jesus: The Early Centuries.* Edited by Oskar Skarsaune and Reider Hvalvik, 463–87. Peabody: Hendrickson, 2007.

Kirk, Alan. *The Composition of the Sayings Source: Genre, Synchrony, & Wisdom Redaction in Q.* NovTSupp 91. Leiden: Brill, 1998.

Klauck, Hans Josef. *Apocryphal Gospels: An Introduction.* Translated by Brian McNeil. London: T&T Clark, 2003.

Klijn, A. F. J. *Jewish Christian Gospel Tradition.* Leiden: Brill, 1992.

Klijn, A. F. J. and Reinink, G. J. *Patristic Evidence for Jewish-Christian Sects.* NovTSup 36. Leiden: Brill, 1973.

Klinghardt, Matthias. "Markion vs. Lukas: Plädoyer für die Wiederaufnahme eines alten Falles." *New Testament Studies* 52.4 (2006): 484–513.

———. "The Marcionite Gospel and the Synoptic Problem: A New Suggestion." *Novum Testamentum* 50.1 (2008): 1–27.

———. *Das älteste Evangelium und die Entstehung der kanonischen Evangelien.* 2 vols. TANZ 60. Tübingen: Francke, 2015.

Kloppenborg, John S. *The Formation of Q: Trajectories in Ancient Wisdom Collections.* Studies in Antiquity and Christianity. Philadelphia: Fortress, 1987.

———. "On Dispensing with Q? Goodacre on the Relation of Luke to Matthew." *New Testament Studies* 49 (2003): 210–36.

———. "Conflated Citations of the Synoptic Gospels: The Beginning of Christian Doxological Tradition." In *Gospels and Gospel Traditions in the Second Century: Experiments in Reception.* Edited by Jens Schröter and Tobias Nicklas, 45–80. BZNW 235. Berlin: de Gruyter, 2018.

Knust, Jennifer and Wasserman, Tommy. *To Cast the First Stone: The Transmission of a Gospel Story.* New Jersey: Princeton University Press, 2019.

Koester, Helmut. *Ancient Christian Gospels: Their History and Development.* London: SCM, 1990.

Köhler, Wof-Dietrich. *Die Rezeption des Matthäusevangeliums in der Zeit vor Irenäus.* Tübingen: Mohr Siebeck, 1987.

Kok, Michael J. *The Gospel on the Margins: The Reception of Mark in the Second Century.* Minneapolis: Fortress, 2015.

———. *The Beloved Apostle? The Transformation of the Apostle John Into the Fourth Evangelist.* Eugene: Cascade, 2017.

———. "Did Papias of Hierapolis Use the *Gospel according to the Hebrews* as a Source?" *Journal of Early Christian Studies* 25.1 (2017): 29–53.

———. "Classifying Cerinthus's Christology." *Journal of Early Christian History* 9.1 (2019): 30–48.

———. "Re-naming the Toll Collector in Matthew 9:9: A Review of the Options." *Journal of Gospels and Acts Research* 4 (2020): 24–34.

Körtner, U. H. J. *Papias von Hierapolis: Ein Beitrag zur Geschichte des frühen Christentums,* FRLANT 133. Göttingen; Vandenhoeck & Ruprecht, 1983.

Köstenberger, Andreas and Snout, Stephen O. "'The Disciple Jesus Loved' – Witness, Author, Apostle: A Response to Richard Bauckham's *Jesus and the Eyewitnesses.*" *Bulletin for Biblical Research* 18 (2008): 209–31.

Köster, Helmut. *Synoptische Überlieferung bei den apostolischen Vätern.* TU 65. Berlin: Akedemie-Verlag, 1957.

Kraus, Thomas J. "'Uneducated,' 'Ignorant,' or even 'Illiterate'? Aspects and Background for an Understanding of ΑΓΡΑΜΜΑΤΟΙ (and ΙΔΙΩΤΑΙ) in Acts 4:13." *New Testament Studies* 45 (1999): 434–49.

Kruger, Michael J. *The Question of Canon: Challenging the Status Quo in the New Testament Debate.* Nottingham: IVP, 2013.

Kürzinger, Josef. *Papias von Hierapolis und die Evangelien des Neuen Testaments.* Regensberg: Verlag Friedrich Pustet, 1983.

Lane, William L. *The Gospel of Mark.* NICNT. Grand Rapids: Eerdmans, 1974.

Langer, Ruth. *Cursing the Christians: A History of the Birkat HaMinim.* Oxford: Oxford University Press, 2012.

Larsen, Matthew. *Gospels before the Book.* Oxford: Oxford University Press, 2018.

Larsen, Matthew D. C. "Correcting the Gospel: Putting the Titles of the Gospel in Historical Context." In *Rethinking "Authority" in Late Antiquity: Authorship, Law, and Transmission in Jewish and Christian Tradition.* Edited by A. J. Berkovitz and Mark Letteney, 78–104. New York: Routledge, 2018.

Larsen, Matthew D. C. and Letteney, Mark. "Christians and the Codex. Generic Materiality and Early Gospel Traditions." *Journal of Early Christian Studies* 27.3 (2019): 383–415.

Lessing, Gotthold Ephraim. "New Hypothesis on the Evangelists as Merely Human Historians." In *Gotthold Ephraim Lessing: Philosophical and Theological Writings.* CTHP. Translated and Edited by H. B. Nisbet, 148–71. Cambridge: Cambridge University Press, 2005.

Lieu, Judith M. *Marcion and the Making of a Heretic: God and Scripture in the Second Century.* Cambridge: Cambridge University Press, 2015.

Lightfoot, Joseph Barber. *Essays on the Work Entitled Supernatural Religion.* London: Macmillan, 1893.

Lindars, Barnabas. "Matthew, Levi, Lebbaeus, and the Value of the Western Text." *New Testament Studies* 4 (1957–58): 220–22.

Lindemann, Andreas. *Paulus in ältesten Christentum.* BHT 58. Tübingen: Mohr Siebeck, 1979.

Litwa, M. David. *The Refutation of All Heresies.* Atlanta: SBL, 2016.

Lührmann, Dieter. "Die Geschichte von einer Sünderin und andere Apokryphe Jesusüberlieferungen bei Didymos von Alexandrien." *Novum Testamentum* 32 (1990): 289–312.

———. "Sayings of Jesus or Logia." In *The Gospel Behind the Gospels: Current Studies on Q.* Edited by Ronald A. Piper, 97–116. New York: Brill, 1995.

Luomanen, Petri. *Recovering Jewish-Christian Sects and Gospels*. Leiden: Brill, 2012.

————. "The Nazarenes: Orthodox Heretics with an Apocryphal Canonical Gospel?" In *The Other Side: Apocryphal Perspectives on Ancient Christian "Orthodoxies."* NTOA 117. Edited by Candida R. Moss, Tobias Nicklas, Christopher Tuckett, and Joseph Verheyden, 55–74. Göttingen: Vandenhoeck & Ruprecht, 2017.

Luz, Ulrich. *Matthew 8–20*. Translated James E. Crouch. Hermeneia. Minneapolis: Fortress, 2001.

MacDonald, Dennis. *Two Shipwrecked Gospels: The Logoi of Jesus and Papias's Exposition of Logia about the Lord*. Atlanta: SBL, 2012.

————. *From the Earliest Gospel (Q+) to the Gospel of Mark: Solving the Synoptic Problem with Mimesis Criticism*. Lanham: Lexington Press, 2020.

MacDonald, Lee Martin. *The Biblical Canon: Its Origin, Transmission, and Authority*. Grand Rapids: Baker Academic, 2007.

MacEwan, Robert E. *Matthean Posterity: An Exploration of Matthew's Use of Mark and Luke as a Solution to the Synoptic Problem*. London: Bloomsbury T&T Clark, 2015.

Manor, T. Scott. "Papias, Origen, and Eusebius: The Criticisms and Defense of the Gospel of John." *Vigiliae Christianae* 67.1 (2013): 1–21.

Manson, T. W. *Studies in the Gospels and Epistles*. Manchester: Manchester University Press, 1962.

Marcus, Joel. *Mark 1–8*. AB. New Haven: Yale University Press, 2000.

————. *"Birkat Ha-Minim* Revisited." *New Testament Studies* 55.4 (2009): 523–51.

Maaren, John van. "Does Mark's Jesus Abrogate Torah? Jesus' Purity Logion and its Illustration in Mark 7:15–23." *Journal for the Jesus Movement in its Jewish Setting* 4 (2017): 21–41.

Martin, Ralph P. *Mark: Evangelist and Theologian*. Grand Rapids: Zondervan, 1978.

Marx, Werner G. "Money Matters in Matthew." *Bibliotheca Sacra* 136.542 (1979): 109–28.

Mason, Steve. *Josephus, Judaea, and Christian Origins: Methods and Categories*. Peabody: Hendrickson, 2009.

Massaux, Édouard. *The Influence of the Gospel of Saint Matthew on Christian Literature before St. Irenaeus*. 3 vols. Translated by Norman J. Belval and Suzanne Hechte. Edited by Arthur J. Bellinzoni. Macon: Mercer University Press, 1990.

Matthews, Christopher R. *Philip: Apostle and Evangelist: Configurations of a Tradition*. Leiden: Brill, 2002.

Matthews, Shelly. "Does Dating Luke-Acts into the Second Century Affect the Q Hypothesis?" In *Gospel Interpretation and the Q-Hypothesis.* Edited by Mogens Müller and Heike Omerzu, 253–64. LNTS 573. London: T&T Clark, 2018.

McNichol, Allan J., David L. Dungan, and David B. Peabody. *Beyond the Q Impasse: Luke's Use of Matthew: A Demonstration by the Research Team of the International Institute for Gospel Studies.* Philadelphia: Trinity Press International, 1996.

———. *One Gospel from Two: Mark's Use of Matthew and Luke: A Demonstration by the Research Team of the International Institute for Gospel Studies.* Philadelphia: Trinity Press International, 2002.

Meier, J. P. *The Vision of Matthew: Christ, Church and Morality in the First Gospel.* New York: Paulist, 1978.

Menken, M. J. J. *Matthew's Bible: The Old Testament Text of the Evangelist.* BETL CLXXIII. Leuven: Leuven University Press, 2004.

Metzger, B. M. *The Canon of the New Testament: Its Origin, Development, and Significance.* Minneapolis: Fortress, 1985.

Milavec, Aaron. *The Didache: Text, Translation, Analysis, and Commentary.* Collegeville: Liturgical, 2003.

———. "Synoptic Tradition in the *Didache* Revisited." *Journal of Early Christian Studies* 11.4 (2003): 443–80.

Mimouni, Simon Claude. "Les Nazoréens Recherche Étymologique Et Historique" *Revue Biblique* 105.2 (1998): 208–62.

———. *Early Judaeo-Christianity: Historical Essays.* Translated by Robyn Fréchet. Leuven: Peeters, 2012.

Minns, Dennis. *Irenaeus: An Introduction.* New York: T&T Clark, 2010.

Mitchell, Margaret. "Patristic Counter-Evidence to the Claim that 'The Gospels were Written for all Christians.'" *New Testament Studies* 51 (2005): 36–79.

Moll, Sebastian. *The Arch-Heretic Marcion.* WUNT 250. Tübingen: Mohr Siebeck, 2010.

Mommsen, Theodor. "Papianisches." *Zeitschrift für die Neutestamentliche Wissenschaft* 3 (1902): 156–59.

Morris, Leon. *The Gospel according to Matthew.* Grand Rapids: Eerdmans, 1992.

Moss, Candida. "A Note on the Death of Judas in Papias." *New Testament Studies* 65.3 (2019): 388–97.

———. "Fashioning Mark: Early Christian Discussions about the Scribe and Status of the Second Gospel." *New Testament Studies* 67.2 (2021): 181–204.

Mullins, Terrence Y. "Papias on Mark's Gospel." *Vigiliae Christianae* 14 (1960): 221–23.

Munck, Johannes. "Presbyters and Disciples of the Lord in Papias: Exegetic Comments on Eusebius, Ecclesiastical History, III, 39." *Harvard Theological Review* 52.4 (1959): 223–43.

Mutschler, Bernhard. "John and His Gospel in the Mirror of Irenaeus of Lyons: Perspectives of Recent Research." In *The Legacy of John: Second-Century Reception of the Fourth Gospel.* Edited by Tuomas Rasimus, 319–43. Leiden: Brill, 2010.

Nagel, Titus. *Die Rezeption des Johannesevangeliums im 2. Jahrhundert: Studien zur vorirenäischen Auslegung des vierten Evangeliums in christlicher und christlich-gnostischer Literatur.* ABG 2. Leipzig: Evangelische Verlagsanstalt, 2000.

Nautin, Pierre. "Théodore Lecteur et sa 'réunion de différentes Histoires' de l'Église." *Revue des Études Byzantines* 52 (1994): 213–43.

Neirynck, F. "The Symbol Q (=Quelle)." *Ephemerides theologicae Lovanienses* 54.1 (1978): 119–25.

Niederwimmer, Kurt. *The Didache.* Hermeneia. Translated by Linda M. Maloney. Edited by Harold W. Attridge. Minneapolis: Fortress, 1998.

Nolland, John. *The Gospel of Matthew.* NIGTC. Grand Rapids: Eerdmans, 2005.

Nolte, Johann Heinrich. "Ein Excerpt aus dem zum größen Theil noch ungedruckten Chronikon des Georgius Hamartolus." *Theological Quarterly* 44 (1862): 464–68.

Norelli, Enrico. *Papia di Hierapolis: Esposizione Degli Oracoli Del Signore I frammenti.* Figlie di San Paolo: Paoline, 2005.

North, J. L. "MARKOS HO KOLOBODAKTYLOS: Hippolytus, Elenchus, VII.30." *Journal of Theological Studies* 29 (1977): 498–507.

Oliver, Willem H. "The Catechetical School in Alexandria." *Verbum et Ecclesia* 36.1 (2015): 1–12.

Olson, Ken. "The Lord's Prayer (Abridged Edition)." In *Marcan Priority without Q: Explorations in the Farrer Hypothesis.* Edited by John C. Poirier and Jeffrey Peterson, 101–18. London: Bloomsbury T&T Clark, 2015.

Orchard, Bernard and Longstaff, Thomas R. W. *J. J. Griesbach: Synoptic and Text-Critical Studies 1776–1976.* Cambridge: Cambridge University Press, 1978.

Orchard, Bernard and Riley, Harold. *The Order of the Synoptics: Why Three Synoptic Gospels?* Macon: Mercer University Press, 1987.

Osborn, Eric Francis. *Justin Martyr*. BHT 47. Tübingen: Mohr Siebeck, 1973.

Paget, James Carleton. *Jews, Christians and Jewish Christians in Antiquity*. WUNT 251. Tübingen: Mohr Siebeck, 2010.

Parvis, Paul. "Justin Martyr." In *Early Christian Thinkers: The Lives and Legacies of Twelve Key Figures*. Edited by Paul Foster, 1–14. London: SPCK, 2010.

Parvis, Sara and Foster, Paul. Editors. *Justin Martyr and His Worlds*. Minneapolis: Fortress, 2007.

Patterson, Stephen J., James M. Robinson, and Hans-Gebhard Bethg. *The Fifth Gospel: The Gospel of Thomas Comes of Age*. New edition. London: Bloomsbury T&T Clark, 2012.

Patzia, Arthur G. *The Making of the New Testament: Origin, Collection, Text & Canon*. Downers Grove: IVP, 1995.

Peel, Malcolm L. "The Treatise on the Resurrection (I,4)." In *The Nag Hammadi Library in English*. Third Revised Edition. Edited by James M. Robinson, 52–57. San Francisco: Harper & Row, 1988.

Perumalil, A. C. "Are Not Papias and Irenaeus Competent to Report on the Gospels?" *Expository Times* 91 (1980): 332–37.

Pesch, Rudolf. "Levi-Matthäus (Me 2.14/Mt 9.9; 10.3). Ein Beitrag zur Lösung eines alten Problems." *Zeitschrift für die neutestamentliche Wissenschaft* 59 (1968): 40–56.

Petersen, Silke. "Die Evangelienüberschriften und die Entstehung des neutestamentlichen Kanons." *Zeitschrift für die neutestamentliche Wissenschaft* 97 (2006): 250–74.

Pilhofer, Peter. "Justin und das Petrusevangelium." *Zeitschrift für die neutestamentliche Wissenschaft* 81 (1990): 60–78.

Piper, Otto. "The Nature of the Gospel according to Justin Martyr." *The Journal of Religion* 41.3 (1961): 155–68.

Poirier, John C. and Peterson, Jeffrey. Editors. *Marcan Priority without Q: Explorations in the Farrer Hypothesis*. London: Bloomsbury T&T Clark, 2015.

Pokorny, Petr. *From the Gospels to the Gospel: History, Theology and Impact of the Biblical Term Euangelion*. BZNW 195. Berlin: De Gruyter, 2013.

Powers, B. Ward. *The Progressive Publication of Matthew: An Exploration of the Writing of the Synoptic Gospels*. Nashville: B&H Publishing Group, 2010.

Pritz, R. A. *Nazarene Jewish Christianity: From the End of the New Testament Period Until Its Disappearance in the Fourth Century*. Jerusalem: Magnes Press, 1988.

Pryor, John W. "Justin Martyr and the Fourth Gospel." *Second Century* 9 (1992): 153–69.

Rebenich, Stefan. *Jerome.* The Early Church Fathers. London: Routledge, 2002.

Reed, Annette Yoshiko. "ΕΥΑΓΓΕΛΙΟΝ: Orality, Textuality, and the Christian Truth in Irenaeus's *Adversus Haereses.*" *Vigiliae Christianae* 56 (2002): 11–46.

Rigg, Horace A. "Papias on Mark." *Novum Testamentum* 1 (1956): 161–83.

Robinson, James M., Paul Hoffmann, and John S. Kloppenborg. *The Sayings Gospel Q in Greek and English with Parallels from the Gospels of Mark and Thomas.* BBET 30. Leuven: Peeters, 2002.

Robinson, Will and Llewelyn, Stephen R. "The Fictious Audience of 1 Peter." *Heythrop Journal* 61.6 (2020): 939–50.

Rodriguez, Jacob A. "Justin and the Apostolic Memoirs: Public Reading as Covenant Praxis." *Early Christianity* 11.4 (2020): 496–515.

Rollens, Sarah E. *Framing Social Criticism in the Jesus Movement: The Ideological Project in the Sayings Gospel Q.* Tübingen: Mohr Siebeck, 2014.

Roth, Dieter T. *The Text of Marcion's Gospel.* NTTSD 40. Leiden: Brill, 2015.

———. "Marcion's Gospel and the Synoptic Problem in Recent Scholarship." In *Gospel Interpretation and the Q-Hypothesis.* Edited by Mogens Müller and Heike Omerzu, 267–82. LNTS 573. London: T&T Clark, 2018.

Runesson, Anders and Gurtner, Daniel M. "Introduction: The Location of Matthew-within-Judaism Perspective in Past and Present Research." In *Matthew within Judaism: Israel and the Nations in the First Gospel.* Edited by Anders Runesson and Daniel M. Gurtner, 1–25. Atlanta: SBL, 2020.

Sanders, E. P. and Davies, Margaret. *Studying the Synoptic Gospels.* London: SCM, 1989.

Sandt Huub Van and Flusser, David. *The Didache: Its Jewish Sources and Its Place in Early Judaism and Christianity.* Minneapolis: Fortress, 2002.

Schiffman, Lawrence. *Who Was a Jew? Rabbinic and Halakhic Perspectives on the Jewish-Christian Schism.* Hoboken: Ktav, 1985.

Schildgen, Brenda Deen. *Power and Prejudice: The Reception of the Gospel of Mark.* Detroit: Wayne State University Press, 1999.

Schleiermacher, Friedrich. "Über die Zeugnisse des Papias von unsern beiden ersten Evangelien," *TSK* 5 (1832): 735–68.

Schmidt, P. L. "'Und es war geschrieben auf Hebräisch, Griechisch und Lateinisch' Hieronymus, das Hebräer-Evangelium und seine mittelalterliche Rezeption." *Filologia Mediolatina* 5 (1998): 49–93.

Schmidtke, Alfred. *Neue Fragmente und Untersuchungen zu den judenchristlichen Evangelien: Ein Beitrag zur Literatur und Geschichte der Judenchristen.* TU 37.1. Leipzig: Hinrichs, 1911.

———. "Zum Hebräerevangelium." *Zeitschrift für die neutestamentliche Wissenschaft* 35 (1936): 24–44.

Schoedel, William R. *The Apostolic Fathers, A New Translation and Commentary: Polycarp, Martyrdom of Polycarp, Fragments of Papias.* 5 vols. Edited by R. M. Grant. Camden: Thomas Nelson, 1967.

———. *Ignatius of Antioch: A Commentary on the Letters of Ignatius.* Hermeneia. Edited by Helmut Koester. Philadelphia: Fortress, 1985.

———. "Papias." In *Aufstieg und Niedergang der römischen Welt* 2.27.1. Edited by Wolfgang Haase, 235–70. Berlin: De Gruyter, 1993.

Schoeps, Hans-Joachim. *Jewish Christianity: Factional Disputes in the Early Church.* Translated by Douglas A. Hare. Philadelphia: Fortress, 1969.

Schreiner, Patrick. *Matthew, Disciple and Scribe: The First Gospel and Its Portrait of Jesus.* Grand Rapids: Baker Academic, 2019.

Shanks, Monte A. *Papias and the New Testament.* Eugene: Pickwick, 2013.

Shotwell, Willis A. *The Biblical Exegesis of Justin Martyr.* London: SPCK, 1965.

Siegert, Folker. "Unbeachtete Papiaszitate bei armenischen Schriftstellern." *New Testament Studies* 27 (1981): 605–14.

Sim, David C. "The Gospel of Matthew, John the Elder and the Papias Tradition: A Response to R. H. Gundry." *HTS Teologiese Studies* 63.1 (2007): 283–99.

Skarsaune, Oscar. "The Ebionites." In *Jewish Believers in Jesus: The Early Centuries.* Edited by Oskar Skarsaune and Reider Hvalvik, 419–62. Peabody: Hendrickson, 2007

———. "Justin and His Bible." In *Justin Martyr and His Worlds.* Edited by Sara Parvis and Paul Foster, 53–76. Minneapolis: Fortress, 2007.

Skeat, T. C. "Irenaeus and the Four-Gospel Canon." *Novum Testamentum* 34 (1992): 194–99.

———. "The Origin of the Christian Codex." *Zeitschrift für Papyrologie und Epigraphik* 102 (1994): 263–68.

Sloan, David B. "What if the Gospel of the Hebrews was Q?" Paper presented to the Q Section at the Annual Meeting of the Society of Biblical Literature, Boston, November 2017.

———. "A Better Two-Document Hypothesis: Matthew's and Luke's Independent Use of Mark and the Gospel according to the Hebrews." Paper presented at the annual SBL Conference, San Diego, 2019.

———. "The Widow at Nain, the Sinful Woman who Loved Much, and the Extent of Q." Paper presented at Eastern Great Lakes Bible Society, Annual Meeting, 2021.

Smith, Daniel A. "Marcion's Gospel and the Resurrected Jesus of Canonical Luke 24." *Zeitschrift für Antikes Christentum* 21.1 (2017): 41–62.

———. "Marcion's Gospel and the Synoptics: Proposals and Problems." In *Gospels and Gospel Traditions in the Second Century: Experiments in Reception*. Edited by Jens Schröter, Tobias Nicklas, Joseph Verheyden, and Katharina Simnovic, 129–73. BZNW 235. Berlin: de Gruyter, 2018.

Stanton, Graham. *Jesus and Gospel*. Cambridge: Cambridge University Press, 2004.

Stein, Robert. *Studying the Synoptic Gospels: Origin and Interpretation*. Second Edition. Grand Rapids: Baker Academic, 2001.

Stevens, Luke J. "Did Eusebius Read Papias?" *Journal of Theological Studies* 70 (2019): 163–83.

Stewart-Sykes, Alistair. "*Taxei* in Papias: Again." *Journal of Early Christian Studies* 3 (1995): 487–92.

Streeter, Burnett Hillman. *The Four Gospels: A Study of Origins, Treating of the Manuscript Tradition, Authorship, & Dates*. Revised Edition. Eugene: Wipf & Stock, 2008.

Taylor, Joan E. "Missing Magdala and the Name of Mary Magdalene." *Palestine Exploration Quarterly* 146.3 (2014): 205–23.

Taylor, R. O. P. "The Ministry of Mark." *Expository Times* 54 (1943): 136–38.

Trobisch, David. *The First Edition of the New Testament*. Oxford: Oxford University Press, 2000.

Tuckett, Christopher M. *Nag Hammadi and the Gospel Tradition: Synoptic Tradition in the Nag Hammadi Library*. Edinburgh: T&T Clark, 1986.

———. "Synoptic Tradition in the Didache." In *The New Testament in Early Christianity*. Edited by Jean-Marie Sevrin, 197–230. BETL 86. Leuven: Leuven University Press, 1989.

———. *Q and the History of Early Christianity*. London: T&T Clark, 2004.

———. "The *Didache* and the Writings that Later Formed the New Testament." In *The Reception of the New Testament in the Apostolic Fathers*. Edited by Andrew Gregory and Christopher Tuckett, 83–127. Oxford: Oxford University Press, 2005.

Turner, Nigel. "Q in Recent Thought." *Expository Times* 80 (1968–69): 324–28.

Tyson, Joseph B. *Marcion and Luke-Acts: A Defining Struggle*. Columbia: University of South Carolina Press, 2006.

Vielhauer, Philipp and Strecker, Georg. "Jewish Christian Gospels." In *New Testament Apocrypha I: Gospels and Related Writings*. Translated by R. McL. Wilson. Edited by Wilhelm Schneemelcher, 134–78. Louisville: Westminster John Knox, 1991.

Vincent, Markus. *Christ's Resurrection in Early Christianity and the Making of the New Testament*. Farnham: Ashgate, 2011.

———. *Marcion and the Dating of the Synoptic Gospels*. Studia Patristica Supplements 2. Leuven: Peeters, 2014.

———. "Marcion's Gospel and the Beginnings of Early Christianity." *Annali Di Storia Dell'Esegesi* 32.1 (2015): 55–87.

Verheyden, Joseph. "Epiphanius on the Ebionites." In *The Image of the Judaeo-Christians in Ancient Jewish and Christian Literature*. Edited by Peter J. Tomson and Doris Lambers-Petry, 182–208. WUNT 158. Tübingen: Mohr Siebeck, 2003.

———. "Justin's Text of the Gospels: Another Look at the Citations in *1 Apol.* 15.1–8." In *The Early Text of the New Testament*. Edited by Charles E. Hill and Michael J. Kruger, 313–35. Oxford: Oxford University Press, 2012.

Voorst, R. E. Van. *The Ascent of James: History and Theology of a Jewish Christian Community*. SBLDS 112. Atlanta: Scholars Press, 1989.

Waitz, Hans. "Das Evangelium der zwölf Apostel: (Ebioniteevangelium)." *Zeitschrift für die neutestamentliche Wissenschaft* 13.4 (1912): 338–48.

———. "Das Evangelium der zwölf Apostel: (Ebioniteevangelium)." *Zeitschrift für die neutestamentliche Wissenschaft* 14.2 (1913): 117–32.

———. "Neue Untersuchung über die sogen. Judenchristlichen Evangelien." *Zeitschrift für die neutestamentliche Wissenschaft* 36 (1937): 60–81.

Watson, Francis. *Gospel Writing: A Canonical Perspective*. Grand Rapids: Eerdmans, 2013.

Weiss, Christian Hermann. *Die evangelische Geschichte kritisch und philosophisch bearbeitet*. 2 vols. Leipzig: Breitkopf und Härtel, 1838.

Wenham, John. *Redating Matthew, Mark & Luke: A Fresh Assault on the Synoptic Problem*. New Edition. Eugene: Wipf & Stock, 2020.

Williams, Travis B. "Delivering Oracles from God: The Nature of Christian Communication in 1 Peter 4:11a." *Harvard Theological Review* 113.3 (2020): 334–53.

Witherington III, Ben. *Matthew*. Macon: Smyth & Helwys, 2006.

Wright, Arthur. "*Taxei* in Papias." *Journal of Theological Studies* 14 (1913): 298–300.

Yadin-Israel, Azzan. "'For Mark was Peter's Tanna': Tradition and Transmission in Papias and the Early Rabbis." *Journal of Early Christian Studies* 23.3 (2015): 337–62.

Yarbrough, Robert W. "The Date of Papias: A Reassessment." *Journal of the Evangelical Theological Society* 2 (1983): 181–91.

Young, Stephen E. *Jesus Tradition in the Apostolic Fathers: Their Explicit Appeals to the Words of Jesus in Light of Orality Studies*. WUNT 2.311. Tübingen: Mohr Siebeck, 2011.

Zahn, Theodor. *Geschichte des neutestamentlichen Kanons: Erster Band: Das Neue Testament vor Origenes Erste Hälfte*. Erlangen: Deichert, 1889.

———. *Einleitung in das Neue Testament: Zweiter Band*. Leizpig: Deichert, 1897.

Zelyck, Lorne. "Irenaeus and the Authorship of the Fourth Gospel." In *The Origins of the Fourth Gospel*. Edited by Stanley Porter and Hughson T. Ong, 239–58. Leiden: Brill, 2016.

Zuiddam, B., F. J. Van Rensburg, and P. J. Jordaan, "Λόγιον in Biblical Literature and Its Implications for Christian Scholarship." *Acta Patristica et Byzantina* 19 (2008): 379–94.

Zwierlein, Otto. *Petrus in Rom, die literarischen Zeugnisse: Mit einer kritischen Edition der Martyrien des Petrus und Paulus auf neuer handschriftlicher Grundlage. Untersuchungen zur antiken Literatur und Geschichte*. Bd. 96. Berlin: De Gruyter, 2009.

INDEX OF NAMES

INDEX OF ANCIENT SOURCES

Old Testament Apocrypha and Pseudepigrapha

New Testament